D0787332

Theory of Accounting and Control

SHYAM SUNDER

Richard M. Cyert Professor of Management and Economics
Carnegie Mellon University

SOUTH-WESTERN College Publishing

An International Thomson Publishing Company

Accounting Team Director: Mary H. Draper
Sponsoring Editor: David L. Shaut
Developmental Editor: Ken Martin
Production Editor: Jason M. Fisher
Production House: Trejo Production
Internal Design: Michael Stratton
Cover Design: Michael Stratton
Marketing Manager: Steve Hazelwood

I⊤P
International Thomson Publishing
South-Western College Publishing is an ITP Company.
The ITP trademark is used under license.

Cataloging-in-Publication Data
Shyam Sunder, 1944–
        Theory of accounting and control / Shyman Sunder.
            p.   cm.
        Includes bibliographical references and index.
        ISBN 0-538-86686-1
        1. Managerial accounting.   I. Title.
        HF5657.4.S48   1997
        658.15'11--dc20   96-17545
                                                                          CIP

To Yuji Ijiri and Robert S. Kaplan

"Where shall we find a form of association which will defend and protect with whole common force the person and the property of each associate, and by which every person, while uniting himself with all, shall obey only himself and remain as free as before?

J. J. Rousseau, *The Social Contract*

Preface

●●●

This book originated in the mid-seventies because of my curiosity about the functions of accounting and control in organizations and in society at large. Although these functions might be obvious to some, to a young engineer working within the social science culture of the 1970s business schools, it was difficult to understand the big picture. Over the years, I struggled to organize what I knew, saw, read, and taught into a coherent whole. I came to believe that economic self-interest is the organizing principle I had been looking for. The contract theory of accounting is based on the idea that much of accounting practice is shaped by economic forces.

My introduction to accounting was simple enough. When my sister left home for college, my father turned to this sixth grader for assistance in keeping the farm and household accounts. Once a week or so I would write down the journal entries (debits to the right, credits to the left, as is the Indian convention) as he dictated them from his pocket notebook. Most entries were cash expenditures and payroll accruals for farmhands. Sales of farm products were in bulk and infrequent. Land, buildings, and equipment were owned outright and did not appear on the balance sheet. No depreciation was charged against revenue to compute our farm income for the year.

Management classes in engineering school and subsequent work in factories introduced me to the need for keeping track of what it costs to make a railroad car through manufacturing accounts, job order costing, allocation of costs, and overheads. The impersonal nature of huge factories and division of responsibility among managers created a need for budgets, performance evaluations, and variance analysis. Every batch of engine blocks was escorted through the factory by an invisible accountant in the form of a red job order sheet. At each stop, data on resources expended were recorded.

While working on a masters in industrial administration at Carnegie Mellon University, I learned another form of accounting, called Quantitative Controls for good reason. Large, professionally run corporations, with diffuse ownership of stock, extensive use of short- and long-term credit, complex production processes and financial instruments, and independent audits exemplified the complexity of accounting in its extensive and mature form. Although accounting was hardly mentioned in courses on organizational behavior, I was fortunate to have Yuji Ijiri explain the human motivations that drive the need for and the form of control systems. To this point, I felt quite at ease with what I had learned of business, organizations, and controls. I had in my mind a reasonably coherent picture of the functions of accounting in simple and in complex organizations. And then I was introduced to accounting research.

The specialized nature of most accounting research forces a tight focus on specific functions of accounting in narrowly defined environments. Some have received more attention than others. The role of accounting in valuation of securities, in providing information for evaluation of performance, and in motivating members of an organization are three such functions. Although detailed study of these specific functions is important, it is easy to miss the forest for the trees. My disorientation in the forest of accounting research arose from my inability to synthesize various functions of accounting into a coherent picture. This book is a step in that direction.

Who else might be interested in these thoughts? Originally, this material was developed in the form of lecture notes for a second-year MBA elective and was used in conjunction with cases I developed. Subsequently, I used the notes for a senior seminar in accounting theory, again supplemented by cases and articles from the financial press. These notes, supplemented by selected books and journal articles, have also been used to arouse the curiosity of first-year Ph.D. accounting students about the challenges of accounting research and teaching. Management and other social scientists are often curious about how accounting and control, apparently rigid and insulated from other disciplines, are linked to their own view of how organizations function. This book suggests some of these links. Finally, and most ambitiously, businesspeople may find in this book a way of organizing what they already know.

Acknowledgments

•••

Although this book carries my name, it includes ideas from innumerable sources. I am aware of only some of these sources. My debts are more numerous than I can count. But let me try.

My father taught me the discipline of accounting. My elder brother urged me to take leave from an engineering job in India to attend Carnegie Mellon University to broaden my horizons.

In 1970, Carnegie Mellon's Graduate School of Industry Administration (GSIA) may have been the only business school that mailed a list of faculty working papers and reprints to the students admitted to their master's program and encouraged them to request copies of the papers. I had read the works of Taylor, Gilbreth, and their contemporaries in our management classes at the engineering school in India. The list of working papers made me realize that the world of management had moved on beyond Taylorism.

I had the good fortune to learn from inspiring teachers such as Kalman Cohen, Claude Colantoni, Yuji Ijiri, Robert Kaplan, Thomas Morton, and Gerald Thompson. Both inside and outside the classroom, the GSIA environment was infused with the spirit of learning and experimentation. Soon after I joined the master's program, Claude Colantoni suggested that I consider joining the Ph.D. program. I did.

GSIA had one workshop for presentation of all scholarly work. These workshops sparkled with the excitement of learning, scholarship, and open discussion of all issues among the participants, who included Egon Balas, Martin Bronfenbrenner, David Cass, Richard Cyert, William Cooper, Lester Lave, Robert Lucas, Timothy McGuire, Allan Meltzer, Allan Newell, Edward Prescott, Richard Roll, and Herbert Simon. For us graduate students, it was an exhilarating experience, especially because in this world of ideas, there was no rank. As in most other successful Ph.D. programs, we had lively debates to defend our ideas. I was fortunate to overlap with an especially talented group that included Costas Azariadis, B. Balachandran, Bob Forsythe, Charlie Holt, Hiroyuki Itami, Finn Kydland, Ram Rao, and V. Srinivasan.

Over the years, I have had the good fortune to have Amin Amershi, Rick Antle, Andrew Bailey, Srikant Datar, Sidney Davidson, Joel Demski, John Dickhaut, Nick Dopuch, Jerry Feltham, George Foster, Nick Gonedes, David Green, Chandra Kanodia, Baruch Lev, Bob Magee, Ramon Marimon, Charlie Plott, Prem Prakash, Al Rappaport, and Dan Simunic as my friends and colleagues, and they have helped shape my thinking in many ways.

This book includes a great deal of what I learned from my undergraduate, masters, and Ph.D. students, especially Gary Biddle, Jim Donegan, Rong-Ruey Duh, Suk Sig Lim, Karim Jamal, Dhananjay Gode, Anish Shah, and Carolyn Levine.

I started writing the book as lecture notes for a master's class that Dean Peter Lusztig asked me to teach during my 1982–83 visit to the University of British Columbia. The Accounting Department secretary, Barbara Strouts, did a wonderful job typing the notes on short notice. Daniel Coloumbe, Masko Darrough, and Karim Jamal participated in the class and critiqued my first draft. Over the years, Andrew Bailey, Stan Baiman, Ron Dye, Yoshi Fukui, Jon Glover, Dhananjay Gode, Michael Hechter, Sok-Hyon Kang, Baruch Lev, Bob Magee, Richard Mattessich, Jim Ohlson, Katherine Schipper, Shiva Sivaramakrishnan, Gordon Walter, Hidetoshi Yamaji, Steve Zeff, and Jerry Zimmerman have spent hours reading the manuscript and sharing their constructive comments with me.

The main burden of manuscript preparation and fixing my English was carried by Gerry Hoag, Betty Cosnek, Traci Radzniak, and Ann Nelson. Debra Hovland and Li Zhang painstakingly tracked down the hundreds of references and many quotations for accuracy.

Dave Shaut of South-Western College Publishing has been a constant source of support for this project. Developmental Editor Ken Martin and Production Editor Jason Fisher of South-Western have made my task an easy and painless one.

I have worked on this book at four great universities—University of British Columbia, University of Minnesota, Carnegie Mellon University, and Kobe University. I am grateful for their financial, secretarial, and collegial support that made this work possible. Financial support from the Honeywell Foundation at the University of Minnesota, from Richard M. and Margaret Cyert Family Funds at Carnegie Mellon University, and from the Japanese Ministry of Education at Kobe University were especially valuable.

Manjula, my wife, has read the manuscript almost as many times as I have, and she patiently guided various revisions during the fourteen years since I wrote the first draft. She and our children, Richa and Neal, have given me their love and support to complete this project.

Yuji Ijiri and Robert Kaplan taught me the two half-semester courses in accounting. To them, this book is dedicated.

Contents

4

Managers and Accounting Decisions   49

Hierarchy of Accounting Decisions 49 • Certain Features of Control Systems 54 • Managerial Consequences of Accounting Decisions 57 • Observable Behavior of Managers 60 • Summary 61 • *Notes* 61 • *Additional Reading* 62

5

Income and Its Management   65

Law of Conservation of Income 67 • Functions of Income in a Firm 67 • Attitudes of Agents Toward Income 68 • Management of Income 73 • Summary of Empirical Findings 77 • Summary 79 • *Notes* 79 • *Additional Reading* 80

6

Investors and Accounting   83

Description of the Investor Class 83 • Investor Attitudes and Preferences 88 • Accounting Choice Mechanisms for Investors 89 • Consequences of Accounting Policy for Investors 92 • Summary 94 • *Notes* 95 • *Additional Reading* 95

7

Accounting and the Stock Market   97

The Limited Role for Valuation Rules 97 • The Role of Information Intermediaries 98 • Questions About Accounting and the Stock Market 99 • Problems of Inference 106 • Summary 109 • *Notes* 109 • *Additional Reading* 110

8

Auditors and the Firm   113

The Function of the Audit in the Firm 114 • Auditor Decisions 116 • Institutional Structure of the Audit Profession 120 • Summary 128 • *Notes* 128 • *Additional Reading* 129

PART ONE

Contract Theory of the Firm

’1’

Introduction to the Theory of Accounting and Control

• •

Three ideas are central to understanding accounting and control in organizations. First, all organizations are sets of contracts among individuals or groups of individuals. Second, provision of shared information among the contracting parties helps design and implement these contracts. Finally, control *in* organizations is a sustainable balance or equilibrium among the interests of its participants. It should be distinguished from control *of* organizations, which suggests manipulation or exploitation of some participants by others. We start this overview by stating these ideas briefly, leaving most definitions and details for the following chapters. We conclude with a summary of ideas about micro and macro aspects of accounting and control presented in the book.

Organizations as a Set of Contracts

Organizations are many things to many people. Business firms, for example, are employers to those who work for them; customers to the purveyors of goods and services; suppliers to their own customers; benefactors to those who receive their charity; investments to those who save; taxpayers to the government; a threat to the livelihood of their competitors; impersonal bureaucracies to the powerless; and pillars of free enterprise to the believers. Organizations are variously seen as complex networks of human relationships, production functions, hierarchies, even garbage cans. They are praised for being storehouses of culture and civilization, and for being engines of change. They are also pilloried as sources of vulgarity and as roadblocks to progress in society.

We take no issue with these and other ways of looking at organizations. However, for our limited purpose of trying to explain the nature of accounting and control in organizations, we will use an appealing old idea supported by such scholars as Cyert and March, Simon, Barnard, and Rousseau: an organization is simply a set of contracts among agents.[1] Contracts are mutual understandings, whether formal or informal. Both an apartment lease and a lunch date with a friend are contracts. Agents are either individuals or other organizations. We assume agents to be rational: they do not knowingly choose what they do not like.

Shared Facts for Conflict Resolution

Disputes waste resources; provision of shared knowledge helps avert and settle disputes. Unsettled conflicts among agents weaken, or even wreck, the complex fabric of socioeconomic exchanges from which so much of our prosperity is derived. Industrial strikes and lockouts are an example. The practice of carefully collecting and sharing information arises to meet this fundamental demand for a means to preserve our socioeconomic system. Sharing of knowledge and expectations is a large part of acculturation and socialization.

Many conflicts in families, neighborhoods, the workplace, and trade are averted or settled with the help of shared information. The judicial system relies on written documents and the testimony of witnesses—both forms of shared information. However, only a minuscule proportion of all conflicts ever enter the courts of law. Most conflicts are promptly and inexpensively resolved through systematic provision of shared information outside any formal system of conflict resolution.

Defining executable contracts among agents requires *common knowledge*. Information X is common knowledge between agents A and B if A knows X, and B knows X, and A knows that B knows X, and B knows that A knows X, and A knows that B knows that A knows X, and so on.[2] In the English fable, when the boy shouted that the emperor had no clothes, everybody already knew that the emperor had no clothes; he only made it common knowledge.

When variables that are not common knowledge are used in contracts, contention or deception can arise. Common knowledge is more than the observability of an event by all parties. It also requires that every party be aware of its observability to the others. When everybody knows about the event, but not about others' knowledge of it, some may be tempted to use such information to their own advantage, and create avoidable conflict. Common knowledge helps reduce such conflict and the concommitant losses.

Accounting and control in organizations produce common knowledge to help define contracts among the agents. However, common knowledge is a theoretical abstraction. Translating it into practice is as difficult as making a mathematical point visible on a chalkboard. No physical representation of a point can be dimension-free, although freedom from dimensions is the essence of the mathematical definition of a point. Yet we can teach geometry, design and build bridges, and gain myriad other advantages that flow from abstractions without insisting that the physical and practical analogs be true to the fundamental concepts in all respects. The concept of common knowledge, likewise, has no exact representation in the practical world.

When deciding what to do, we may face two kinds of uncertainty. We decide under *imperfect* information if the rules or structure are common knowledge, only we do not know about events and actions of others. Roulette, for example, is a game of imperfect information because the players do not know where the ball will stop on the wheel. They all know the rules of the game, and the chances of various outcomes. Similarly, when we think of accounting as an information system for decision making, we assume that all parties know the rules of the game and accounting only provides information about various events and the actions of others.

If we do not know the rules or structure of the situation, we decide under more difficult circumstances, called *incomplete* information. In *The Wizard of Oz*, Dorothy faces a game of incomplete information. She does not know the rules nor the players in the game who keep popping up to surprise her. Accounting, as a system for implementing contracts or as an accountability system, must function effectively in an environment of not only imperfect but also incomplete information. In the less certain and more complex environment of incomplete information, accounting informs not only about events and the actions of others, but also about the structure of the game and the relative positions of players in that game. Some parts of accounting and control (e.g., public disclosure of financial statements) may appear to be redundant until we look at organizations as games of incomplete information.

Control in Organizations as Balance and Equilibrium

Conflict and cooperation coexist in economic exchanges. The desire to pursue what we want promotes contradictory instincts of cooperation and conflict. In an economic exchange, the gain from exchange or the total surplus is the difference between the maximum amount the buyer is willing to pay and the minimum amount the seller is willing to accept. This sum of consumer and producer surpluses is the organizational glue that drives agents toward cooperation, trust, goodwill, and sharing.

The actual transaction price determines the division of the total surplus between the buyer and the seller. This division engenders conflict, competition, and fear, and threatens to pull organizations apart. Control in organizations moderates this centrifugal force by helping mitigate and resolve conflicts. When conflict overpowers cooperation, the organization disintegrates. Pan American Airlines, the greatest airline in the world at one time, folded because the conflict between the employees and the shareholders could not be resolved to the satisfaction of both.

The idea of control *in* organizations is distinct from control *of* organizations. The former connotes balance and equilibrium among interests of agents; the latter suggests manipulation, even exploitation, of some agents by others. Control *of* organizations implies that the organization is an instrument of an agent or a group who uses it to attain its objectives, emphasizing the disparity in the relative bargaining powers of the controlling agent and the others. Under the concept of control *in* organizations, we look at organizations more symmetrically, from the point of view of various participants. In a modern corporation, even the chief executive officer does not control the rest of the organization because the CEO also is subject to the control system of the firm. We will focus attention on the larger and more general problem of control *in* organizations.

The accounting antecedents of this book lie in the work of Yuji Ijiri. He looked at accounting as a "system to facilitate smooth functioning of *accountability* relationships among interested parties," and distinguished this way of looking at accounting from the then-prevalent decision-usefulness approach along three dimensions:

1. significance of the process as well as the output of accounting,
2. the accounting system as an equilibrium outcome of the game among the parties involved and not something chosen arbitrarily by the accountant, and
3. the symmetry of the accountee–accountor (that is, principal–agent) relationship as opposed to the asymmetry inherent in the master–servant metaphor.[3] This last idea echoes Barnard's and Simon's analyses of authority relationships[4] and, historically, Rousseau's analysis of the relationship between the ruler and the ruled.[5] Consent of the ruled is as important as the ability of the ruler in these relationships.

Throughout this book we will assume that individuals choose actions to achieve their goals, within the constraints of their environment, knowledge, and capacity, and that they are rational in the sense that they do not deliberately choose courses of action whose outcomes are undesirable to them. The rationality assumption links people's goals to their actions.

This book is organized in three parts. The contract model of the firm, and functions of accounting and control in implementing the contract set are laid out in the next chapter. The six chapters of Part Two examine the attitudes and the actions of three major classes of agents—investors, managers, and auditors—under the label of microtheory of accounting. Attention is focused on the attitudes and actions of each class of agents, while the attitudes and actions of the remaining agents are assumed to remain fixed. In Part Three, under the label of macrotheory, we look at the problems of social choice, role of government, interaction between law and accounting, institutional structure of accounting, and problems of control in public goods-producing organizations. The remainder of this introductory chapter summarizes the main ideas of the book.

Microtheory of Accounting and Control

Organizations consist of individuals, each obligated to contribute resources and entitled to receive compensation in exchange. Individuals' pursuit of self-interest can induce conflict as well as cooperation. Accounting and control systems are designed to ensure that the centrifugal forces of conflict do not overcome the cooperative instinct. This is accomplished through five functions in implementing and enforcing the organization's contract set: (1) measuring everybody's contributions; (2) measuring and disbursing entitlements to each participant; (3) reporting to the participants about the extent of contract fulfillment; (4) distributing information to potential participants to maintain liquidity of the various factor markets from which the organization draws its resources; and (5) distributing certain information as common knowledge to help reduce the cost of negotiating contracts. Chapter 2 looks at how various forms and aspects of accounting can be understood in terms of these five functions.

Contracts that define the rights and obligations of each individual in an organization vary, depending on the nature of the resources each party has to offer and is willing to accept in exchange. As mentioned earlier, rational agents participate in an organization only as long as they receive, or expect to receive, greater compensation from the organization than they can get elsewhere in exchange for the resources they have to offer. Some resource flows can be measured more easily or more precisely than others (e.g., cash versus managerial effort). Contractual links of the agent to the firm, and the accounting and control mechanisms to carry out the contracts, are chosen to fit one another. That is why the contractual forms of shareholders, managers, factory workers, sales people, and customers take such diverse forms. Their participation in the accounting and control of the organization also varies accordingly.

Managers and Income

Managers are the most important group of agents whose interests and behavior are key to understanding the structure of an organization and its accounting and control. Their contribution to the firm is difficult to measure. Control systems are designed so organizations can operate efficiently without directly measuring managers' input. In order to induce managers to deliver on their obligations, their compensation, promotion, and retention are linked to those output data that are observable as well as informative about their contribution. Accounting and control systems are designed to produce these data.

Top managers and their subordinates directly negotiate the latter's contracts. Unlike public financial reports, design and enforcement of managerial contracts is not governed by across-firm standards. Top managers' performance, however, is monitored by investors and auditors who deal simultaneously with many firms. Since financial reports of business firms are also used for evaluating the top managers and investments, such reports are partially standardized.

Managers tend to pick accounting methods that suit their own interests. Managerial contracts are designed to withstand such self-serving behavior. Many puzzles about accounting choices (e.g., LIFO, leases, troubled loans, and research and development costs) can be understood within this context.

Income, often considered the singlemost important number in financial reports, serves several functions. It is a measure of the resource entitlement of the shareholders, and is a basis for rewarding managers whose input cannot be measured directly. Most important, income is the residual left after the cost of all production factors except equity is subtracted from revenue. This residual nature of net income renders it a valuable signal about the continued viability of the firm. When income becomes negative for reasons that are not thought to be temporary, all participants in the organization are put on notice that their existing contract set must be modified or dissolved in the not-too-distant future. The use of income figures in managerial compensation and in stock valuation also motivates managers to expend resources to opportunistically "manage" income to their own advantage.

Shareholders, Stock Markets, and Auditors

Shareholders constitute the second important group of contracting agents. Their contract has four major characteristics:

1. shareholders as a class are precommitted to the firm in the sense that they put their money down long before they can expect to receive any returns;
2. their resource entitlement is a residual (i.e., whatever is left after entitlements of all other agents have been set aside);
3. their contractual rights are transferable, and the market for shares of larger firms are often quite liquid; and
4. the shareholders as a class have the right to choose managers and auditors and to dissolve the organization.

The protection afforded to the shareholders through items (3) and (4) compensates them for the risks imposed by items (1) and (2).

Managers control the information generated in the firm and are tempted to disseminate it selectively. Shareholders need information to protect their interests against managerial incompetence or malfeasance. To limit selective screening of information, publicly held firms engage the services of independent auditors and require disclosure of verified information. Managers present their reports to auditors and give them access to the corporate records so the reports can be verified independently. The auditors provide verified reports to the investors and other participants in the firm so they can make their own decisions about continuing participation in the firm.

The audit fee is the price shareholders pay to reduce the chance of being misled by erroneous reports from managers, and to buy insurance against auditors' negligence or complicity with the managers. Without verification, managers would have an incentive to try to conceal unsatisfactory performance and to exaggerate good performance. Auditors receive fees for their professional services and for the risk of attesting to reports produced by managers.

Managers' role in the process is more complex. The audit fees reduce the net income of the firm available for the shareholders, as well as the financial remuneration of the managers. Enhanced credibility of managers' reports in the eyes of investors compensates the managers for this loss.

All agents—shareholders, managers, and auditors—seek accounting systems that will make them better off. They resist adverse changes and adjust their behavior to fare the best when changes do occur. This adjustment to others' behavior is a poorly understood, complex, dynamic process that continues until the system reaches equilibrium and no agent can increase his or her welfare by changing his or her behavior. Accounting theory is the study of this decision and adjustment process and the nature and conditions of accounting equilibrium.

Macrotheory of Accounting and Control

Conventions of accounting are distinguishable from its economic features. Conventions are those features that derive economic value entirely from coordination among agents. None of their value arises from the specific choice of the convention per se. For example, it is valuable to use the convention that debits be placed on the left and credits on the right. If the placement of debits and credits were reversed, the convention would be just as useful. All other features of accounting (such as entity, valuation, double entry, and accrual) have direct economic consequences and should not be called conventions. Some other basic features (such as uniformity and comparability) have doubtful theoretical support in contract theory. They are often used as rhetorical devices in accounting debates.

Social Choice Criteria, Mechanisms, and Standardization

Standardization of certain aspects of accounting captures gains from social coordination. But it is hard enough to tell what is good for an individual, let alone what is good for society as a whole. Consequences of decisions are often uncertain and spread over time. To arrive at a standard, somebody must collect data about individual preferences and then combine these data to find out what is best for society. Both steps are difficult. Even if the physical collection of data is cheap, getting people to reveal their private tastes and information is not easy. And if we know what each individual wants, it is not clear what is best for society as a whole, unless everybody prefers the same option. A variety of social decision mechanisms (e.g., markets, elections, courts, and bureaucracies) have evolved to handle, but not necessarily solve, this problem. Selection of accounting standards uses all these mechanisms in various stages.

There are two ways of thinking about rules and standards: constraints or reward/ punishment functions. If we think of them as constraints, rules tell us what we can and can-not do. If we think of them as reward/punishment functions, rules simply attach a reward or punishment to whatever choices we make without prohibiting anything. The former implies an unrealistic assumption that rules can be enforced perfectly; the latter interpretation is consistent with the economic perspective.

There are several levels of accounting standards, and a variety of motivations lie behind standardization. The mechanisms chosen for setting standards, the types of standards chosen, and the magnitude of sanctions used to enforce them all have significant effects on the contractual systems firms choose, on the structure of the auditing profession, and on accounting education.

Government and Public-Good Organizations

Government plays three important accounting roles. First, government is a contracting agent in ordinary firms, sometimes as a customer or vendor, and almost always as a tax collector. Since the government must simultaneously deal with millions of taxpayers, the economics of tax collection dictates relatively objective, nonjudgmental methods of accounting for the determination of tax liability of individual taxpayers. The bilateral monopoly between the federal government as a customer and defense contractors as vendors of weapon systems generates custom-designed accounting systems for enforcing defense procurement contracts.

Second, the government acts as a super-firm in setting the laws, rules, and regulations in certain areas of accounting. This effort produces template contracts that can form the starting point of negotiations among the agents participating in an organization. These templates save negotiating effort, search costs, and time, just as preprinted lease forms do for tenant and landlord. The template contracts are fleshed out in negotiations among the participating agents. The imposition of mandatory audit requirements on publicly held firms and the laws governing the training and licensing of auditors are examples of such template contracts.

Finally, government itself is an organization. It, too, is a set of contracts among a large number of agents. These contracts also need to be implemented and enforced efficiently. Accounting and control systems of government and many not-for-profit organizations differ significantly from those of business organizations. These differences can be understood in terms of the economic characteristics of the output of various organizations. Customers of private goods must be enticed to buy them in arm's length transactions. These customers impose a market discipline on the managers. This discipline is weak in natural monopolies and absent in public-good-producing organizations. Additional constraints on managerial behavior and lower levels of discretionary freedom granted to such managers is an attempt to provide an equilibrium system of controls for them. The differences in the accounting and control systems, and indeed, in their organizational structure, can be understood in terms of the economic characteristics of the output of natural monopolies and government and not-for-profit organizations.

Summary

A theory of accounting must cover all important aspects of accounting activity in an integrated framework. The contract model of organization provides such a simple but comprehensive framework. The thumbnail sketch of contract theory of accounting and control given in this chapter is fleshed out in the remainder of this book.

Notes

[1]Richard M. Cyert and James March, *A Behavioral Theory of the Firm* (Englewood Cliffs, N.J.: Prentice-Hall, 1963); Herbert A. Simon, *Administrative Behavior* (New York: Macmillan, 1947); Chester I. Barnard, *The Functions of the Executive,* 30th anniversary ed. (Cambridge, Mass.: Harvard University Press, 1968); J. J. Rousseau, *The Social Contract* (New York: Hafner Publishing Co., 1947).

[2]Robert J. Aumann, "Agreeing to Disagree," *The Annals of Statistics*, Vol. 4, No. 6 (1976), pp. 1236–39.

[3]Yuji Ijiri, *Theory of Accounting Measurement. Studies in Accounting Research, No. 10* (Sarasota, Fla.: American Accounting Association, 1975).

[4]Chester I Barnard, *The Functions of the Executive*, 30th anniversary ed. (Cambridge, Mass.: Harvard University Press, 1968); Herbert A. Simon, *Administrative Behavior*, (New York: Macmillan, 1947).

[5]J. J. Rousseau, op. cit.

,2,

Accounting and the Contract Model of the Firm

• •

Accounting helps make a firm work. To understand accounting, the firm itself must be understood. What is the nature of the firm? What are its components, and how do they fit together? How does it operate, and what is the role of accounting in making it work? We pursue these questions in this chapter.

Much of the discussion of firms is applicable to organizations in general. Accounting is an essential aspect of the working of government, not-for-profit, and even religious organizations. Some of these organizational forms and the special features of accounting needed to help operate them are discussed in Chapter 13.

There are many ways of looking at the firm, each suited for a different purpose. The neoclassical model of microeconomic textbooks sees the firm as a monolithic profit-maximizer. This model is designed to explain equilibrium in markets for inputs and outputs of the firm, and not its internal workings. It is no more reasonable to expect the neoclassical model to help describe and analyze the accounting system of a firm than it is for microeconomic consumer theory to explain the structure and dynamics of a family. The neoclassical model of the firm with perfect markets has no people, organization, or need for information, and therefore has no role for accounting in operating a firm.

The beginnings of a model of the firm that can help analyze the role of accounting lie in the work of Berle and Means, Coase, Barnard, Simon, and Cyert and March. In 1932, Berle and Means documented the separation of managerial control from stock ownership in major corporations of the United States. They argued that the interests of shareholders and managers diverge significantly, and therefore the behavior of modern corporations differs significantly from the behavior of entrepreneur-run firms of the neoclassical models.[1] Implicit in their critique of the modern corporation (as an efficient device for resource use and allocation in society) is the need for mechanisms that align the diverse interests of stockholders and managers. Accounting helps carry out this function.

In 1937, Coase asked why firms grow beyond the elemental unit of a single person firm, and why they do not grow indefinitely until all economic activity in the society is conducted by a single firm. His answer: It is costly to use markets.[2] Cheung identified four types of these costs: cost of discovering the relevant prices, cost of knowing the characteristics of products, cost of measurement, and cost of identifying the contribution of individuals to collaborative effort.[3] Contracts based on market transactions are internalized by the firm when it is cheaper to do so. In this book we shall see how accounting and control of firms helps reduce the costs of carrying out these contracts.

Barnard thought of organizations as "system(s) of consciously coordinated activities or forces of two or more persons."[4] Stability of the organization, he argued, depends on its ability to provide sufficient incentives or inducements to individuals so they find it more desirable to participate in the organization than to quit. A mere six years after Berle and Means labored to document the separation of share ownership and control in large publicly held firms, it is interesting to find Barnard, a telephone company executive (apparently unaware of their work), taking it for granted that it is the executive and not the shareholder who plays a critical role in the survival of organizations.

Cooper recognized the inadequacy of the entrepreneurial theories of the firm for the purpose of understanding the organization.[5] Simon refined Barnard's view of organizations, making it formal and precise.[6] Simon's representation of an organization as a set of arrangements among various factors of production, each motivated by personal, though not necessarily egoistic, considerations, provides the basic framework on which the accounting theory of this book is erected. Cyert and March saw the firm as a coalition of multiple, conflicting interests using standard rules and procedures.[7] The existence of diverse interests within the firm, and visualization of the firm as a set of contracts among these interests, are the two ideas in the contract model of the firm presented in the next section. The following chapters analyze a variety of accounting phenomena using this model.

In the half-century since publication of these seminal works, much has been done to clarify, refine, revise, and develop the relevant ideas. Alchian and Demsetz, Williamson, Jensen and Meckling, and Fama are some of the important contributors to this literature, reviewed by Cyert and March and Moe.[8]

The Firm as a Set of Contracts

To understand accounting, the firm can be seen as a set of contracts among rational agents. Contracts can be explicit or implicit, short-term or long-term. Agents can have different preferences and different endowments of capital, skills, and information. Agents are rational in the sense that, within the constraints of their opportunities and information, they do not knowingly pick less desirable courses of action over the more desirable ones.

Figure 2.1   **The Firm as a Set of Contracts Among Agents**

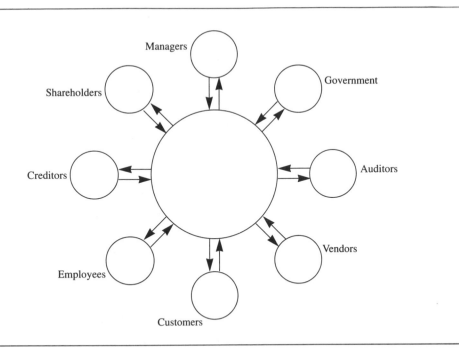

Agents enter into contracts to improve their lot. Contracts obligate each agent to contribute resources—capital, skills, or information—to the organization's pool and, in return, entitle each agent to receive resources from the pool. The form, amount, and timing of resources an agent gives and receives is a matter for bargaining among agents. We use the terms *entitlements*, *incentives*, and *inducements* interchangeably for resources agents receive or expect to receive (see Figure 2.1).

Contributions and inducements can be economic or noneconomic, and a general theory of organizations must consider both, as Barnard and Simon do.[9] Accounting deals mostly with quantifiable economic resource flows in organizations, such as money and machinery. We therefore limit the discussion here to economic variables. A simple theory of accounting can be based on a simple model of organizations, excluding variables that accounting does not usually handle (such as sincerity and enthusiasm of an employee). The price of simplicity is the incompleteness of the theory, because the control system is influenced by these omitted variables.

Whether an agent joins a firm depends on what the agent has to offer, what he or she wants to get, and what alternative courses of action are available. A rational agent does not enter a contract that promises less than the best alternatives known and available. An agent could consume the resources he or she has, use them to

Table 2.1	Contributions and Entitlements of Various Agents		
Type of Agent		**Contribution**	**Entitlement**
Shareholder		Equity capital	Dividend, residual value
Manager		Skills	Salary, bonus, benefits
Employee		Skills	Salary, wages, benefits
Vendor		Goods, services	Cash
Customer		Cash	Goods, services
Lender/creditor		Loan capital	Interest, principal
Government		Public goods	Taxes
Auditor		Services	Fees

produce something else, or enter a contract with other agents. The last course of action amounts to "joining" a firm and accepting a package of obligations and entitlements. Rationality means that the agent would do so only if this package is more desirable than the alternatives available. A person looking to buy a suit "joins" the firm of Hart Schaffner & Marx as a customer only if he likes their suits and service and does not know of a place where he can do better.

Who are these agents? Agents are people with personal tastes and economic resources. Homogenous groups of agents with similar tastes and endowments can be thought of as a single agent for our purposes. An industrial firm, for example, could be thought of as a set of contracts among agents who provide equity and debt capital, trade credit, labor, managerial skills, auditing services, raw materials, cash, utilities, infrastructural facilities, and security, and buy products and services from the firm. Self-motivated mutual cooperation of these agents makes the firm possible. Other types of organizations can be similarly defined as contracts among an appropriate set of agents (see Table 2.1).

Defining the exact boundaries of a firm is neither feasible nor necessary. As in any modeling effort, which agents and which contracts are included in the analysis depends on its purpose. The contract model of the firm has the flexibility to help study a rich variety of accounting phenomena. A general model of the firm includes contracts involving all transacting agents. To explain a particular aspect of the behavior of the firm, attention can be focused on the relevant subsets of agents. For example, in examining the separation of ownership and control, Berle and Means and Jensen and Meckling focus on the behavior of two classes of agents—shareholders (the suppliers of equity capital) and managers (the suppliers of managerial skills).[10] In analysis of financial accounting, three classes of agents—investors, managers, and auditors—play the critical roles and receive most of the attention. For tax accounting, government is also an important agent; for payroll and benefits accounting, employees are an important class of agents.

An individual may be an agent in several firms. No single firm might need all the resources the person has to offer, or provide all the person needs. Examples include investors holding diversified equity portfolios; independent auditors; part-time or moonlighting employees; and a welder who works for one firm, buys a car from a second, and invests savings in shares of a third. Indeed, participation in multiple organizations is a norm, not an exception. This point is well made by Barnard:

> I select at random a man who is chiefly identified by his connection with the organization with which I am also ordinarily identified. He is an engineer whose career and living for many years have depended upon that organization. Without special enquiry, I know he has the following organization connections also: He is (1) a citizen of the United States, the State of New Jersey, the County of Essex, and the City of Newark—four organizations to which he has many inescapable obligations; he is a member of (2) the Catholic Church; (3) the Knights of Columbus; (4) the American Legion; (5) the Outanaway Golf Club; (6) the Democratic Party; (7) the Princeton Club of Newark; (8) he is a stockholder in three corporations; (9) he is head of his own family (wife and three children); (10) he is a member of his father's family; (11) he is a member of his wife's family; (12) to judge from his behavior he belongs to other less formal organizations (but often seems not be aware of it) which affect what he wears, how he talks, what he eats, what he likes to do, how he thinks about many things; and (13) finally he gives evidence of "belonging" also to himself alone occasionally. Lest it be thought that his "major" connection is predominant, and the others trivial, it may be stated that he devotes to it nominally less than 25 percent of his approximately 8760 hours per annum; and that actually while he thinks he is working, and despite his intentions, he dreams of fishing, reflects on family matters, and replays a part of the previous evening's bridge, etc.[11]

Therefore, the term *agent* refers to a particular aspect of a person's behavior and not to the person himself (see Figure 2.2).

A firm consists of a *set of relationships or contracts*, explicit or implicit, that link its shareholders, managers, and employees, and so on, into certain patterns of expectations and behavior. The gap between the concept of contract in law and the lay concept of promise and mutual expectations is not as wide as it may appear to be. Texaco paid several billion dollars in damages to Pennzoil because the court found that Texaco had interfered in the verbal promise made to Pennzoil by a third party. However, the willingness of courts to enforce contracts is less than total, and certainly falls short of the popular impressions of such willingness. MacNeil states:

> A less than total commitment to the keeping of promises is reflected in countless ways in the legal system. The most striking is the modesty of its remedial commitment; contract remedies are generally among the weakest of those the legal system can deliver. But a host of doctrines and techniques lies in the way even of those remedies: impossibility, frustration, mistake, manipulative interpretation, jury discretion, consideration, illegality, duress,

Figure 2.2   Multiple Roles of an Individual as Agent in Various Organizations

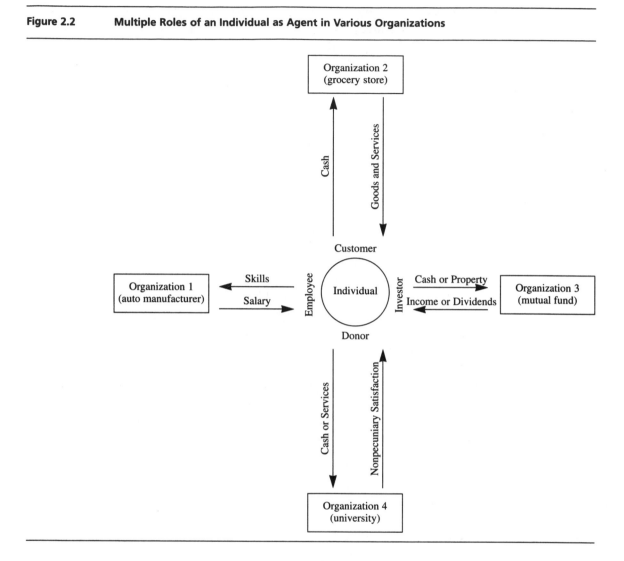

undue influence, unconscionability, capacity, forfeiture and penalty rules, doctrines of substantial performance, severability, bankruptcy laws, statutes of frauds, to name some; almost any contract doctrine can and does serve to make the commitment of the legal system to promise keeping less than complete.[12]

A firm does not consist of the agents themselves. Molecules that constitute an organism come and go, but the pattern of arrangement of molecules—the organism—persists. Similarly, individuals who participate in an organization come and go, often replaced in their positions by others with similar tastes and endowments; the pattern of contractual arrangements that persists is the firm. Of course, persistence is not permanence; organisms as well as organizations may grow, transform, reproduce or die.

The contract model of the firm differs from the neoclassical model in micro-economic textbooks. In the neoclassical model, the firm is an *actor*, operated by the entrepreneur–manager who has a well-defined objective, usually profit. From this perspective, all other economic agents are outsiders. In the contract model, the firm itself is not an economic actor, has no objective or motivation of its own, and is not identifiable with any agent. Instead, it is seen as an arena in which self-motivated economic agents play by mutually agreed upon or implied rules to achieve their respective objectives. This arrangement itself is labeled *firm* for convenience. A firm is not a purposive entity.

Stripping purpose from the concept of firm might appear to be a major departure from Barnard and Simon, who emphasize the purpose of organizations. However, a closer scrutiny makes it clear that most of what they call organizational purpose consists of the purposes of some subset of agents participating in the organization, usually shareholders, managers, or customers.[13] Simon recognizes this arbitrariness[14] but discards it altogether in his 1952 article and treats all agents symmetrically.

> In the F-theory, a single participant, the entrepreneur, is explicitly treated as a rational individual. The other participants—employees, customers, suppliers—enter into the theory only implicitly and only as passive "conditions" to which the entrepreneur adjusts in finding the solution that is optimal to him. . . . In the O-theory, the participants are generally treated in a more symmetrical fashion. Each participant is offered an *inducement* for his participation in the organization. Through his participation, he makes a *contribution* to the organization. The participant's contributions may be regarded as "factors," the inducements offered to him as "products."[15]

Cyert and March state:

> Ultimately it makes only slightly more sense to say that the goal of a business organization is to maximize profit than to say that its goal is to maximize the salary of Sam Smith, Assistant to the Janitor.[16]

Most organizations do, however, post a "statement of objectives" in their charter. It is tempting to argue on the basis of such statements that the objective of Chrysler Corporation, for example, is to manufacture and sell cars to the public. The irrelevance of such statements of objectives for our purpose can immediately be seen by asking: Would the Chrysler Corporation still manufacture cars if all participating agents felt that *each of them* would be better off if Chrysler produced, say, blue jeans instead?

In the contract model, objectives attach to people, not organizations. When applied to organizations, they are simply a description of the activity that the participants agree to engage in. For example, operating a blood bank is an activity that agents participating in the Red Cross may agree to for a variety of motivations. The Red Cross's statement of objectives, which may include operation of a blood bank, has little power to explain the behavior of these agents who may, one day, decide to abandon blood banks in favor of organ banks or ambulance services.

Demsetz writes: "The chief mission of neoclassical economics is to understand how the price system coordinates the use of resources, not to understand the inner working of real firms."[17] Let us explore the usefulness of the contract model to understand the internal workings of the firm—that is, its accounting and control.

Accounting and the Firm

Accounting helps implement and enforce contracts that constitute the firm. Accounting performs five functions to make the firm work.

1. It measures the input of each agent to the firm's pool of resources.
2. It determines and disburses the contractual entitlement of each agent.
3. It informs appropriate agents about the extent to which other agents have fulfilled their contractual obligations and received their entitlements.
4. It helps maintain a liquid market for contractual slots and for the factors of production supplied by their occupants so that the resignation or termination of one agent does not threaten the existence of the firm.
5. Since contracts of various agents are periodically renegotiated, it provides a pool of common knowledge of verified information to all participants to facilitate negotiation and contract formation.

These five functions are key to understanding the nature of accounting. Before analyzing these functions, two caveats must be posted. Accounting is one of several necessary parts of the contract enforcement mechanism of a firm. The other parts are common, civil, and criminal law, along with their enforcement and adjudication systems, and the sociocultural norms. Our analysis is limited to accounting aspects of the enforcement mechanism; analyses of the legal and social systems are available elsewhere. Indeed, the application of methods of economics to analysis of law, organizations, and society by Coase, Posner, Coleman, Hirschmann, and others provided our inspiration for a similar approach to accounting.[18]

To a certain degree, a firm can choose the accounting as well as the legal regime that applies to it. The legal form of the business organization (proprietorship, partnership, cooperative, or corporation) and the place of business and incorporation determine the applicable laws. Agents have some freedom in selecting the accounting regime under which their contract set operates. This overlap between accounting and law is the subject matter of Chapter 12.

Accounting itself is a part of the set of contracts it helps operate and is subject to bargaining among agents. Like a hand that feeds the body of which it is a part, the functioning of the accounting and control of a firm also is recursive.

Measuring Contributions

Accounting and controls are designed efficiently to measure and record the resources contributed by agents and to compare them against their contractual obligations All factor inputs are not equally measurable. The cost of measuring them with equal accuracy may differ, and equal cost measurements may have different accuracy for different resources. Some resources, like physical labor, materials, goods, equipment, and cash can be measured reliably and cheaply. Various parts of accounting, such as attendance registers, time clocks, receiving dock procedures, and cash registers, routinely and inexpensively measure such factor inputs.

The input of managers and certain employees is more elusive. Direct measurement is either too costly (e.g., night guard at the bank) or simply impossible (e.g., chief executive officer). Contracts of such agents have to be such that they can be enforced even without precise measurement of their inputs. A self-enforcing contract is one such device. "In a self-enforcing agreement each party decides unilaterally whether he is better off continuing or stopping his relation with the other parties. He stops if and only if the current gain from stopping exceeds the expected present value of his gains from continuing. No outside party intervenes to enforce the agreement, to determine whether there have been violations, to assess damages, and to impose penalties."[19]

A self-enforcing contract reduces the agent's incentive to shirk, and thus lessens the need to directly measure the agent's contribution. Top managers and outside auditors are examples of such agents. We discuss their contracts in Chapters 4 and 8, respectively. Contractual involvement of customers, vendors, and labor in the firm and its accounting takes relatively simple forms because their contributions and entitlements are easily measurable. On the other hand, deep involvement of the U.S. Department of Defense in the accounting and control of its cost-plus contractors is an interesting exception, caused by the difficulty of measuring the entitlements. We return to this topic in Chapter 12.

Measuring Entitlements

A firm's contract set entitles each participant to receive resources from the firm. The second major function of accounting is to determine who gets what. For example, the accounting system may determine the wages and benefits of factory workers as a function of their measured contributions in time worked or quantity produced. Receivables, payables, purchasing, inventory, and shipping accounts keep track of the entitlements of customers, vendors, and other agents involved in the firm. Loan accounts measure the entitlements of the creditors.

As just stated, when the input of an agent is not easily measurable, entitlements cannot be determined by a simple function of measured input. Rewarding an agent on the basis of a measurable contribution that is poorly related to the actual but unobserved contribution may induce behavior that is unacceptable to other contracting agents. This is especially true of top managers and auditors. When the direct measure of an agent's input is difficult, entitlements are either fixed in advance and thus made independent of measured input or are made to depend on surrogate measures, such as some measure of output. The former method is used for auditors; a combination determines the compensation of top managers.

Shareholders contribute capital and bear risk. Cash contributions are easy to measure but the value of in-kind contributions must be estimated before entry into capital accounts. Shareholders invest in the firm without a guarantee that they will receive a return on it.

Shareholders do not bear *all* the risk, only a relatively large part of it. Risk arises either from acts of nature or when one or more contracting agents behave differently than what others expected of them: customers may fail to return to buy the firm's products, employees may demand higher wages and go on strike, managers may prove to be extraordinarily shortsighted or incompetent, and the auditors may prove to be negligent or worse in their duties. Such unexpectedly bad performance on the part of any agent drains the pool of wealth represented by the firm from which all agents draw their share, just as unexpectedly good performance increases the wealth. Some agents may be shielded from short-term variations in the size of this pool of wealth, but sooner or later, all are affected to some degree. For example, customers risk not being able to obtain spares, employees may lose jobs, auditors lose clients and reputations, and managers lose both jobs and reputations.

Perhaps the key difference between shareholders and other agents is not that the former bear the residual risk of the firm. The shareholders have little flexibility, having bought the stock, to improve their contractual terms with other agents, and thereby to affect the total size of the pool of wealth. (They can, of course, dump the stock and lower the price, but they themselves end up bearing the brunt of such loss of wealth.) In this sense, the equity holders as a class are almost completely *precommitted* with respect to this set of contracts and are therefore passive bystanders after the primary issue of the stock is completed. This resource precommitment, or the relinquishment of the right to periodically recontract, is combined with the right to choose managers. These features of the shareholders' contract distinguish them from all other agents.

The precommitment of capital by shareholders is coupled with their status as residual claimants. Given the size of the total wealth pool of the firm, and n classes of agents, at most n-1 entitlements can be determined independently. The nth entitlement is determined by the first n-1, and is not directly linked to the corresponding input. This lack of a direct link between input and entitlement, necessary because there are only n-1 degrees of freedom in allocating wealth to n agents, is accepted by the group of shareholders as a *quid pro quo* for rights to all residual wealth. Double-entry bookkeeping is designed to measure the entitlement of the shareholders as a residual. Once the entitlement of the shareholders *as a group* has been determined, the allocation of this entitlement among the individual shareholders is proportional to their contributions.

Distribution of Information About Contract Fulfillment

Agents want to know if they have received what they contracted for. Some agents know their contributions and their entitlements without the help of the firm's accounting system, especially if their entitlements are independent of others'. Creditors, vendors, and customers are examples of such agents. They are interested in the firm's accounting and control to help minimize and promptly resolve any disputes through provision of shared information. Preparation of bills, invoices, and other documents helps efficient settlements.

Other agents, such as hourly or weekly workers and many salaried employees, often depend on the accounting and control to measure their input and entitlements, even though their entitlements are largely independent of the inputs and entitlements of others. The payroll accounting system provides enough data to these agents so they can verify if the terms of their contract have been fulfilled. They are interested in the accuracy of accounts. They are also interested in the overall financial performance of the firm because it determines the prospects for continued employment. Financial data become especially important when a labor contract is renegotiated.

It is hardly surprising that shareholders, agents who depend on the inputs and entitlements of other agents for their own entitlements, exhibit keen interest in ensuring that others fulfill their contract. Accounting is designed efficiently to provide shareholders with information about the fulfillment of contracts by other agents. Much of the cost accounting system, which includes job order or process costing, cost allocation, transfer pricing, and budgeting, is designed to enable managers in a decentralized firm to evaluate contract fulfillment by other managers at subordinate levels of the organization. Accounting also enables the top managers to determine if they themselves have received the compensation due to them.

Shareholders are not obligated to contribute more resources. However, creditors use the accounting system to monitor if shareholders withdraw more resources than their contractual due in the form of dividends or stock repurchases. Shareholders themselves, being most vulnerable to excess withdrawals by other agents, use the accounting and control to monitor, through the board of directors and with the help of outside auditors, that the top managers do not take more than their due and are worth what they receive.

Finally, the client's accounting and control, which is the object of verification by auditors, cannot, in principle, be the instrument to determine whether the auditors have fulfilled their contract. Therefore, the auditors' fees are set outside the firm's accounting system and verification of their input is governed by laws on auditors' responsibility. Critics of the current structure of the audit industry often object when auditors are retained for recruitment of managers and other advisory services. To the extent the information and revenue related to audit and non-audit services are interdependent, the sale of both types of services from auditor to the client contaminates the incentives of the auditor and diminishes the effectiveness of the independent audit. Chapter 8 includes a more detailed discussion of the audit industry.

Liquidity of Markets for Contractual Slots

Individuals or groups who occupy contractual slots in a firm occasionally wish to vacate their positions. If the law and the existing contracts permit, they sell their slots to other agents who might be willing to accept or renegotiate the terms of the contract associated with that slot. Although shareholder and creditor positions in firms are easily capitalized and frequently sold, they are not the only ones. Exclusive contracts to supply goods and services to a firm can sometimes be sold to other suppliers. Exclusive contracts to buy goods and services from a firm, called *distributorships*, are also sold. Even the top management positions can be "sold"—in a negotiated corporate merger, the top executives of the acquired corporation are sometimes handed "golden parachutes," which are financial bonuses for relinquishing their positions. If the capitalized value of the slot is negative, the agent will have to *pay* a price. For example, Westinghouse Electric Corporation bought itself out of long-term contracts to supply nuclear fuel to certain electric power utilities by paying hundreds of millions of dollars.

Owners of salable contractual slots have an interest in creating and maintaining a liquid market for them. Firms distribute information about the rights, obligations, and record of profitability of each slot to the potential buyers. Fear of manipulation or selective release of information can make potential buyers skeptical of the reliability of such information. Arrow suggests that asymmetric distribution of information diminishes the efficiency of market outcomes.[20] To attract new contracting agents, firms release audited accounting information about past performance. They may also include their assessment of future prospects of shareholder and creditor slots in the firm to the potential entrants.

Such information about future prospects can be self-serving. Williamson uses the term *information impactedness* to describe a "derivative condition that arises mainly because of uncertainty and opportunism."[21] He suggests that "the reason why outsiders are not on a parity with insiders is usually because outsiders lack firm-specific, task-specific, or transaction-specific experience. Such experience is a valuable resource and can be used in strategic ways by those who, being awarded initial contracts, have acquired it."[22] Only verifiable information can be *effectively* communicated to potential buyers.

Even if the current occupants of contractual slots in the firm cannot sell them, they often have an interest in making their contributions to the firm known to other potential buyers of the resources they have to offer. The "free" distribution of accounting information of a firm to nonparticipating agents is particularly important for suppliers of skills that are difficult to measure. Managers, auditors, or consultants carry much of their earning capacity in the form of reputation and are, therefore, interested in various aspects of the accounting system that help create a market for their services.

Finally, the agent interested in leaving the firm is not the only one interested in creating a market for these slots. All other participants in the firm are also interested in promptly filling a vacated slot if leaving it vacant reduces their own welfare. Indeed, much of the risk of participation in a firm arises from the unexpected departure of coparticipants. Departure of customers lowers sales, departure of employees lowers production, departure of managers lowers efficiency, and departure of auditors lowers the credibility of the accounting and control. The remaining agents are adversely affected if nonredundant vacated slots are not filled. Corporate restructuring, a popular U.S. practice in the mid-nineties, aims to cut the redundant workforce and plant. In amateur hands, the knife can cut out meat along with fat, killing the patient.

It is in the participants' interest to create and maintain a liquid market for the inputs the firm needs. The accounting and control is designed, in part, to help create such markets for equity and loan capital, managerial and other human skills, equipment, materials and supplies, and products and services. It helps to create security markets as well as to recruit managers and engineers, and it assures vendors and customers that the firm is a reliable business partner. A substantial part of the print order of annual reports of large publicly held corporations is distributed to nonparticipating agents. W.R. Grace, for example, prints four times as many annual reports as it has shareholders and advertises the report in financial publications.[23] The importance of the role played by financial analysts, the business press, and other information intermediaries in accounting is explained by the help they provide in maintaining the liquidity of markets for the inputs and outputs of the firm.

Common Knowledge for Renegotiation of Contracts

The length of individual contracts in a firm varies in time as well as in the number of transactions covered. A contract to buy or sell could be a one-time deal or a long-term commitment. The same is true of employment and borrowing. The audit contract is usually negotiated each year. With the exception of shareholders, whose commitment is open-ended, all contracts are periodically renegotiated.

The fifth function of accounting is to provide information in the form of common knowledge in order to facilitate contract renegotiation among current participants. Although agents may also use additional private information, availability of a common verified database helps eliminate certain types of strategic bargaining that may make some participants worse off without improving the lot of any.

The practice of negotiated renewal of contracts is an intermediate solution between (1) starting a fresh search for potential participants in the appropriate factor market at the conclusion of each transaction, and (2) entering long-term or permanent, comprehensive contracts. Uncertainty, changing environment, and boundedness of human foresight rule out rigid, long-term comprehensive contracts.[24] The magnitude of the incremental costs of conducting frequent transactions in many factor markets renders the first option uneconomical. In addition, participants in the firm learn about local conditions, tasks, and techniques from their past experience in their contract slots. Their increased efficiency makes it attractive for other participants to want to retain them in the contract set. However, the special knowledge an agent acquires on the job is not available either to the manager who may negotiate the agent's contract on behalf of the firm, or to the potential replacements of the agent drawn from the appropriate factor market. Existing participants seek to exploit this special knowledge by demanding a larger share of resources. Competition among many such participants reduces their ability to increase their compensation. But contract renewal negotiation can give rise to prolonged conflicts.

The basic theme that the efficiency of economic relations depends on the ability of agents to renew contracts by adjusting them to the changing environment occurs through-out economics. Commons emphasized the role of organizations in promoting continuity of relationships by reducing actual or potential conflict.[25] Hayek insisted on the importance of rapid adaptation to changes in "particular circumstances of time and place."[26] Arrow analyzed the importance of minimizing the cost of bargaining among agents in organizations.[27]

Wiggins and Libecap provide a dramatic illustration of how large the deadweight losses to social welfare can be when asymmetric distribution of information prevents economic agents from arriving at mutually beneficial arrangements.[28] Owners of leases that cover a single underground pool can extract oil and gas independently, or can form a partnership and operate the field as a single unit. Unitization of oil fields yields large gains, as much as 100 or 200 percent, in the value of extractable hydrocarbons. Yet, for a majority of oil fields in the United States, lease owners are unable to conclude negotiations for unitization of their leases. Recovery of oil from independently operated leases leads to inefficient utilization of the underground pressure of gas to get the oil out and reduces the extent of secondary recovery. This loss frequently amounts to hundred of millions of dollars. However, since the lease owners and their engineers have superior information about the value of their own leases rather than of the value of other leases, negotiations often break down because the parties fail to agree on the relative shares of the net profits from the unitized operation of the field. It is interesting to note that the same lease owners apparently have no difficulty in sharing the cost of exploratory drilling on neighboring lease tracts, because there is no information asymmetry at that stage of negotiations. Most of the unitization that does take place in the United States occurs during the secondary recovery phase of oil fields. By that time most of the information about the relevant characteristics of various leases has passed into public domain, and it becomes easier to reach an agreement.

Accounting includes some precommitments to reduce information asymmetries among contracting parties by sharing a common base of information in the form of public disclosure. Public financial statements, disclosure of accounting policies and significant details in footnotes, management's analysis of financial statements and results, and even financial forecasts have the effect of reducing surprises at the time of contract renegotiation. The losses to society from such surprises and the confrontational attitudes they engender can be so large and have such significant externalities that securities laws in the United States and in many other countries require public disclosure by publicly held firms. In the later half of the nineteenth century, state regulators in the United States used public disclosure as an instrument to reduce confrontation between railroads and a suspicious public.[29]

Private disclosure to those who request information is deemed insufficient. If information were only privately available, many agents may have reason to doubt that others have received the information and, therefore, may be tempted to behave strategically.[30] Public disclosure laws abate such behavior by making financial statements common knowledge.

Correspondence Between Organizational and Accounting Forms

Accounting adapts to the size and form of organization or contract set it serves. To illustrate this point, consider three stylized forms of business organizations and the kind of accounting that serve each form.

Bookkeeping

The corner grocery store or fruit stand, operated by its proprietor with little or no outside help, is an elemental business organization. The owner may use personal savings or borrow to finance the operation, may lease the premises, and buy daily or weekly from wholesalers on credit and sell for cash to the customers. Few of these agents, other than the tax collectors and, perhaps, the grocer's creditors, depend on the grocer's accounts to carry out exchanges with the firm. Most of the grocer's accounting effort goes into recording transactions as a memory aid. Much of it could be dispensed with if the grocer's memory were better. This form of business organization, without managerial hierarchy and with a closely held residual interest, is the oldest and, even today, most numerous. Accounting that serves such an organization, largely as a record to aid memory and convenient organization of data, has long been known as bookkeeping. This is the classical model of accounting.

Managerial Accounting

If the grocery store grows until the grocer cannot perform all the managerial work alone, a second organizational form comes into being. The residual interest in such a firm is still closely held, but it is decentralized and has a managerial hierarchy. The problems accounting must solve in such an organization are more complex.

The aid-to-memory role of classical bookkeeping is still necessary, but not sufficient. The contribution of managers cannot be measured directly. A more complex system is designed to evaluate and control the performance of such agents in the firm. Budgets, transfer prices, and interdepartmental and interperiod allocations of costs and revenues are some of the devices used for this purpose in such organizations. Note that these tools of managerial accounting are rarely used or useful in the mom-and-pop grocery store. This more complex form of accounting can be labeled the managerial accounting or stewardship model. It includes bookkeeping as an important component.

Financial Reporting

Finally, consider a third firm that is internally decentralized and in which the number of shareholders has become so large that they can no longer exercise direct control over the activities of the managers. At this stage, the firm's system expands to the financial reporting model. Either because of the diffusion of ownership, or because of heterogeneity of interests among the nonmanagement agents, agents find it worthwhile to pay for the services of an independent auditor to verify the information provided by management. The demand for audited reports by banks and other creditors is an example of this latter phenomenon.[31] The presence of a third party to attest to the veracity of the information produced by management characterizes the financial reporting model. Financial accounting always includes bookkeeping and almost always includes managerial accounting, depending on the degree of internal decentralization.

Distinctions between bookkeeping and accounting, and between financial and managerial accounting, have long been a matter of discussion among accountants. Bookkeeping is said to be procedural or mechanical, while accounting is judgmental or discretionary. Managerial and financial accounting are differentiated on the basis of internal and external use of the data provided by them. Such distinctions have become deeply ingrained in the organization of accounting curricula and textbooks.

In contrast, the correspondence between forms of accounting and organizations does not divide the accounting of a firm into several parts. Instead, it relates the entire system of accounting to the organizational form. Accounting scholars have long recognized and analyzed this connection. Hatfield recognized the separation of ownership and control and the diffusion of ownership as the two important breakpoints in organizational forms that drive accounting.[32] Yamey traced the historical evolution of organizational and accounting forms.[33] Skinner also identified a similar correspondence between accounting and organizational forms.[34] Littleton described this relationship as follows:

> Accounting has always been primarily a service tool of enterprise management. Morality is clearly involved here. As long as an owner–operator was the only person concerned, accounting could only be operative in a very pri-

vate and personal way. If deception was involved, it was self-deception, except, of course, where an embezzling bookkeeper would try to falsify the records. Wherever partners operated a business, there was need for a factual record to which certain differences of opinion could be referred. Accounting, however, was still a personal service, although it must be said that a partner had more opportunity than a bookkeeper to falsify the facts into a deceptive picture. When we think of limited liability corporations of today, with hired managers and large numbers of absentee stockholders, it becomes evident that the moral scope of accounting has been vastly expanded. Many people, wholly out of touch with the physical aspects of enterprise operation, depend upon future representations of managerial actions, of results of actions, and of potentialities for future actions. As the size of enterprises increases and the distance between the owner-lenders and the operating managers grows wider, the opportunities expand for the practice of deceit by people of authority.[35]

Summary

Each organization develops accounting suitable to its own unique characteristics so that it may serve as an effective instrument of control. In small business firms, the control function is best served by bookkeeping; in decentralized firms with tight ownership, by managerial accounting; and in decentralized firms with diffuse ownership, by financial accounting. The contract theory of accounting and control helps us integrate this variety of organizational and accounting forms into a unified framework.

Accounting makes contracts work. Accounting affects agents, and is a matter of negotiation and bargaining among them. The choice of accounting is a part of the contracts it helps to implement. The contractual form that ties each agent to the firm depends on the characteristics of the resource the agent contributes and receives. The contractual form, in turn, determines the agent's interest in various aspects of the firm's accounting. In the six chapters of Part Two, we focus attention on the differences among three important types of agents—managers, investors, and auditors. Attention shifts to systemwide issues in the five chapters of Part Three.

Notes

[1] Although this idea can be traced back to Ripley, Veblen, and even to Adam Smith, Berle and Means made the most effective argument. George J. Stigler and Claire Friedland discuss the earlier literature in "The Literature of Economics: The Case of Berle and Means," *Journal of Law and Economics*, Vol. 26 (June 1983), pp. 237–268. See also William Z. Ripley, *Main Street and Wall Street* (Boston: Little Brown & Co., 1927); Thorstein Veblen, *Absentee Ownership and Business Enterprise in Recent Times* (New York: B.W. Huebsch, Inc., 1923), and Adam Smith, *An Inquiry*

Into the Nature and Causes of the Wealth of Nations (London, 1776). Also see A. A. Berle and G. C. Means, *The Modern Corporation and Private Property* (New York: Commerce Clearing House, 1932; Macmillan, 1983).

[2] Ronald H. Coase, "The Nature of the Firm," *Economic*, New series, Vol. 4 (November 1937), pp. 386–405.

[3] Steven N. S. Cheung, "The Contractual Nature of the Firm," *Journal of Law and Economics*, Vol. 26 (April 1983), pp. 1–21.

[4] Chester I. Barnard, *The Functions of the Executive,* 30th anniversary ed. (Cambridge, Mass.: Harvard University Press, 1968), p. 73.

[5] W. W. Cooper, "A Proposal for Extending the Theory of the Firm," *Quarterly Journal of Economics*, Vol. 65 (1951), pp. 87–109.

[6] Herbert A. Simon, *Administrative Behavior* (New York: Macmillan, 1947); and "A Comparison of Organization Theories," *Review of Economic Studies*, Vol. 20 (1952–53), pp. 40–48.

[7] See R. M. Cyert and J. G. March, *A Behavioral Theory of the Firm*, 2nd ed. (Englewood Cliffs, N.J.: Prentice-Hall, 1992).

[8] Armen A. Alchian and Harold Demsetz, "Production, Information Costs and Economic Organization," *The American Economic Review*, Vol. 62, No. 5 (December 1972), pp. 777–795; Oliver E. Williamson, *The Economics of Discretionary Behavior: Management Objectives in a Theory of the Firm* (Englewood Cliffs, N.J.: Prentice-Hall, 1964), *Markets and Hierarchies: Analysis and Antitrust Implications* (New York: Free Press, 1975), *The Economic Institutions of Capitalism* (New York: Free Press, 1985), *Organization Theory: From Chester Barnard to Present and Beyond* (New York: Oxford University Press, 1990); Michael C. Jensen and William H. Meckling, "Theory of the Firm: Managerial Behavior, Agency Costs and Ownership Structure," *Journal of Financial Economics*, Vol. 3, No. 4 (October 1976), pp. 305–360; Eugene F. Fama and Michael C. Jensen, "Separation of Ownership and Control," *Journal of Law and Economics*, Vol. 26 (June 1983), pp. 301–325; and Terry M. Moe, "The New Economics of Organization," *American Journal of Political Science* (November 1984), pp. 739–777.

[9] See Barnard; see Simon.

[10] A. A. Berle and G. C. Means, *The Modern Corporation and Private Property* (New York: Commerce Clearing House, 1932; Macmillan, 1983); and Michael C. Jensen and William H. Meckling, "Theory of the Firm: Managerial Behavior, Agency Costs and Ownership Structure," *Journal of Financial Economics*, Vol. 3, No. 4 (October 1976), pp. 305–360.

[11] Barnard, 1938 ed., pp. 71–72.

[12] I. R. Macneil, "The Many Futures of Contracts," *Southern California Law Review*, Vol. 47 (May 1974), pp. 691–816.

[13] Barnard; and Simon.

[14] Simon, p. 113.

[15] Ibid., p. 41.

[16] Cyert and March, p. 34.

[17] Harold Demsetz, "The Structure of Ownership and the Theory of the Firm," *Journal of Law and Economics*, Vol. 26 (June 1983), p. 377.

[18] See Ronald H. Coase, "The Problem of Social Cost," *Journal of Law and Economics*, Vol. 3 (October 1960), pp. 1–44; R. B. Posner, *Economic Analysis of Law* (Boston: Little Brown & Co., 1972); James S. Coleman, *The Asymmetric Society* (Syracuse, N.Y.: Syracuse University Press, 1982); and B. Hirschmann, *Exit, Voice, and Loyalty* (Cambridge, Mass.: Harvard University Press, 1970).

[19] Lester Telser, "A Theory of Self-enforcing Agreements," *Journal of Business*, Vol. 53 (1981), p. 27.

[20] Kenneth J. Arrow, "The Organization of Economic Activity," *The Analysis and Evaluation of Public Expenditure: The PPB System.* Joint Economic Committee, 91st Congress, first session, 1969, pp. 59–73.

[21] Oliver E. Williamson, *Markets and Hierarchies: Analysis and Antitrust Implications* (New York: Free Press, 1975), p. 31.

[22] Ibid.

[23] Peter Verrengia and Roberta Reynes, "Hello and Good Buys," *Management Focus* (PPM) (July–August 1984), p. 14.

[24] See Simon (1947) on bounded rationality and Roy Radner, 1978, on the impracticality of comprehensive contracting. Williamson (1975, 1985) builds the detailed case for incomplete renewable contracts as a characteristic of organizations.

[25] John R. Commons, *Institutional Economics* (Madison: University of Wisconsin Press, 1934).

[26] F. A. Fayek, "The Use of Knowledge in Society," *American Economic Review*, Vol. 35 (September 1945), pp. 519–530.

[27] See John R. Commons, *Institutional Economics* (Madison: University of Wisconsin Press, 1934); F. A. Hayek, "The Use of Knowledge in Society," *American Economic Review*, Vol. 35 (September 1945), pp. 519–530; and Kenneth J. Arrow, *The Limits of Organization* (New York: W. W. Norton and Company, Inc., 1974).

[28] Steven N. Wiggins and Gary D. Libecap, "Oil Field Utilization: Contractual Failure in the Presence of Imperfect Information," *American Economic Review*, Vol. 75, No. 3 (June 1985), pp. 368–385.

[29] Hidetoshi Yamaji, *Kaikei Jouhou Koukai Ron (Theory of Accounting Information Disclosure)* (Kobe: The Research Institute for Economics and Business Administration, Kobe University, 1983); and "Modern Functions of Accounting Information Disclosure," in Yuji Ijiri and Isao Nakano, eds. *Business Behavior and Information* (Pittsburgh: Carnegie Mellon University Press, 1992).

[30] Amin Amershi and Shyam Sunder, "Failure of an Efficient Market to Discipline Managers in a Rational Expectations Economy," *Journal of Accounting Research* (Autumn 1987), pp. 177–195, provide an example of suboptimal resource allocations when the common knowledge assumption is weakened. Strategic behavior implies acting in one's

own best interest after taking into account how others might behave in a given situation.

[31] George J. Benston, *Corporate Financial Disclosure in the UK and the USA* (Lexington, Mass.: Lexington Books, 1976).

[32] Henry Rand Hatfield, "An Historical Defense of Book-keeping," *Journal of Accountancy*, Vol. 34, No. 4 (April 1924), pp. 241–253, reprinted in W. T. Baxter and Sidney Davidson, eds., *Studies in Accounting* (London: Institute of Chartered Accountants in England and Wales, 1977).

[33] B. S. Yamey, "Some Topics in the History of Financial Accounting in England, 1500–1900," in W. T. Baxter and Sidney Davidson, eds., *Studies in Accounting* (London: Institute of Chartered Accountants in England and Wales, 1977).

[34] R. M. Skinner, *Accounting Principles: A Canadian Viewpoint* (Toronto: Canadian Institute of Chartered Accountants, 1972).

[35] A. C. Littleton, *Structure of Accounting Theory* (Sarasota, Fla.: American Accounting Association, 1953).

Additional Reading

Anderson, Gary M., and Robert D. Tollison. "Adam Smith's Analysis of Joint-Stock Companies." *Journal of Political Economy*, Vol. 90 (1982), pp. 234–260.

Aumann, Robert J. "Agreeing to Disagree." *The Annals of Statistics*, Vol. 4, No. 6 (1976), pp. 1236–1239.

Baiman, Stanley. "Agency Research in Managerial Accounting: A Survey." *Journal of Accounting Literature*, Vol. 1 (1982), pp. 154–213.

Butterworth, John E., Michael Gibbins, and Raymond D. King. "The Structure of Accounting Theory: Some Basic Conceptual and Methodological Issues." In Sanjoy Basu and J. Alex Milburn, ed., *Research to Support Standard Setting in Financial Accounting: A Canadian Perspective.* Toronto: Clarkson Gordon Foundation, 1982.

Demski, Joel S., and David E. Sappington. "Sourcing with Unverifiable Performance Information." *Journal of Accounting Research*, Vol. 31, No. 1 (Spring 1993), pp. 1–20.

Dye, Ronald. "Optimal Length of Contracts." *International Economic Review* (1985).

Eldenburg, Leslie, and Naomi Soderstrom. "Accounting System Management by Hospitals in a Changing Regulatory Environment." *Accounting Review*, Vol. 71, No. 1 (January 1996), pp. 23–42.

Fama, Eugene F. "Agency Problems and the Theory of the Firm." *Journal of Political Economy*, Vol. 88, No. 2 (April 1980), pp. 288–307.

Hart, Oliver, and B. Holmstrom. "A Theory of Contracts." In T. Bewley, ed., *Advances in Economic Theory*, Cambridge, England: Cambridge University Press, 1987.

Hermalin, B. "Adverse Selection and Contract Length." Mimeo, Massachusetts Institute of Technology, 1986.

Gjesdal, F. "Accounting for Stewardship." *Journal of Accounting Research*, Vol. 19 (Spring 1981): pp. 208–231.

Liberty, Susan E., and Jerold L. Zimmerman. "Labor Union Contract Negotiations and Accounting Choices." *Accounting Review*, Vol. 61, No. 4 (October 1986), pp. 692–712.

Milgrom, P., and John Roberts. *Economics, Organizations & Management.* Englewood Cliffs, N.J.: Prentice-Hall, 1992.

Perrow, C. *Complex Organizations: A Critical Essay.* New York: Random House, 1986.

Simon, Herbert A. "A Formal Theory of Employment Relationship." *Econometrica* Vol. 19 (1951), pp. 293–305.

Tirole, J. "Hierarchies and Bureaucracies: On the Role of Collusion in Organizations." *Journal of Law, Economics, and Organization*, Vol. 2 (Fall 1986): pp. 181–214.

Tirole, J. *The Theory of Industrial Organization.* Cambridge, Mass.: MIT Press, 1988.

Microtheory of Accounting and Control

Contracting for Managerial Skills

●●●

Managers play the most prominent and visible role in designing, implementing, and enforcing the contracts of a firm. They contribute a variety of managerial skills. Let us look at the relationship between managers and other agents. What are the special characteristics of managers as economic agents? How do these features affect the managers' role in the firm and in its accounting and control?

Characteristics of Managers

The characteristics of managers are the basis for understanding their role in accounting and control. First, managers' wealth takes the form of human capital, and their services for the firm stream out of this capital stock. Second, the quality and quantity of the flow of managers' services are difficult to measure, and this difficulty becomes acute at the higher levels of the managerial hierarchy. Third, managers are continually in contact with other agents, and they are not permitted to work simultaneously for two or more competing firms or organizations in a managerial capacity.

Human Capital

Human capital is inalienable. It is physically impossible to detach the *stock* of human capital from its holder, so there can be no market for such a resource in its capitalized form. Long-term contracts for the *flows* of human capital are legally unenforceable by the buyer in most societies. Such contracts must be designed to be self-enforcing. Defined in Chapter 2, self-enforcing contracts are such that agents find it in their own best interests to do what others expect them to do.

Managerial capital is used on the job, but it does not get used up. On the contrary, much of it is acquired as a byproduct of doing the job. No more than a small part of this capital can be acquired off-the-job, for example, by getting a degree in management. Senior managers, with their large stock of human capital, get paid a great deal more than new entrants—the difference between new MBA and new undergraduate salaries is small in comparison.

Managers receive from firms not only the salary, bonus, fringe benefits, and perquisites, but also the work experience. Experience adds to their human capital and to their future earning power. Accretion of human capital is especially important to younger managers. The accounting and control is relevant to the determination of both the components. Accounting data are an important part of managers' track records and reputations.

The supply of managerial capital is inelastic in the short run because it must be accumulated through on-the-job experience. The supply of senior managers who need more experience is more inelastic. This inelasticity allows managers (as a class) to extract rents from favorable changes in the firm's legal and accounting environment. It also encourages managers to work for favorable changes.

Managerial human capital cannot readily be converted into cash, property, or some other form of human capital. For example, a manager cannot exchange marketing skills for violin playing skills. This barrier to exit from the managerial market makes managers vulnerable to expropriation of their wealth by a firm's legal and accounting environmental changes that are unfavorable to managers as a class. It also induces them to resist such changes. For example, in the mid-nineties, managers in the United States were virtually unanimous in their opposition to recognizing the economic value of stock options as compensation expense, as we will discuss later.

Since precommitment of human services is legally unenforceable by the buyer, it is not feasible to write employment contracts in which the job slot can be explicitly sold by the holder to another person. The absence of direct transactions in managerial positions weakens the market for such skills. Transactions in managerial skills, both inter- and intrafirm, rely largely on the reputation of individuals from their past performance. Accounting provides performance data through cost allocations, transfer prices, cost and profit centers, budgets, and rates of return in the intrafirm market and through financial statements, market surveys, and industry compilations in the interfirm market.[1]

Finally, a large proportion of the total wealth of professional managers is tied up in their managerial skills. The human capital part of their portfolio cannot be diversified. The market price of their services is determined by past performance data because others cannot directly observe their skills. Due to this lack of diversification and observability, managers' welfare is highly sensitive to small changes in current performance data. These data tend to be extrapolated by others to evaluate the current value of their future services. Managers, therefore, try to smooth their performance data.

Measuring Managerial Contribution

Managerial contribution is different from other skills or contributions. Parts assembled, sales made, and touchdowns scored can all be measured, but there is no direct way of measuring management. The higher you go in the managerial hierarchy, the less observable the contribution becomes. The number of hours spent in the office may be devoted to making work rather than doing it, while hours spent away may bring valuable business to the firm. A folder full of carefully drafted memoranda may not be worth more than an idea scribbled on the back of an envelope. Personal rapport with colleagues and subordinates may be worth more in employee morale than many meetings and company picnics. The extreme difficulty in directly observing managerial contribution to the firm renders it difficult to define the manager's contract. How should the manager be rewarded so as to be motivated to contribute the time, attention, and skills expected by other agents? This problem is solved by designing the managerial contracts in terms of observable outputs of their domain of control, a topic to which we shall return later in this chapter.

No matter how the managerial contract is defined, we can expect rational managers to choose their actions to increase their welfare under the contract. Individual rationality need not be myopic. If optimum behavior relative to a contractual form leads to collapse of the firm, and the manager has a stake in the firm's survival, that stake must be explicitly included in defining managerial rationality. If the firm still collapses, the contractual form is unstable. We should not expect to observe such contractual forms in practice frequently.

Self-enforcing contracts try to minimize the shortfall created when an imperfect surrogate is substituted for unobservable managerial input. Accounting and control plays a major role in such contracts.

Contact with Other Agents

Managers work with other agents to plan, coordinate, renegotiate, implement, and readjust plans when surprises occur. Acts of nature and the unanticipated behavior of agents (e.g., suppliers of raw materials, government, labor, or other managers) are the two sources of surprises. As a class, managers work in direct contact with more people than any other class of agents. Most other agents deal directly with the managers and not with other classes of agents. Neither labor nor customers nor vendors of a firm have contact with the shareholders. Because of their coordinating role, the managers occupy the hub in the procedural scheme of the firm (see Figure 3.1).

Occupying a central position in the operating scheme of the firm is not the same as occupying a central position in the economic scheme of the firm (shown in Figure 2.1). By its definition, neither the managers nor any other agents occupy a central position in the contract model of the firm used here. The firm is merely a set of contracts among rational vendors of various factors of production. Man-

Figure 3.1   **Procedural Scheme of the Firm**

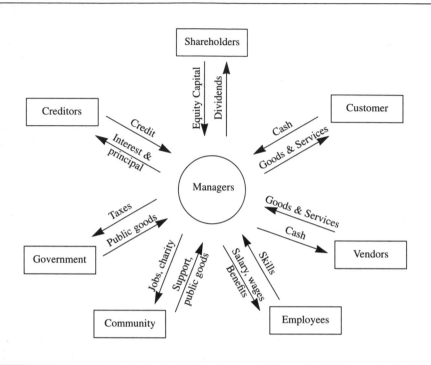

agers occupy the hub in the operating chart of the firm, but not in the economic chart. The functioning of factor markets rearranges the lines from the procedural to the economic chart.

Procedurally, managers negotiate the purchases and labor contracts and write out the checks to pay employees and vendors. Economically, however, they negotiate with each agent on behalf of all the rest and not on their own. The economic burden of payments to each agent falls not on the manager alone, but on all remaining agents. In the Alchian and Demsetz' model of a classical owner-managed firm, the entrepreneur is placed at both the procedural and the economic hub.[2] Our discussion, however, is directed to the accounting and control of larger, publicly held firms.

The managers' position at the procedural hub of the firm gives them privileged access to information about the contractual obligations and rights of various agents, actual and expected levels of fulfillment of these rights and obligations, future demand for factor inputs provided by each agent, and future changes in their entitlements. This access to inside information, often in the form of accounting reports, creates the problems of adverse selection and moral hazard on the part of managers.

The problem of adverse selection arises because managers know things about the work environment that others, especially the shareholders, do not know. Adverse selection is the opportunity managers have to use this information for their personal advantage. The problem of moral hazard arises because other agents cannot see most of what managers do. Moral hazard allows managers to shirk their responsibilities.

In addition to adverse selection and moral hazard, managers could sell such inside information to competing firms for personal gain. Therefore, managers are prohibited from sharing their services among competing firms. A factory manager may preside over the neighborhood club, but is not allowed to manage the factory of a competitor. The former problem of self-dealing on the part of the manager is handled by the design of an accounting system with a built-in hierarchy of internal controls, supplemented by an external audit by independent agents and public disclosure of financial reports.

Forms of Contracts for Managers

The nature of managers' work, human capital, and intimate involvement in the contracts of other agents renders external enforcement of the manager's contract difficult. External enforcement of contracts through the legal system is possible when shared information about agents' contributions, entitlements, and contract fulfillment is available. Legal disputes are resolved on the basis of shipping documents, invoices, written contracts, and so on. This is easy to do for vendors, customers, and, to some degree, for nonmanagerial employees. Little hard evidence is available about managers' contributions to the firm. How can the managerial contracts be made to be self-enforcing?

A flat salary contract is simple. It does not depend on either the efforts or the results of the manager's effort. It is utilized, as we argue in Chapter 13, in compensating managers in public-good organizations when even the outputs of managerial effort are not easy to measure.

Such a contract is a poor motivational instrument, however, because it does not link pay to performance. Most private-good organizations can improve a flat wage contract by making at least a part of the compensation contingent on some measure of results produced by the manager.

How can the results be measured? No single measure of results is perfect. No production statistics (e.g., stock price, earnings per share, return on investment, product market share, cash flow, growth in sales, or cost reduction) measure managerial effort perfectly. They all depend, at least in part, on factors well outside the control of specific managers. A second and equally significant problem is that the relationship between the managerial efforts and the measured results is at least partially controlled by the managers, and is therefore subject to manipulation. Inclusion of results or output in compensation functions does not always serve as an effective motivating device for managers.

The formal part of managerial contracts does not state conditions under which a manager is terminated. Being fired is accompanied by the loss of compensation, fringe benefits, perquisites, and possibly reputation, which means reduced earning power. Managerial jobs rarely carry the security of tenure, severance pay for most managers is not large, and the notice period frequently is no longer than a few days. Even the "golden parachutes" that came into vogue during the 1980s do not provide tenure to senior executives. Large severance benefits promised under such managerial contracts are a device to induce top managers to behave in a desirable manner when the firm is a target for acquisition and their job is in imminent danger. Continuing to perform their duties in the firm under such uncertain circumstances is the first of these desirable behaviors. Giving up their job in exchange for the golden parachute, rather than use their privileged access to inside information to wage a scorched-earth battle against the outsiders in order to hang on to the job, is the second. How effective this innovation is in attaining its purported objective is an open question.

Other agents in the firm have the power to unilaterally terminate a manager's contractual relationship with the firm without giving reason. This power is known and accepted by managers, and helps balance the power managers have through their access to virtually all the information in the firm.

Accounting plays an important part in such contracts. Many of the planning, coordinating, and control tasks of managers are carried out through accounting procedures (e.g., budgeting). In addition, the accounting system determines their resource entitlement and thus affects their welfare. The following analysis of the role of accounting in contracts for managers provides a basis for understanding how managers choose accounting systems.

Managers' Preferences

Managers' preferences include pecuniary variables (such as salary, bonus, benefits, and options) as well as nonpecuniary variables (such as status, opportunities for growth, job flexibility, risk, and challenge). Some of the nonpecuniary variables determine future pecuniary compensation.

Salary is the part of compensation that is contingent only on continuation of the employment relationship. It is a rare managerial contract in which salary does not account for a significant part of pecuniary compensation. A Towers-Perrin survey revealed that, on average, salary accounts for about half of the total pecuniary compensation of the chief executive officers of large firms in the United States.[3]

The salary component in managers' compensation attests to the difficulty of measuring their contribution. The benefit component, on the other hand, is driven by the consideration of tax law and by the complex interaction of human preferences for goods and services versus money. This interaction is not well understood. The proportion of total pecuniary compensation represented by fringe benefits has grown considerably during the post–World-War-II period, largely due to the favorable provisions of the federal income tax law. Some other benefits (e.g., financial planning for managers) can be understood in terms of search costs and economies of scale associated with the purchase of services whose quality is difficult to ascertain. Yet a third class of benefits (e.g., country club membership) may be desirable not so much for their direct pecuniary worth, but as a signal of how valuable top managers think one's services are to the company and what kinds of promotions and assignments one might expect in the future.

Even though the cost of benefits is not difficult to determine, not all benefits are valued for pecuniary reasons. Interactions among human preferences for money, goods, and services are not clearly understood, and the behavior of the economic person in corporate managers is occasionally intruded upon by emotions, a sense of self-worth, and other variables not easily incorporated into economic analysis. Few college professors would be both willing to pay an extra $50 a month for a larger office and willing to accept an extra $50 a month in exchange for moving to a smaller one. Knetsch, Thaler, and Kahneman give some interesting examples of such variables.[4]

For chief executives of the firms listed on the New York Stock Exchange, the American Stock Exchange, and the NASDAQ National Market System, the median total compensation in 1992–93 was $520,000. The median salary, bonus, and stock options were $280,000, $63,000, and $13,000 respectively. Ninety-one percent of these firms had stock option plans for chief executives. In 1995, the chief executive officer of US West, Inc. received $760,000 in salary, $450,000 in bonus or short-term incentive compensation (based on net income, cash flow, operating income, strategic accomplishments, and qualitative measures), restricted stock worth $2,083,292 with a two-year restriction, and 140,000 at-money stock options with a ten-year term.[5] Holthausen found that bonus formulas are often truncated by a maximum and a minimum and do not usually make explicit references (with the exception of GAAP) to accounting methods used to compute the accounting numbers used in the compensation plan.[6]

The distinction between salary and bonus is not quite as clearcut as it might first appear to be. In the sense that managers with unsatisfactory performance get fired from their jobs, salary itself can be thought of as a performance-based reward. In addition, even in the absence of a bonus, improved performance can carry the promise of a higher salary and promotion to a more responsible position. However, neither the loss of a job nor promotion and higher salary is specified as an explicit function of some performance variable known to the manager. Thus, the difference between salary and bonus is a matter of degree to which the link between compensation and performance is explicitly specified by a function that may be *common knowledge* among the managers. Bonus functions popularly used are piece-wise linear in performance measures.

Managers' bonuses depend on performance and environmental variables. The value of a variable for this purpose depends on how much information it has about the unobserved effort of managers. Generally speaking, variables that are affected by such effort are the best. Such variables can be said to be controlled by managers. For example, sales volume carries information about the efforts of the marketing manager. However, the growth in GNP, which is not controlled by the marketing manager, also carries information about the manager's effort when evaluated in conjunction with the sales volume. If a marketing manager holds the decline in sales to 10 percent during a recession when industry sales decline by 20 percent, one may justifiably reach a favorable conclusion about the unobservable effort of that manager. Thus, for the purpose of determining the bonus, uncontrolled variables such as GNP and competition can be labeled as environmental variables.

The amount of information a performance variable carries about the managerial effort can be assessed by the correlation between effort and results when the environmental variables are held constant. The informational value of an environmental variable, on the other hand, can be assessed by the change in this correlation when the value of the environmental variable is changed.

Environmental variables are not used to evaluate managers as frequently as they could be. However, development of portfolio theory has introduced new environmental variables (e.g., market performance, market risk of the portfolio) to the process of evaluating the performance of portfolio managers. The effect of this change has been a revolution in the way mutual funds are run, because fund managers are now evaluated not on the basis of their total return but on the basis of how this return compares with the return on other portfolios of comparable risk.

This development notwithstanding, however, there has been little progress in statistically evaluating the usefulness of various variables in assessing managerial performance. Most schemes for evaluating managers are developed by intuition and judgment. Frequently used accounting variables include sales, production, cost, profit, rates of return, earnings per share, market share, and the rates of change in these variables. Stock price and the change in stock price are the popularly used market-based variables.

Although "bonuses" are rarely negative, managers do share an element of the risk associated with the operations of the firm through variability of bonuses. Participation in a stock option plan has a similar effect. Risk sharing with managers might have only a negligible effect on the risk borne by the shareholders, but the motivational effects of risk sharing on managerial behavior are substantial. Risk-sharing features of managerial contracts are driven not so much by the shareholders' desires to reduce their own risk as by the need to elicit creative effort from managers.

There is a limit, however, to which giving ownership rights to managers helps align their motivations with the shareholders' motivations. A large undiversifiable and illiquid shareholding in the hands of managers may deter them from taking risks that are acceptable to the shareholders. This problem can be mitigated by giving out-of-money stock options to managers. If the stock price exceeds the specified price, managers can reap the benefits by exercising their options without having to bear the losses associated with price declines on shares of stock held outright.

In addition to the explicit components (e.g., salary, bonus, and benefits), managerial employment contracts may include implicit elements that can be just as important to managers. First, the conditions of termination are rarely specified. Second, the opportunity for personal growth and advancement means higher compensation and benefits in the future. These are as important as the current compensation to far-sighted managers, and therefore affect the choice among alternative contracts. Challenging assignments and the opportunity to exercise discretion and creativity provide managers with the chance to build their reputations. Reputation is the currency of internal and external managerial markets. Jobs that help develop transferable skills are attractive because they make it easier to find another job. Power—the opportunity to direct the actions of others—may also attract some to a job. However, in business firms, compensation and power are so closely related that it is difficult to determine which is the principal, and which is the surrogate, variable.

Some aspects of managerial contracts are driven by tax laws, not incentives. Through careful tailoring of compensation plans, a firm can effectively transfer to the government a part of the burden of paying the managers.[7] Nonqualified stock options, restricted stock, phantom stock, stock appreciation rights, or a performance-related bonus have received favorable tax treatment under the federal income tax laws at various times. Firms have tax reasons to use such plans, even if they provide no assistance in motivating and evaluating managers.

On the other hand, firms have no economic reason to use most insurance plans that are tax neutral and deferred wage/salary payment plans that are tax disadvantageous unless they are justified by incentive consequences. Therefore, one can assume that certain compensation schemes have been chosen for their incentive considerations only if they do not offer tax advantages.

Contracts of Top, Middle, and Lower-Level Managers

Just as a firm can be seen as a set of contracts, each subsidiary, division, or plant of a firm can also be seen as a smaller set of contracts or a subfirm. The position of the head of a subfirm is structurally similar to the position of the CEO of the firm. While the equity capital of the firm is supplied by a diffuse body of shareholders, the position of the supplier of capital, usually all capital, in the subfirm is occupied by the immediate superior of the head of the subfirm. A subsidiary of a publicly held corporation is like a privately held firm in its own right. The superior of the subsidiary's manager occupies the position of the controlling shareholders and the bankers of this subfirm. The entire firm can be thought of as a nested set of hierarchies, each being parallel to, and included in, the managerial hierarchy of the firm (see Figure 3.2).

The subfirm (the domain of responsibility of the lower-level managers) draws many of its resources directly from outside markets, and the cost of these resources is readily determinable. Labor wages, utility rates, and materials prices are examples of these costs. Some outputs of the subfirm may also go directly to ex-

Figure 3.2   Hierarchy of Managers and Subfirms in a Firm

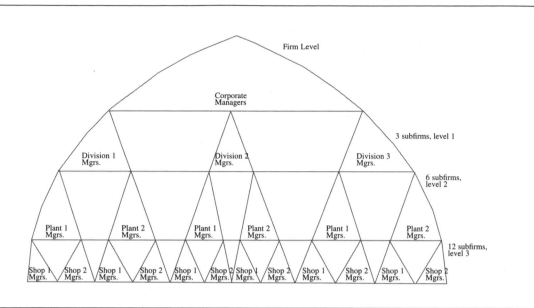

ternal markets, where market prices are available to assess their value. When there are transfers of resources among the subfirms, their value must be assessed either in terms of physical measures, such as sales or production units, or by internally generated pseudo-prices.

The problem of poor observability of managerial contributions is present at the subfirm level also. Assessment of the performance of these managers also requires specification of a measurable variable or variables that can be used as a surrogate for managerial effort. A large part of the managerial accounting system is designed to meet this goal. Product costing, transfer pricing, and budgeting are some aspects of accounting used to measure the performance of managers of the subfirms. Let us illustrate with a few examples.

Consider the head of Division 1 in Figure 3.2. Suppose this division buys labor and materials to produce auto parts and ships these parts to Division 2. To examine the system of control for the managers of Divisions 1 and 2, we must first address the question of why these two divisions are not run as independent, freestanding firms. We can analyze the control system only in the context of a valid answer to that question.

First, suppose that the parts manufactured by Division 1 are traded in a perfectly competitive market. Following Coase's explanation for the nature of the firm, there is no *economic* reason for the two divisions to be included within a single firm under these circumstances, because no market transaction costs are saved and eliminated through replacement of market exchange by administrative action.[8] Indeed, Hirschleifer proposed market price as a solution to the problem of determining the transfer price (price at which the product is sold by Division 1 to Division 2).[9] This solution is applicable only in circumstances when the problem is economically trivial.

Second, suppose that the market for parts manufactured by Division 1 has significant imperfections and incompleteness. If the cost of engaging in market exchanges for these parts (e.g., selling, advertising, negotiation, purchasing, credit investigation) can be reduced by replacing the market transaction by administrative action, we would have an economic rationale for integrating the two organizations into divisions of a single organization. Of course, the cost of administration won't be zero. Instead of incurring costs of market exchange, the firm will now incur the costs of central administration and the collection of information from divisions and communicating to them. The firm must pay the cost of devising and administering a system of control for the managers who run the two divisions. Most important, division managers will use information they have to their own advantage, and it is not possible to guarantee that they will always make decisions in the best interests of the firm as a whole, inflicting the cost of suboptimality on the firm. There is an economic rationale for combining the two divisions into a single firm when the sum of all these costs is exceeded by the savings in the cost of market exchanges brought about by internalization of the two divisions.

The transfer pricing problem is often stated in a manner that ignores the circumstances that give rise to the problem in the first place. Why let the two divisions act independently in a decentralized setting if it has already been determined that it is not the most economical mode of operation for them? Integration of the two divisions into a single firm is predicated on the cost of market exchanges between them being greater than the administrative and agency costs. After integrating two divisions under this rationale, one cannot then turn around and wish the administrative and agency costs away through an appeal to a costless but nonexistent system of market exchanges.

Managerial accounting systems generate pseudo-prices for the purpose of tracking resource flows to and from the domain of control of various managers. Attaching prices to resource flows makes it possible to aggregate heterogeneous resources to construct performance measures of the individual managers.

The dependence of performance measures of individual managers on pseudo-prices (rather than market prices) varies. The construction and use of pseudo-prices in managerial control is a practical solution for the problem of imperfection and incompleteness in the relevant factor markets when using the price system is costly. The major subjective factor in evaluation of these managers is the extent to which their production or results are attributable to factors beyond their control.

Formal analyses of simple one-period agency models reveal situations in which it is Pareto superior (better for some but worse for none) to include uncontrolled variables in determining a manager's rewards when such variables contain information about the local environment faced by the managers. Such results have been used to criticize controllability as a valid criterion for selecting managerial compensation function. They have also been criticized for generalization to complex situations not covered by the simple agency.[10] There is some truth to both arguments. One rarely encounters managerial compensation functions based solely on individual performance. Even a super-efficient foundry manager of a sinking firm is unlikely to receive a generous bonus. On the other hand, textbook arguments for controllability have to be viewed as arguments for greater emphasis on controllability, and not as arguments for complete elimination of uncontrolled variables from the compensation function.

Because the products or services of the firm are sold in external markets, the value of the production of the domain controlled by the top managers is readily determined from the transaction data. However, it is difficult to separate the contribution of the top managers to this production from the contribution of their subordinates. This difficulty in evaluating the individual performance of top managers is met by making them completely responsible for the hiring, firing, promotion, and evaluation of their subordinate managers and by evaluating the top managers on the basis of such gross measures of production as sales, profit and, to a degree, the share price. Their discretionary control over the accounting system that measures sales and profit, and so on, is limited by the outside independent audit.

Evaluation of the middle managers is most difficult because neither the resources that enter into their domain of responsibility (from the lower-level managers) nor the resources that leave this domain (that they provide to the top managers) are usually measured through external markets. The effect of the effort of an individual manager on the total income and share price of the firm is small, and incentives based on such measures alone induce a free-rider problem. It is a challenge to design a self-enforcing environment for such managers. Transfer pricing and divisional performance evaluation schemes, such as return on invested capital, are designed to seek this end by providing accounting substitutes for the missing market variables.

Summary

Managers occupy a special position in contracts. As agents, they have important characteristics. The difficulty of measuring their contribution and the direct contact they have with all other classes of agents lead to distinct contractual forms for managers. The internal control system of the firm is driven by the need to design implementable contracts for each manager in the hierarchy.

In the following chapter we examine the role of managers in making accounting decisions. Measurement of income and its relationship to managerial contracts is discussed in Chapter 5.

Notes

[1]Eugene Fama discusses these markets in detail in "Agency Problems and the Theory of the Firm," *Journal of Political Economy*, Vol. 88, No. 2 (April 1980), pp. 288–307.

[2]Armen A. Alchian and Harold Demsetz, "Production Costs and Economic Organization," *The American Economic Review*, Vol. LXII, No. 5 (December 1972), pp. 777–795.

[3]"The Need for Greed," *The Economist* (4 May 1996), p. 80.

[4]J. Knetsch, R. Thaler, and D. Kahneman, "Reluctance to Trade: An Experimental Refutation of Coase's Theorem," Presented at Public Choice, Economic Science Association Meetings, Tucson, Arizona, March 1987.

[5]Anish Shah, "Determinants of Managerial Compensation: A Focus on Industry Effects and Shareholding Patterns," Carnegie Mellon University Working Paper (1996).

[6]Robert W. Holthausen, "Evidence of the Effect of Bond Covenants and Management Compensation Contracts on the Choice of Accounting Techniques: The Case of Depreciation Switchback," *Journal of Accounting and Economics*, Vol. 3 (1981), pp. 73–109.

[7]Merton H. Miller and Myron S. Scholes, "Executive Compensation, Taxes and Incentives," in William F. Sharpe and Cathryn M. Cootner, eds., *Financial Economics: Essays in Honor of Paul Cootner* (Englewood Cliffs, N.J.: Prentice-Hall, 1982), pp. 179–201.

[8]Ronald H. Coase, "The Nature of the Firm," *Economica*, New Series Vol. 4 (November 1937), pp. 386–405.

[9]Jack Hirschleifer, "Economics of the Divisionalized Firm," *Journal of Business* (April 1957), pp. 96–108.

[10]Joel S. Demski, "Uncertainty and Evaluation Based on Controllable Performance," *Journal of Accounting Research*, Vol. 10 (Autumn 1976), pp. 230–245; S. Baiman and Joel S. Demski, "Economically Optimal Performance Evaluation and Control Systems," *Journal of Accounting Research* (Supplement 1980), pp. 184–220; S. Baiman, "Agency Research in Managerial Accounting: A Survey," *Journal of Accounting Literature*, Vol. 1 (1982), pp. 154–213; and Robert S. Kaplan, *Advanced Management Accounting* (Englewood Cliffs, N.J.: Prentice-Hall, 1982).

Additional Reading

Antle, Rick, and Joel S. Demski. "The Controllability Principle in Responsibility Accounting." *The Accounting Review*, Vol. 63 (October 1988), pp. 700–718.

Baiman, Stanley, David F. Larcker, and Madhav V. Rajan. "Organizational Design for Business Units." *Journal of Accounting Research*, Vol. 33, No. 2 (Autumn 1995), pp. 205–230.

Baker, George, Michael Gibbs, and Bengt Holmstrom. "Hierarchies and Compensation: A Case Study." *European Economic Review*, Vol. 37 (1993), pp. 366–378.

Baker, George, Michael Gibbs, and Bengt Holmstrom. "The Internal Economics of the Firm: Evidence from Personnel Data." *Quarterly Journal of Economics* (forthcoming).

Banker, Rajiv, and Srikant Datar. "Sensitivity, Precision, and Linear Aggregation of Signals for Performance Evaluation." *Journal of Accounting Research*, Vol. 27, No. 1 (Spring 1989), pp. 21–39.

Chen, Kevin C. W., and Chi-Wen Jevons Lee. "Executive Bonus Plans and Accounting Trade-Offs: The Case of Oil and Gas Industry." *Accounting Review*, Vol. 70, No. 1 (January 1995), pp. 91–112.

Clinch, Greg. "Employee Compensation and Firms' Research and Development Activity." *Journal of Accounting Research*, Vol. 29 (1991), pp. 59–78.

Cyert, Richard M., and Praveen Kumar. "On the Determination of Top Management Compensation." Carnegie Mellon University Working Paper, 1996.

Demski, Joel S., and D. Sappington. "Hierarchical Structure and Responsibility Accounting." *Journal of Accounting Research*, Vol. 27 (Spring 1989), pp. 40–58.

Ellig, B. *Executive Compensation: A Total Pay Perspective*. New York: McGraw-Hill, 1982.

Garner, S. P. *Evolution of Cost Accounting to 1925*. Montgomery: University of Alabama Press, 1954.

Gibbons, R., and Kevin Murphy. "Optimal Incentive Contracts in the Presence of Career Concerns: Theory and Evidence." *Journal of Political Economy*, Vol. 100 (1992), pp. 468–505.

Gibbs, Michael. "Incentive Compensation in a Corporate Hierarchy." *Journal of Accounting and Economics*, Vol. 19 (1995), pp. 247–277.

Grossman, Sanford J., and Oliver Hart. "An Analysis of Principal-Agent Problem." *Econometrica*, Vol. 51 (January 1983): pp. 7–45.

Groves, T., and M. Loeb. "Incentives in a Divisionalized Firm." *Management Science*, Vol. 25 (March 1979): pp. 221–230.

Harris, Milton, and Artur Raviv. "Some Results on Incentive Contracts with Application to Education and Employment, Health Insurance, and Law Enforcement." *American Economic Review*, Vol. 68 (March 1978): pp. 20–30.

Harris, Milton, Charles Kriebel, and Artur Raviv. "Asymmetric Information, Incentives and Intrafirm Resource Allocation." *Management Science*, Vol. 28 (June 1982): pp. 604–620.

Healy, Paul M., S. Kang, and K. G. Palepu. "The Effect of Accounting Procedure Changes on CEO's Cash Salary and Bonus Compensation." *Journal of Accounting and Economics*, Vol. 9 (1987): pp. 7–34.

Hewitt Associates. *An Overview of Productivity-Based Incentives*. Lincolnshire, Ill.: Hewitt Associates.

Hirshleifer, Jack. "On the Economics of Transfer Pricing." *Journal of Business* (July 1956), pp. 172–184.

Holthausen, Robert W., David F. Larcker, and Richard G. Sloan. "Business Unit Innovation and the Structure of Executive Compensation." *Journal of Accounting and Economics*, Vol. 19 (1995), pp. 279–313.

Jensen, Michael C., and Kevin Murphy. "It's Not How Much You Pay But How." *Harvard Business Review* (May–June 1990), pp. 138–153.

Lambert, Richard A., and David F. Larcker. "Golden Parachutes, Executive Decision-making, and Shareholder Wealth." *Journal of Accounting and Economics*, Vol. 7 (1985), pp. 179–203.

Lambert, Richard A., and David F. Larcker. "An Analysis of the Use of Accounting and Market Measures of Performance in Executive Compensation Contracts." *Journal of Accounting Research*, Vol. 25 (Supplement 1987), pp. 85–125.

Lawler, E., III. *Pay and Organizational Effectiveness: A Psychological View*. New York: McGraw-Hill, 1971.

March, James G., and Herbert A. Simon. *Organizations*. New York: Wiley, 1958.

Melumad, Nahum, D. Mookherjee, and S. Reichelstein. "Hierarchical Decentralization of Incentive Contracts." Working Paper, 1991.

Melumad, Nahum, D. Mookherjee, and S. Reichelstein. "A Theory of Responsibility Centers." *Journal of Accounting and Economics*, Vol. 15, No. 4 (1992), pp. 445–484.

Milkovich, George T., and Alexandra K. Wigdor, eds. *Pay for Performance: Evaluating Performance Appraisal and Merit Pay*. Washington, D.C.: National Academy Press, 1991.

Mintzberg, H. *The Nature of Managerial Work*. New York: Harper and Row, 1973.

Murphy, Kevin. "Corporate Performance and Managerial Remuneration." *Journal of Accounting and Economics*, Vol. 7 (1985), pp. 11–42.

Murthy, K. R. S. *Corporate Strategy and Top Executive Compensation*. Cambridge, Mass.: Harvard University Press, 1977.

Natarajan, Ramachandran. "Stewardship Value of Earnings Components: Additional Evidence on the Determinants of Executive Compensation." *Accounting Review*, Vol. 71, No. 1 (January 1996), pp. 1–22.

Rosen, Sherwin. "Authority, Control and Distribution of Earnings." *Bell Journal of Economics*, Vol. 13 (1982), pp. 311–323.

Rosen, Sherwin. "Contracts and the Market for Executives." In L. Wernin and H. Wijkander, eds. *Contract Economics* (Oxford: Basil Blackwell, 1992).

Scholes, Myron, and Mark Wolfson. Taxes and Business Strategy: A Planning Approach. Englewood-Cliffs, N.J.: Prentice-Hall, 1992.

Shah, Anish. "Directors' Incentives and CEO Compensation." Carnegie Mellon University Working Paper, 1996.

Simon, Herbert A. *Centralization versus Decentralization in Organizing the Controller's Departments*. New York: Controllorship Foundation (now Financial Executives Research Foundation), 1954.

Sloan, Richard G. "An Empirical Examination of the Role of Accounting Earnings in Top Executive Compensation Contracts." University of Rochester Working Paper, 1991.

Solomons, David. *Divisional Performance: Measurement and Control*. New York: Financial Executives Research Foundation, 1965. 2nd ed., Markus Weiner Publishing Inc. 1985.

Stedry, Andrew C. *Budget Control and Cost Behavior*. Englewood Cliffs, N.J.: Prentice-Hall, 1960.

Stern, Joel, G. Stewart, and D. Chew, ed. *Corporate Restructuring and Executive Compensation*. Cambridge, Mass.: Ballinger, 1989.

Vancil, Richard F. *Decentralization: Managerial Ambiguity by Design*. Homewood, Ill.: Dow Jones-Irwin, 1979.

U.S. General Accounting Office. *A Two Year Appraisal of Merit Pay in Three Agencies*. Washington, D.C.: U.S. Government Printing Office, 1984.

Wallace, M. *Reward and Renewal: America's Search for Competitive Advantage Through Alternative Pay Strategies*. American Compensation Association, 1990.

Waller, William S., and Rachel A. Bishop. "An Experimental Study of Incentive Pay Schemes, Communication, and Intrafirm Resource Allocation." *Accounting Review*, Vol. 65, No. 4 (October 1990), pp. 812–836.

Whyte, W. *Money and Motivation*. New York: Harper and Row, 1955.

4

Managers and Accounting Decisions

• •

Accounting and control extends from the grassroots data collection throughout the firm, to performance reports for various managers, to public disclosures and audited financial reports. When the promoters of a firm choose a form of organization (e.g., proprietorship, partnership, cooperative, or private or publicly held firm with limited liability), they also choose the applicable legal and accounting regimes. A decision to go public in the United States, for example, implies a willingness of the firm's agents to conform its accounting and control to the requirements of the Securities and Exchange Commission.

Within the boundaries defined by its organizational form, a firm's managers shape the details of its accounting and control. Other agents participate in the process indirectly. Managers' choices affect other agents, and the latter's reactions affect the managers themselves. Therefore, managers must take into account the effect of their choices on other agents. In addition, managers actively participate in the process of changing the applicable accounting and legal regimes at local, national, and international levels.

In this chapter we examine the range of accounting decisions managers make, and review some prominent features of accounting in terms of contract theory. In addition, we look at the consequences of accounting decisions for managers, and at the part of managerial behavior that is observable to other agents in the firm. Interactions between accounting choices and regulation are discussed in Chapters 11 and 12.

Hierarchy of Accounting Decisions

At the bottom end of the hierarchy of accounting decisions are the frequent decisions on classification of specific transactions, such as expensing versus capitalization of a major repair job in the factory. At the other end are infrequent decisions with long-run implications, such as decisions about managers' roles in setting the accounting and auditing standards. Let us review the context of a range of such decisions.

Discretionary Decisions on Expensing–Capitalization of Costs

Managers have unique access to information about the likely causes and consequences of expenditures. Since other agents do not know, managers create "facts" when they classify transactions that do not unambiguously fall in one or another of the limited number of accounts in the firm's books. Classification questions arose early in the history of publicly held corporations in the United States. In the mid-eighteenth century, railroad managers could exercise broad discretion on which construction costs were charged to expense and which operating costs were capitalized.[1]

Managers also choose the accounting classification of unusual or infrequent trans actions for which the firm has no defined policy. It is difficult to clearly demarcate capital improvements, repairs, overhauls, rebuilding, salvaging, and maintenance from one another. Managers have discretion over the exact timing of recognizing a transaction. Even small transaction decisions can have a large cumulative effect on financial statements.

Managers' expensing–capitalization choices depend on the form of their contracts, their decision horizons, and their places in the managerial hierarchy. Under the clean surplus rule, all changes in owners' equity except transactions with the shareholders must flow through the income statement, and the Law of Conservation of Undiscounted Accounting Income holds (see Chapter 5). Expensing a cost item instead of capitalizing it shifts accounting income from the current period to some future accounting period without changing the total income over the lifetime of the firm. It also lowers the accounting valuation of assets in the subfirm, and lowers the accounting rate of return on investment for the current period in exchange for a higher return in the future. Managers whose compensation is contingent on short-term income or rate of return are therefore likely to favor capitalization of costs within their range of discretion.

Three countervailing forces reign in the managerial proclivity to capitalize. First, compensation plans induce managers to smooth the measures of their performance over time, and a flat-out policy of capitalizing costs deprives them of one instrument of smoothing income. Second, compensation plans seek to lengthen the decision horizon of managers using such devices as restricted stock options near the top of the managerial hierarchy and multiperiod budgeting at the lower levels. Postponement of expense recognition becomes less important as the decision horizon becomes longer. Third, internal and external auditing limit what managers can capitalize.

Accounting Estimates

Managers estimate many economic magnitudes for the books of account. The allowance for bad debt, costs of warranty obligations, net realizable value of byproducts, service life, and salvage value of equipment and plant are examples of such estimates. Once entered into the books, some estimates cannot be changed without substantial justification, which limits managerial flexibility. Other estimates allow a great deal of flexibility for the managers.

The U.S. savings and loan industry's crisis in the mid-eighties, brought about by large bad debts combined with inadequate allowances made to cover such debts in their financial statements, is a good example. In other industries, independent auditors may be relied upon to provide effective restraints on such occurrences. Responsibility for oversight of U.S. banks is shared by the Federal Reserve Bank, the Controller of Currency, Federal Deposit Insurance Corporation, state regulators, the Securities and Exchange Commission, and independent auditors. This diffusion of responsibility was blamed for the glaring inadequacy of bad debt allowances in the banking industry. However, equally severe problems exist in the recognition of bad debt allowances in Japanese banks during the mid-nineties. The basic considerations that motivate managers in choosing accounting estimates are the same as in discretionary items.

Accounting Principles

Generally accepted accounting principles (GAAP) allow firms to choose from a menu of accounting methods and disclose such choices in a footnote on accounting policy. The timing of revenue recognition and methods of accounting for depreciation, inventory, and costs of pension plans are examples of such decisions. Managers can choose some accounting methods even if they are not included in the set recommended by the law or published accounting standards. However, managers must carefully weigh the gains from such deviations from the norm against the costs they impose on the firm. Even if a firm switches from one generally accepted accounting principle to another, it invites auditor qualification. Section AU 546.01 of the American Institute of Certified Public Accountants' (AICPA) *Professional Standards* applies even if a change is recommended by the Financial Accounting Standards Board or the Securities and Exchange Commission.[2] Other participating agents, especially the investors, view deviations from the norm and changes in accounting principles with unease or even suspicion. Publicly held firms do not, therefore, change accounting principles frequently.

Disclosure Policy

Managers decide what information, beyond the specific requirements of law and accounting standards, is publicly disclosed. Disclosure could appear as additional detail in the financial statements, in the footnotes and schedules, in management's review, in the letter to the shareholders, or in press releases. Major purchase or sale contracts, capital investment plans, research, development and exploration, new product introduction, budgets, and financial forecasts are examples of such disclosures. Honest disclosure of additional information in public affords other participating agents a better assessment of managerial input and the value of their own interest in the firm. However, managers may be tempted to disclose information selectively, withholding information that casts them in a bad light. Such manipulation reduces the credibility of disclosures. Such "soft" information is costly, even impossible, to verify. In choosing disclosure of additional information and its independent verification, managers trade off credibility and the cost of verification in order to enhance their welfare.

Disclosure can also affect the actions and strategies of creditors and shareholders. Public disclosure is equally accessible to participating and nonparticipating agents, and places them on equal footing as bargaining agents. It enhances the liquidity of the factor markets from which the firm draws its resources, and this increased liquidity benefits the participating agents as well as potential participants.

Disclosure of performance forecasts by managers has been debated since the 1930s. The Securities and Exchange Commission (SEC), created in 1934 in the wake of the stock market crash, considered such forecasts potentially mislead-ing to investors and steadfastly opposed them. The SEC changed its attitude in the early seventies, however, and tried to persuade publicly held firms to issue such forecasts. Many firms voluntarily issue public performance forecasts, but managers oppose imposition of a legal requirement to do so. They are afraid of giving away proprietary information to competitors and of being held liable to investors for any forecast errors or misuse of information. (In Chapter 11 we discuss the problems that arose in requiring firms to disclose their oil and gas reserves.)

A firm's competitors might benefit from the forecasts, but product market competition among publicly held firms is a two-way street: Each benefits from the other's disclosure. Shareholders and often employees (through their pension funds) tend to be well-diversified across firms, so a disclosure requirement should not hurt them. The desire to curb the opportunistic use of information by managers is the major source of demand for additional disclosure.

Of course, the reciprocity argument will not hold if publicly held firms have to compete against privately held firms (not subject to disclosure requirements) in technologically innovative industries (where a great deal of high-value proprietary information exists). The theory suggests that, other things being equal, we should expect the resistance to mandatory disclosure requirements to be strongest in such industries.

Even without mandates there are limits to managerial discretion in making disclosures, however. Failure to disclose, when disclosure is expected by others on the basis of past experience, may do more damage to the manager than revealing the bad news. Indeed, some firms win plaudits from the financial community for bluntly admitting setbacks and mistakes. Most announcements of corporate restructuring and large write-offs during the early nineties were followed by a jump in the corporation's stock price.

Internal Controls

Managers exercise broad discretion in designing the accounting and controls. Since the passage of the Foreign Corrupt Practices Act in 1977, managers of publicly held firms are legally required to maintain an adequate internal control system. However, the law provides little specific guidance in designing the system. The Cost Accounting Standards Board wrote accounting standards to help the U.S. government enforce its contracts with its vendors. Most of these contracts implement the bilateral monopoly relationship between the government as the sole buyer and defense contractors as the sole suppliers of specific weapons systems. These standards are designed for this special case, and do not apply to most business relationships. As the firm changes or expands, managers, especially the controllers, continually redesign its accounting system.

A self-enforcing contract environment is created for each manager by simultaneously placing the manager in two agency relationships. In one relationship the manager is the principal in relation to subordinates; in the other, an agent with respect to superiors in the managerial hierarchy. Thus, the organization of managers in a firm can be represented as overlapping principal–agent relationships between various pairs of managers. Low-level managers at the bottom of the hierarchy supervise nonmanagerial employees. At the top, the chief executive officer is answerable to the board of directors.

In stewardship or principal–agent relationships, each manager has exclusive or preferential access to some information, resources, or skills. Each believes that he or she can be better off working within this relationship rather than by abandoning it. Neither knows for sure the actions of the other. The complex design of the managerial control system of the firm is an attempt to solve the problem of providing a set of self-enforcing contracts for all managers in the firm. We will discuss some features of managerial control systems and their economic rationale shortly.

Accounting Standards

U.S. accounting standards for publicly held firms are set by the SEC and the Financial Accounting Standards Board (FASB) through a participative process. Managers are second only to professional auditors in their level of participation in this process. Managers usually claim to speak on behalf of their firms, and rarely in their personal capacity. As with disclosure decisions, it is difficult to untangle the extent to which positions espoused by managers advance their own interests as opposed to the common interests of all agents who participate in the firm. Unless we observe managers espousing proposals that favor agents at large at the expense of managers' personal interests, we are inclined to assume that managers, like others, seek personal goals.

To illustrate, in 1982 bank managers persuaded the FASB not to require recognition of loss at the time of restructuring of troubled debt. Their persuasive argument was couched in terms of potential damage to the interests of others: bank borrowers, depositors, and shareholders. This goes to the heart of the dilemma that accounting rule makers face. If forcing the banks to recognize huge loan losses precipitates bank failures and loss of public confidence in the banking system, such action would be self-defeating. Accounting does not merely seek to represent reality; it may also *create* reality. Appealing as the idea of representational faithfulness is to the advocates of realism in accounting, the reflexivity of accounting and economic reality also cannot be ignored by the auditors when they examine a firm whose continuity is in doubt. Is an adverse audit opinion that erases the doubt by forcing the firm into bankruptcy representationally faithful?

Yet the managers who made these arguments stood to benefit handsomely from the FASB's acquiescence. Because so many of their skills are industry-specific, a fired bank manager suffers an economic loss. The top bank managers had economic incentives to fight the potentially damaging requirement of immediate recognition of loss associated with troubled debt restructuring. Similar incentives led managers to fight against recognizing the economic value of managerial stock options as part of a firm's compensation expense, as will be discussed later in this chapter.

Although managers can, and often do, use participation in the standard-setting process to their own advantage, their exclusion from the process would only leave the field open to auditors to do the same thing. Serious errors in standard setting can be minimized by balanced representation of various interests in the standard-setting body, not by excluding agents who may have an ax to grind or personal stakes to protect. We return to the problem of designing institutions for setting accounting standards in Chapter 11.

Certain Features of Control Systems

Electronic computers make it cheaper to include additional details in accounting records. However, the costs of identifying the additional details, classifying them into appropriate categories, and converting them into machine-readable form must be incurred first. For example, a magazine publisher may decide that computerizing subscriber accounts should be accompanied by collecting demographic and renewal data to support marketing and advertising. The firm would have to redesign its accounting system, identify additional pieces of data needed, specify procedures for collecting it, enter it into the system, and process it after entry. To justify such efforts, the expected benefits from improved marketing would have to exceed the costs of redesign and implementation.

Auditors' demands for verification of accounting systems often require the use of otherwise redundant, even inefficient, accounting procedures. Optimizations of accounting systems reckon not only the direct costs of accounting, but also the cost of auditing and the indirect costs that follow from errors and failure of internal controls.

Transfer Pricing

According to Coase, a firm replaces market transactions with administrative organization when the cost of the latter is less than the cost of the former.[3] When two stages of production are organized within a firm and managed by a single person, the need for a transfer price vanishes. However, if each stage is managed by a separate manager, a transfer price can be used to split the transaction cost savings between the two managers. Ideally, this price should align their individual incentives with the interests of the firm as a whole.

The standard textbook solution to this problem (use of the market price as the transfer price) is a nonsolution. When a well-defined market price exists for the transferred good, there is no economic rationale for the two divisions to be part of a single firm. This is a common problem with computing transfer prices by assuming that a central planner knows all the facts. But information asymmetry in favor of subordinates is an essential driver for decentralization. Decentralization brings its own costs in the form of decisions that may serve the interests of the subordinate, but not the interests of the larger firm. One of the toughest problems of organization design is to make this trade-off between the benefits (decisions optimized for superior local information) and costs (global suboptimality of local decisions). Ignoring this fundamental trade-off does not yield useful organization designs or transfer pricing schemes. Organizations tend to address the problem by defining a process rather than a specific solution. Accounting and organizational practices for determination of transfer prices (e.g., cost plus, negotiated, and full cost, etc.) are best seen in this light. Such practices often appear to be suboptimal in narrowly constructed scenarios that leave out the essential trade-off that lies at the heart of organizational design.

Cost Allocations

It is often cheaper for a firm to have two or more managers share a plant or facility that was created by incurring a fixed cost. After a plant has been acquired, it seems irrational to allocate the sunk cost of the facility among the managers who utilize it. Charging the managers may only result in suboptimal utilization of a plant whose costs have already been paid for by the firm.

Plant use after its purchase is only a part of the problem. The other part of the problem, frequently ignored in the cost allocation literature, concerns the critical decision to acquire the plant and incur the cost in the first place. A decentralized firm needs an accurate and efficient method of finding out how much of the capacity of the shared facility each division needs. This information is in the hands of the division managers. If they know that the use of the facility, once it is installed, is free, they will demand more capacity than they can productively use. This will result in economic waste for the firm. On the other hand, charging managers a high price for using the facility will induce them to underestimate their demand, again hurting the firm. Allocation of costs creates a pseudo-marginal price for the services of the plant and helps improve the quality of the firm's decision to buy the capacity.

After capacity is installed, it is inefficient to charge the users of the capacity if the opportunity cost of such capacity is zero. On the other hand, if no price were charged, managers would learn to anticipate this policy and provide inflated estimates of demand that would result in too large a capacity being installed by the firm. If they had to pay on the basis of their estimated demand for the use of the proposed facility, managers will tend to understate their projected use. Inefficiency after installation is the unavoidable price that a decentralized firm must pay in order to gain other benefits of decentralization. Cost allocation schemes balance the efficiency of plant acquisition against the efficiency of plant utilization.

Participative Budgeting

Traditionally, participative schemes have been explained by the satisfaction agents receive from the act of participation or power sharing. However, it is also possible to understand the value of participation in terms of the fundamentally dispersed nature of information in any economy or organization.[4] Nobody, not even the boss, knows everything. It is impossible to get others to share the information they have without giving them a say in decision making. They decide what information they will share and how precisely and how truthfully they share it. This influence of others on decisions made is the price paid for information. All participation in decisions, in budgeting and elsewhere, involves a trade-off between (1) the value of information gathered from the participants through better informed decisions, and (2) shading of the decisions in favor of the participants through the information they choose to share.

This trade-off is eternal. However, in management consulting circles, the participative style of decision making is a fad that waxes and wanes in cycles. There are two reasons for this instability. First, participation is often sold by management gurus as a good thing in itself, and not in terms of the economic trade-off just described. When the manager does not make sure that the gains outstrip the losses in the implementation of participation, the experiment fails, consultants are fired, and the boss returns to the office to brood.

A second cause of failure lies in the expectations of those invited to participate in the process. Human beings are not blank slates. They carry a history of their experiences in the form of expectations. Under conditions of uncertainty, we all act relative to these subjective expectations. When invited to participate in budgeting or other forms of decision making, people act in light of their past experiences. If they have played out a failed round of a participation game in the past, the chances of success diminish with each subsequent experience. If people do not trust the boss to do right with them when they share information, they will not share information.

Standards and Variance Analysis

The use of budgets or standards in managerial contracts suggests the existence of a discontinuity in the managerial reward function. In other words, managerial rewards change in some qualitative manner if the performance falls above or below some specified standard. Variance analysis implies a search for additional information by the principal when performance of the agent falls in some prespecified range. Whatever policy the manager uses to set budgets, standards, or investigations, it is reasonable to assume that, sooner or later, subordinates will learn about this policy and adjust their behavior in light of this knowledge. Most standards and variance analysis systems have complicated nonlinear dynamics, making it difficult to predict the end point of this action–reaction sequence between the manager and subordinates.

Managerial Consequences of Accounting Decisions

Accounting and managerial welfare are intertwined. Let us discuss a few examples of the consequences of accounting decisions.

The LIFO Puzzle

When the unit costs of inventory rise and the unit volume is stable or increasing, the use of the last-in-first-out (LIFO) cost-flow assumption to calculate the cost of goods sold lowers the income of the firm. This method is acceptable for income tax purposes in the United States. It offers nongovernment participants of firms that satisfy the unit cost and volume conditions an opportunity to enlarge their share of the corporate pie at the expense of the government. Most U.S. firms satisfy these conditions. Yet, a majority of publicly held corporations do not use LIFO. Why this reluctance to save taxes?

Managers are more likely to choose income-enhancing accounting methods if their compensation is tied to income. Managers' bonuses are often linked to accounting income. They assume that adopting LIFO, unless accompanied by an adjustment in the bonus calculation, will reduce their compensation. Although such adjustments are not routinely made, empirical studies reveal that adopting LIFO does *not* decrease executive compensation. The tax savings are so much larger than the compensation costs that only large barriers or costs to renegotiation of managerial contracts could support the absence of adjustment in compensation.

Because LIFO results in lower earnings, adopting LIFO may lower stock prices and, therefore, the short-run wealth of shareholders and managerial compensation. When some managers *believe* that investors value the shares of stock on the basis of accounting income instead of cash flow, even an efficient stock market is not, by itself, sufficient to discipline such managers and correct their beliefs.

Other explanations of firms' reluctance to use LIFO are possible. For example, the complexity of the managerial structure of a firm, the slow speed of innovation in organizations, the differential enforcement policy by tax authorities towards LIFO users, the cost of implementing LIFO accounting, the volatility of earnings under LIFO, and expectations of future rates of price change may influence decisions not to adopt LIFO. In addition, managers may use LIFO as a costly device to send credible signals about future prospects of the firm to the shareholders.

Accounting for Leases

When the FASB issued *Statement No. 13* specifying criteria for capitalization of leases, its action elicited a managerial response that it did not anticipate. Managers redesigned long-term lease contracts to avoid capitalization and the board was kept busy for several years issuing six modifications and seven interpretations of the original statement in an attempt to plug the "loopholes." What do managers gain by avoiding capitalization of leases? Explanations tend to follow those given for LIFO.

The Restructuring of Troubled Loans

When the FASB proposed that banks recognize the loss in economic value of loans when they agree to restructure troubled loans in favor of the creditors, banks took a unified stand against the proposal. Banks succeeded in diluting the requirements of loss recognition. Under *Statement No. 15,* loss is recognized only to the extent that the undiscounted value of all payments to be received under the restructured debt falls below the original face amount. That is, no loss is recognized unless the effective interest becomes negative.

Why did the bank managers, presumably sophisticated in financial analysis and the workings of capital markets, join hands to oppose the recognition of economic reality in financial statements? They argued that recognizing a loss at the time of loan restructuring would result in (1) a loss of deposits for the banks, (2) a loss of investor confidence in the banks, and (3) borrowers being forced into bankruptcy instead of agreeing to restructure their debts. The bankers succeeded in blocking a proposed accounting standard that would have produced a more "realistic" reporting of the financial condition of banks. Whether the banks' stand arose from the interests of banking firms as a whole or from the personal stakes of the bank managers in the issue was not debated.

Cost of Exploration, Research, and Development

FASB *Statement No. 19* required firms to expense the cost of unsuccessful oil and gas exploration. It was subsequently withdrawn under stiff opposition from segments of the oil and gas industry and the Securities and Exchange Commission. Managers of the mostly smaller exploration firms, who capitalized such costs in their books of account, argued that this rule would raise their cost of capital and force them to scale back their exploration efforts.

Since 1974, the FASB's *Statement No. 2* has required immediate expensing of the costs of research and development. It was argued at the time that such a rule would tend to reduce the research and development outlays of publicly held corporations. Horwitz and Kolodny found evidence in support of such an effect,[5] while Dukes, Dyckman, and Elliot looked for, but could not find, such support.[6]

Recognizing Option Value as Compensation Expense

In 1993, the FASB proposed that the economic value of stock options granted to employees, mostly managers, be recognized as part of the firm's compensation expense. The proposal faced determined opposition from corporate managers, especially from the high-technology start-up firms. A relatively large proportion of compensation in such firms is paid in the form of stock options. Speaking on behalf of their firms, these managers argued that the accounting proposal would cripple their ability to attract managerial talent and to raise capital. They also argued that estimating economic value of complex options would be difficult and arbitrary in the absence of a liquid market. In 1995, the FASB gave up and issued *Statement No. 123* that suggests, but does not require, that firms recognize this expense.

Rationality of Apparently Irrational Decisions

Many other examples, in addition to those given here, suggest that managers oppose changes in accounting methods that tend to reduce currently reported income. How do we explain such reluctance, especially if the change produces a substantial increase in the size of the economic pie, as is the case with LIFO?

If everyone knew everything, such reluctance to increase the size of the economic pie would be irrational, and there would be little need for accounting. In the world of business, people cannot know everything. They can't even know all there is to know about. People gather what information they can, and try to infer the rest from what they see of others. An action by a participant in the firm is a substantive economic choice as well as a signal to other agents who can see the action or its consequences. Each agent evaluates the direct consequences of his or her action, as well as how the action will be perceived by others. Others' perceptions determine the agent's reaction, and the effect of such reaction on the agent's own welfare. Common knowledge (see Chapter 1) of this action–reaction sequence is impractical.

This imperfection of information may hold a clue to explaining the LIFO puzzle. Suppose that all agents privately know that a switch to LIFO decreases tax payments without affecting other cash flows. This is not enough to ensure that LIFO will be chosen. In order for LIFO to be a rational decision, not only must the managers who make such a choice believe it to be rational, they must be convinced that others, especially investors, believe it also. If managers doubt that investors can see through the accounting veil, it might not be rational for managers to choose accounting methods that would be preferable if no such doubts exist. It is not irrational for managers to believe that investors do not have the information that they might, in fact, have. Some managerial accounting practices may appear paradoxical simply because we may assume that information is common knowledge when, in fact, it is not.

When a manager's welfare depends on income and a change in accounting method reduces reported income, the manager must ask other participating agents to revise his or her contract just to stay even. Such requests are not necessarily accepted by other agents at their face value. Not everybody is convinced that the change in a manager's contract is simply an effort to retain the status quo. Some agents may see it as a transfer of wealth to the manager. Managers' control of information inside the firm makes it even more difficult to convince others. The reaction of other agents to a perceived transfer of wealth to a manager alters their behavior in a way that is expected to reduce the welfare of the manager. Mistaken as such perceptions might be, the manager might have no effective means of combating them, except to refrain from making the accounting change. Thus, the imperfect communication among agents might prevent them from making Pareto improvements (some are better off but none are worse off) in the firm's contracts.

Observable Behavior of Managers

Managers tend to favor the status quo in accounting methods and resist changes in accounting standards. They use accounting devices to attempt to smooth out sharp changes in income, though not always successfully. Some of their accounting choices can be predicted from characteristics of the firms.

Preference for Status Quo

Accounting changes beget a qualified audit opinion and unfavorable publicity. Even if the change is induced by a new standard from an authority, it means more work, staff training, new software, extra audit fees, an explanation to skeptical directors and investors, and, sometimes, lower compensation for the manager. New standards usually limit the flexibility of the firm in selecting accounting methods. Accounting changes affect the welfare of all agents, yet the accounting system is under the direct control of the managers alone. It is hardly surprising that changes in accounting methods are received with some suspicion by nonmanagerial agents. All agents must incur the costs of adjusting their behavior to the contractual arrangements. If managers have no preference between the status quo and the equilibrium state under the proposed change, these adjustment costs alone are enough to make them prefer the former.

Income Management

Managers use the flexibility in accounting systems and the timing of actual transactions, such as purchases and deliveries, to make their performance look better. Advertising, research, development, exploration, and the write-down of obsolete inventory and equipment have often been cited as areas of substantial discretion to managers. Nonaccounting decisions such as capital budgeting, the sale of equipment, and early debt retirement also afford the manager similar opportunities. Changes in accounting principles with respect to inventory valuation, depreciation, recognition of revenue, and so on, can also be used toward the same end. We return to this topic in the next chapter.

Prediction of Accounting Methods by Firm Characteristics

In Chapter 2 we discussed the approximate relationship between three organizational forms and the three forms of accounting. This process could be refined. Accounting methods chosen or preferred by firms can be linked to their characteristics. For example, the preferences of oil and gas exploration firms for methods of accounting depend on their leverage.[7] The preferences of firms toward proposals for general price-level accounting seem to be related to their size, the existence of a management compensation plan, and their involvement with regulatory agencies of the government.[8]

Summary

Managers' interaction with accounting and control is complex. Being at the procedural hub of the firm, they operate its accounting and control system. Because their contributions cannot be measured directly, a substantial part of their compensation is based on accounting measures of output. The accounting system produces evidence on which their reputation or human capital is built. They also play a premier role in designing the accounting system, modifying it in response to changes in the environment, having its output verified by independent auditors, and even manipulating it to their private advantage. In this system, income is perhaps the single most important number. Not surprisingly, much management as well as investor attention is focused on this aspect of accounting. In the next chapter, we analyze the importance of income and its management.

Notes

[1]Alfred D. Chandler Jr., *The Visible Hand: The Managerial Revolution in American Business* (Cambridge, Mass.: Harvard University Press, 1977), pp. 110–115.

[2]American Institute of Certified Public Accountants, *Professional Standards, Vol. A, U.S. Auditing Standards.* Chicago: Commerce Clearing House, 1986.

[3]Ronald H. Coase, "The Problem of Social Cost," *Journal of Law and Economics*, Vol. 3 (October 1979), pp. 1–44.

[4]F. A. Hayek, "The Use of Knowledge in Society," *American Economic Review*, Vol. 35 (September 1945), pp. 519–530.

[5]Bertrand N. Horwitz and Richard Kolodny, "The Economic Effects of Involuntary Uniformity in the Financial

Reporting of R & D Expenditures," *Studies on Economic Consequences of Financial and Managerial Accounting: Effects on Corporate Incentives and Decisions,* supplement to *Journal of Accounting Research*, Vol. 18 (1980), pp. 38–74.

[6]Ronald E. Dukes, Thomas R. Dyckman, and John A. Elliot, "Accounting for Research and Development Costs: The Impact on Research and Development Expenditures," *Studies on Economic Consequences of Financial and Managerial Accounting: Effects on Corporate Incentives and Decisions*, supplement to *Journal of Accounting Research*, Vol. 18 (1980), pp. 1–37.

[7]Edward B. Deakin III, "An Analysis of Differences Between Nonmajor Oil Firms Using Successful Efforts and Full Cost Methods," *Accounting Review*, Vol. 54, No. 4 (October 1979), pp. 722–734.

[8]Ross L. Watts and Jerold L. Zimmerman, "Towards a Positive Theory of Determination of Accounting Standards," *Accounting Review*, Vol. 53, No. 1 (January 1978), pp. 112–134.

Additional Reading

Abdel-Khalik, A. R. "The Effect of LIFO Switching and Firm Ownership on Executives' Pay." *Journal of Accounting Research,* Vol. 23, No. 2 (Autumn 1985), pp. 427–447.

Abdel-Khalik, A. R., and J. C. McKeown. "Understanding Accounting Changes in an Efficient Market: Evidence of Differential Reaction." *Accounting Review*, Vol. 53 (October 1978), 851–868.

Amershi, Amin H., and Shyam Sunder. "Failure of an Efficient Stock Market to Discipline Managers in a Rational Expectations Economy." *Journal of Accounting Research* (Autumn 1987), pp. 177–195.

Argyris, C. *The Impact of Budget on People.* New York: Controllorship Foundation, 1952.

Atkinson, Anthony. *Intra-Firm Cost and Resource Allocations: Theory and Practice.* Toronto: Canadian Academic Accounting Association, 1987.

Baiman, Stanley. "Agency Research in Managerial Accounting: A Survey." *Journal of Accounting Literature*, Vol. 1 (1982), pp. 154–213.

Baiman, Stanley. "Agency Research in Managerial Accounting: A Second Look." *Accounting, Organizations and Society*, Vol. 15, No. 4 (1990), pp. 341–371.

Baiman, S., and J. S. Demski. "Economically Optimal Per formance Evaluation and Control Systems." *Journal of Accounting Research* (Supplement 1980), pp. 184–220.

Baiman, S., and J. S. Demski. "Variance Analysis Procedures as Motivation Devices." *Management Science* (August 1980), pp. 840–848.

Baiman, Stanley, and J. H. Evans III. "Predecision Information and Participative Management Control Systems." *Journal of Accounting Research*, Vol. 21, No. 2 (Autumn 1983), pp. 371–395.

Becker, Selwyn, and David Green. "Budgeting and Employee Behavior." *Journal of Business*, Vol. 35 (January 1962), pp. 392–402.

Berg, Joyce E., Lane A. Daley, John N. Dickhaut, and John O'Brien. "Moral Hazard and Risk Sharing: Experimental Evidence." In R. M. Isaac, ed., *Research in Experimental Economics*, Vol. 5 (1992).

Bhagat, Sanjai, and Ivo Welch. "Corporate Research & Development Investments: International Comparisons." *Journal of Accounting and Economics*, Vol. 19 (1995), pp. 443–470.

Biddle, Gary. "Allocation of Joint and Common Costs." *Journal of Accounting Literature* (Spring 1984), pp. 1–45.

Biddle, Gary. "Accounting Methods and Management Decisions: The Case of Inventory Costing and Inventory Policy." *Journal of Accounting Research*, Vol. 18 (Supplement 1980), pp. 235–280.

Bowen, Robert M., Larry DuCharme, and D. Shores. "Stakeholders' Implicit Claims and Accounting Method Choice." *Journal of Accounting and Economics*, Vol. 20, No. 3 (December 1995), pp. 255–296.

Christenson, J. "Participative Budgeting: An Agency Approach." Working Paper, Odense University (1980).

Clark, J. Maurice. *Studies in the Economics of Overhead Costs.* Chicago: University of Chicago Press, 1923.

Coase, Ronald H. "The Nature of the Firm." *Economica*, New Series, Vol. 4 (November 1937), pp. 386–405.

Demski, Joel S. "Cost Allocation Games." In S. Moriarty, ed., *Proceedings of the University of Oklahoma Conference on Cost Allocation*, 1981.

Demski, Joel S. "Uncertainty and Evaluation Based on Controllable Performance." *Journal of Accounting Research*, Vol. 10 (Autumn 1976), pp. 230–245.

Demski, Joel S. *Managerial Uses of Accounting Information.* Norwell, Mass.: Kleuwer Academic Publishers, 1994.

Dye, Ron. "Disclosure of Nonproprietary Information." *Journal of Accounting Research*, Vol. 23 (1985), pp. 123–145.

Dye, Ron, and S. Sridhar. "Industry-Wide Disclosure Dynamics." *Journal of Accounting Research*, Vol. 33 (Spring 1995), pp. 157–174.

Dye, Ron, and Robert Verrecchia. "Discretion Versus Uniformity." *The Accounting Review*, Vol. 70 (July 1995), pp. 389–416.

Feltham, G. "Optimal Incentive Contracts: Penalties, Costly Information and Multiple Workers." University of British Columbia Working Paper 588, October, 1977.

Financial Accounting Standards Board. *Statement of Financial Accounting Concepts No. 1: Objectives of Financial*

Reporting by Business Enterprises. Stamford, Conn.: FASB, 1978.

Forsythe, Robert, and Russell Lundholm. "Adverse Selection and Voluntary Disclosure in Financial Markets: Some Experimental Evidence." University of Iowa Working Paper, 1991.

Fremgen, J., and S. Liao. *The Allocation of Corporate Indirect Costs.* New York: National Association of Accountants, 1981.

Gigler, F. "Self-Enforcing Voluntary Disclosures." *Journal of Accounting Research,* Vol. 31 (Autumn 1994), pp. 224–240.

Harris, M., and A. Raviv. "Optimal Incentive Contracts with Imperfect Information." *Journal of Economic Theory,* Vol. 20 (1979), pp. 231–259.

Hines, Ruth D. "Why Won't the FASB Conceptual Framework Work?" Mcquarie University Working Paper, 1987.

Hirshleifer, J. "On the Economics of Transfer Pricing." *Journal of Business* (July 1956), pp. 171–184.

Holmstrom, B. R. "Moral Hazard and Observability." *The Bell Journal of Economics* (Spring 1979), pp. 74–91.

Holmstrom, B., and J. Tirole. "Transfer Pricing and Organizational Form." *Journal of Law, Economics and Organizations,* Vol. 7 (1991), pp. 201–228.

Holthausen, Robert W., and Richard W. Leftwich. "The Economic Consequences of Accounting Choice: Implications of Costly Contracting and Monitoring." *Journal of Accounting and Economics,* Vol. 5 (1983), pp. 77–117.

Hopwood, A. *Accounting and Human Behavior.* Englewood Cliffs, N.J.: Prentice-Hall, 1976.

Hughes, P,. and E. Schwartz. "The LIFO/FIFO Choice: An Asymmetric Information Approach." *Journal of Accounting Research,* Vol. 26 (Supplement 1988), pp. 41–58.

Kanodia, Chandra S. "Effects of Shareholders Information on Corporate Decisions and Capital Market Equilibrium." *Econometrica,* Vol. 48, No. 4 (May 1980), pp. 923–953.

Kanodia, Chandra S. "Stochastic Monitoring and Moral Hazard." *Journal of Accounting Research,* Vol. 23, No. 1 (Spring 1985), pp. 175–193.

Kanodia, Chandra S. "Participative Budgets as Coordination and Motivational Devices." *Journal of Accounting Research,* Vol. 31 (Autumn 1993), pp. 172–189.

Keegan, D. *Transfer Pricing Practices of American Industry.* New York: Price Waterhouse, 1984.

King, Ronald R., and David E. Wallin. "Experimental Tests of Disclosure with an Opponent." *Journal of Accounting and Economics,* Vol. 19 (1995), pp. 139–167.

Kirby, Allison, S. Reichelstein, S. Sen, and T. Paik. "Participation, Slack, and Budget-Based Performance Evaluation." *Journal of Accounting Research,* Vol. 29 (Spring 1991), pp. 109–128.

Lemke, Kenneth, and Michael J. Page. "Economic Determinants of Accounting Policy Choice: The Case of Current Cost Accounting in the U.K." *Journal of Accounting and Economics,* Vol. 15, No. 1 (March 1992), pp. 87–114.

Lev, Baruch, and S. Penman. "Voluntary Forecast Disclosure, Nondisclosure, and Stock Prices." *Journal of Accounting Research,* Vol. 28 (Spring 1990), pp. 49–76.

Locke, E. A., and D. M. Schweiger. "Participation in Decision-Making: One More Look." *Research in Organizational Behavior* (1979), pp. 265–339.

Magee, R. P. "Equilibria in Budget Participation." *Journal of Accounting Research,* Vol. 18 (Autumn 1980), pp. 551–573.

McKinsey, J. *Budgetary Control.* New York: Ronald Press, 1922.

Melumad, N., and S. Reichelstein. "Value of Communication in Agencies." *Journal of Economic Theory,* Vol. 47 (1989), pp. 334–368.

Meyerson, R. B. "Incentive Compatibility and the Bargaining Problem." *Econometrica,* Vol. 47 (January 1979), pp. 61–74.

Newman, Paul, and Richard Sansing. "Disclosure Policies with Multiple Users." *Journal of Accounting Research,* Vol. 31 (Spring 1993), pp. 92–112.

Penno, Mark. "Asymmetry of Pre-decision Information and Managerial Accounting." *Journal of Accounting Research,* Vol. 22 (1984), pp. 177–191.

Rajan, Madhav. "Cost Allocation in Multiagent Settings." *Accounting Review,* Vol. 67 (July 1992), pp. 527–545.

Ramakrishnan, R. T. "Performance Evaluation and Budgeting with Asymmetric Information," MIT Working Paper, April 1980.

Reichelstein, S. "Budgeting and Hierarchical Control," University of California, Berkeley, Working Paper, 1994.

Ronen, Joshua, and G. McKinney, III. "Transfer Pricing for Divisional Autonomy." *Journal of Accounting Research,* Vol. 8 (Spring 1970): pp. 99–112.

Shields, Michael, and S. Young. "Antecedents and Consequences of Participative Budgeting: Evidence on the Effects of Asymmetric Information." *Journal of Management Accounting Research,* (1993), pp. 265–280.

Sunder, Shyam. "The Relationship Between Accounting Changes and Stock Prices: Problems of Measurement and Some Empirical Evidence. *Journal of Accounting Research,* Vol. 11 (Supplement 1973), pp. 1–45.

Sutton, Timothy G. "The Proposed Introduction of Current Cost Accounting in the U.K.: Determinants of Corporate Preference." *Journal of Accounting and Economics,* Vol. 10, No. 2 (April 1988), pp. 127–150.

Swieringa, R., and John Waterhouse. "Organizational Views of Transfer Pricing." *Accounting, Organizations and Society,* Vol. 7, No. 2 (1982), pp. 149–166.

Tang, R. "Transfer Pricing in the 1990s." *Management Accounting* (February 1992), pp. 22–36.

Vatter, William. *Managerial Accounting.* New York: Prentice-Hall, 1950.

Vaysman, I. "A Model of Cost-Based Transfer Pricing." *The Review of Accounting Studies* (Forthcoming).

Vaysman, I. "A Model of Negotiated Transfer Pricing." University of Texas at Austin Working Paper, 1993.

Zimmerman, J. L. "The Costs and Benefits of Cost Allocation." *Accounting Review* (July 1979), pp. 504–521.

Zmijewski, M., and R. Hagerman. "An Income Strategy Approach to the Determination of Accounting Standards." *Journal of Accounting and Economics*, Vol. 2 (1979), pp. 141–161.

5

Income and
Its Management

●●●

To each participating agent, the firm is a source of income. Agents participate if they expect the return on their contribution to the firm to exceed what they can get elsewhere. A measure of income from the firm can be defined for each factor input. Use of the term *income* in this broad sense is not new. Wage income, personal service income, interest income, and income from the sale of goods and services are standard business terms.

A well-known definition of income is:

> The purpose of income calculation in practical affairs is to give people an indication of the amount they can consume without impoverishing themselves. Following out this idea, it would seem that we ought to define a man's income as the maximum value that he can consume during a week and still expect to be as well off at the end of the week as he was at the beginning.[1]

Agents estimate returns on their respective contributions and observe the actual returns. When used without qualification, income has a more restrictive meaning in accounting, referring to shareholders' income. Of all the incomes that accrue to various agents in the firm, what is so special about the income that accrues to the shareholders?

First, the shareholders are entitled to the resources left after the entitlements of all other agents are paid or set aside. In contrast, the entitlement of every other factor of production (with the partial exception of management) is defined independently of the entitlements of the other agents. What they receive is either a direct function of their contribution (e.g., vendors, hourly workers) or a constant (salaried staff). Defining one of the entitlements as the residual is necessary. When a pie is divided into n portions, the size of only $(n-1)$ portions can be independently defined. The size of the nth portion is defined by the size of the first $(n-1)$. Income allotted to equity capital is the nth portion.

Second, the resource entitlements of all agents other than shareholders are transferred to them according to a contractually specified schedule. Disbursements for payroll, bonuses, interest, taxes, accounts payable, and so on are arranged by the firm's treasurer to meet various contractual deadlines. Shipments of goods and delivery of services to customers are arranged according to agreed-upon schedules. Few such payments are deferred beyond a few weeks or months.

In contrast, the wealth that accrues to shareholders is not routinely transferred to them. Only a part of this entitlement is distributed as dividends, and the balance is retained in the firm for reinvestment, thus increasing the agent's commitment of equity capital to the firm. Shareholders, being a diffuse body, cannot directly control the decision about how much of their total accrued entitlement—income—should be taken out of the firm in the form of dividends. The rights issue is a mechanism whereby they could make this decision themselves. The firm could mail out dividend checks in an amount equal to income along with a form that shareholders could use to exercise their rights. Each shareholder could return to the firm an amount he or she wishes to reinvest. However, the U.S. tax law penalizes such a procedure by making the entire dividend immediately taxable. Therefore, the top managers and the board of directors of the firm make the dividend decision, subject to the constraints imposed by debt and other covenants.

Third, income to equity capital cannot be measured as accurately and reliably as income to other factors of production. While the former is easily defined as the resource residual, measuring it in units of money presents severe problems. Modern industrial corporations do not liquidate their assets and hand over the residual to the shareholders at the end of each reporting period. Equity investment—initial commitment plus cumulative amounts retained from periodic income—is carried over from period to period, mostly in the form of physical, human, and reputation capital. Markets for such forms of capital are far from perfect or complete. Therefore, the monetary valuation of physical capital is not unique. It depends both on the assumptions made about the future operation of the contracts that constitute the firm and on the agent whose judgments about the future are relied upon in arriving at valuation. This fundamental indeterminacy in valuation and measurement of periodic income to the shareholders, combined with the managers' responsibility to carry out this measurement, gives rise to the problem of, and opportunity for, income management.

The managers' entitlement depends partly on the income to the shareholders because the managers' input cannot be measured directly. This arrangement may induce managers to use their discretionary powers to manage income in a way that enhances their personal welfare. Managers operate the firm and its accounting and control, but their judgment in resolving the uncertainties of valuation is biased.

Independent audits are used to constrain the managers' tendency to manage income. How much damage income management does to the shareholders is a matter of some debate. In any case, the cost of audits makes total elimination of income management uneconomical. As a consequence, monetary representation of income to shareholders is less accurate and reliable than is the case with income of other agents. In this chapter we discuss the functions of income in a firm, the attitudes of various agents to this measure, and its management.

Law of Conservation of Income

The total lifetime income of a firm is invariant to the changes in accounting methods for the purpose of financial reporting. As long as these changes have no cash-flow effects (e.g., tax implications), changes in accounting methods shift income from one period to another without altering the total that will be recognized over the lifetime of the firm. This *Law of Conservation of Income* always holds as long as income is calculated using a clean surplus rule: All changes in owners' equity, except the transactions with the shareholders themselves, must pass through the income statement.

Since accounting income is measured without subtracting the cost of equity capital, this conservation law holds for undiscounted income. Perhaps it is better to call this the *Law of Conservation of Undiscounted Accounting Income*. It is easily modified to discounted form by subtracting the cost of the book value of the equity capital from accounting income to get the residual income. This calculation yields the *Law of Conservation of Discounted Residual Income.*

The lifetime sum of accounting income, as well as the discounted sum of residual income, are invariant to accounting methods. Both forms of the *Law of Conservation of Income* are derived from accounting identities. There is nothing true or false about them, as long as we the assume no cash-flow consequences and the clean surplus definition of income.

Functions of Income in a Firm

Both the process and the outcome of income measurement play an important role in operating the firm. Income itself measures the entitlement of the shareholders. The processes by which the entitlement of the government and the managers are determined depend on the process of measuring income to the shareholders. Because of its residual nature, income carries valuable clues about the continued viability of the firm. Agents use these clues to plan their own future and to renegotiate their contracts.

Assessing Viability of the Firm

Shareholder income, being a residual statistic, contains valuable information about the continued viability of the firm under its current policies and contracts. Low income (in relation to the equity input) could be the result of poor management, contracts unfavorable to the shareholders, or bad luck. Whatever the reason, poor income unambiguously informs all agents that the firm cannot survive in its current state. If all agents agree that low income resulted from transient bad luck, it is seen as a part of the risk borne by the shareholders. Everyone waits for another period and another turn of chance. If poor management or contracts that are disadvantageous for the shareholders are to blame for the low income, all agents are immediately put on notice that the firm will have to be dissolved unless these causes are repaired.

Shareholders have no reason to continue to participate in the firm if the expected returns on their investment are negative. If the firm is reorganized, all contracts are renegotiated. If the firm is liquidated, participants must look elsewhere for employment of their resources. The firm's income helps participants plan by predicting the demand for their contributions. No other accounting statistic carries information so vital to so many different agents.

Managerial Evaluation and Contract Renegotiation

If they believe that the cause of low income is not transient, shareholders press to renegotiate the contracts with managers, labor, vendors, customers, the government, and so on. All negotiations are conducted under an implicit threat of withdrawal by each agent. Credibility of these threats depends on the information that other agents have about alternative employment opportunities of each resource and the related transaction costs. A worker whose transferable skills are in high demand elsewhere can hardly be intimidated into making concessions by the threat of being laid off. The workers will simply find another job rather than agree to a lower wage. If the physical capital of the firm does not have an alternative use, the shareholders as a *group*, when faced with small, but positive income, have little flexibility. They continue to operate the firm, perhaps searching for better managers at the same time. If, on the other hand, income is negative, they can make credible threats to walk out or to dissolve the firm, even if the firm's physical capital has no alternative use. Wage concessions made by unions in the U.S. auto and steel industries in the early eighties are examples of this phenomenon. Pan American World Airways is an example of the failure of such negotiations and the resulting dissolution of the firm.

If income is higher than what the shareholders *as a group* could earn on alternative uses of the firm's physical capital, there is pressure on the shareholders to share some of the rents with the agents who supply other factors of production. Managers, labor, suppliers, and customers all seek to improve their share of the pie. Their ability to do so depends on the elasticity of supply of the respective resources. Income plays an important role in contract renegotiation among agents.

Attitudes of Agents Toward Income

The attitudes of various types of agents toward income vary, depending on how income affects their interests. We shall confine our discussion to shareholders and managers.

Shareholders

Income measured in units of money is an *estimate* of the shareholders' periodic entitlement from the firm; it is not the entitlement itself. The shareholders' stake in the firm, and changes in this stake, exist in the form of physical capital. For example, if the firm starts a period with five oranges and ten apples, and ends the period with six oranges and eight apples, its income for the period is one orange minus two apples. Translation of this physical-capital income into units of money could be labeled as *first-best valuation* if it were carried out by the proprietor or shareholder of the firm for his or her own information. Even this valuation is not without ambiguity. Changes in relative and nominal prices, and errors in measuring prices, cause errors in valuation.[2]

As much as shareholders would prefer to have income reported to them by the first-best valuation, there is no practical way of accomplishing this. Shareholders must depend on hired managers to translate physical capital income into units of money. Managers have their own interests to look after, and the luxury of forcing managers to report income by the first-best mapping is either not available to the shareholders of large corporations or is not worth the cost. Knowing this imperfection, shareholders do not mistake the income reported to them as the product of first-best valuation. Reported income is a noisy indicator of investors' resource entitlements. The contractual definition of income is in the form of physical capital. The imperfect monetary measure is produced only because the principal cannot be directly observed and conveniently reported.

For the purpose of making short-term trading decisions, individual investors use income as well as other sources of information. They get some direct information from the financial press, while the market process itself is an important source of indirect information. In Chapter 7 we discuss the attitude of equity investors toward accounting and control in the context of the stock market.

Managers

Following Berle and Means, Gordon suggested that managers can be expected to choose and operate an accounting system in a way that enhances their welfare.[3] The welfare of managers increases with job security, job level, compensation, and firm size, and each of these is directly or indirectly linked to higher corporate income. Further, if managers dislike risk, they attain a greater satisfaction when income is smoothed over reporting periods. Therefore, managers can be expected to resist reporting abrupt changes in income.

Consider a manager who is pouring over the preliminary financial statements near the end of the fiscal year and who knows the past income, dividends, sales, gross margins, and so on, as well as the projections of the future values of these variables. The uncertainty of future income and other variables increases with the projection interval. The manager may expect his or her own term of employment with the firm or tenure in his or her current position to be shorter than the planning horizon of the firm.

The manager has an approximate idea of how the board of directors evaluate him or her. If the manager receives a bonus—for example, a percentage of income when income exceeds a specified level—he or she could benefit by maximizing the firm's income. Since money earns interest, the manager prefers to receive a bonus earlier rather than later. The manager risks losing his or her job if income drops, unless some satisfactory explanation—an industry-wide drop in demand, for example—can be found to appease the shareholders and the board of directors. Income reported in the subsequent years may yield scant benefits to the fired manager, even if it is the result of his or her foresight and labor. If the manager's bonus is capped (cannot exceed some specified level), he or she may hide some income in good years and report it in leaner times. If the manager does not earn a bonus unless the income exceeds some minimum level, he or she may dump extra expenses into years that have poor results. In the 1990s, many U.S. firms have reported massive restructuring charges, setting up high earnings growth for subsequent years.

The manager may own stock, stock options, or warrants of the firm. This ownership gives the manager a beneficial interest in the market price of the firm's shares. In addition, evaluation of the manager's own performance may depend partly on the price of these securities. The manager may be interested not only in the current but also in the longer-term price of the firm's stock because his or her contract may not permit selling the stock or exercising stock options until a specified date.

Expectations of future dividends determine the value of stock for the long-term shareholders. However, for the shorter-term shareholders, the value derives only partly from the expectation of dividends. The rest of the value is based on their expectation of what others might be willing to pay for the stock at some time within their short decision horizon. In turn, what others might be willing to pay depends on their expectation of dividends and of what someone else might be willing to pay them for the stock. Thus, the current value of stock depends on the current shareholders' expectations of dividends, as well as on their expectations of the expectations of others. Keynes described the process of stock market valuation as follows:

> Professional investment may be likened to those newspaper competitions in which the competitors have to pick out the six prettiest faces from a hundred photographs, the prize being awarded to the competitor whose choice most nearly corresponds to the average preferences of the competitors as a whole; so that each competitor has to pick, not those faces which he himself finds prettiest, but those which he thinks likeliest to catch the fancy of the other competitors, all of whom are looking at the problem from the same point of view. It is not a case of choosing those which, to the best of one's judgment, are really the prettiest, nor even those which average opinion genuinely thinks the prettiest. We have reached the third degree where we devote our intelligences to anticipating what average opinion expects the average

opinion to be. And there are some, I believe, who practise the fourth, fifth and higher degrees.[4]

Unfortunately, expectations of one person about the expectations of another are not necessarily accurate. Managers know that people form their expectations about the future on the basis of past experience, of which past and current financial statements are an important part. The managers' desires to smooth the income stream arise not only from personal considerations postulated by Gordon,[5] but also from the role of income in forming of the expectations of other participating and potential agents. A variable income stream generates volatile investor expectations about the firm's future. Volatility is compounded when some investors believe that other investors do not fully understand the import of the data on hand and conclude that the price others would be willing to pay for the stock at some future time would be too high or too low compared to what they themselves would consider appropriate. Wealth constraints and the high costs of short-sale transactions prevent these differentials from being completely eliminated through arbitrage.

Low or negative income carries the possibility that the firm's contract set will be dissolved and all agents will be forced to incur the transaction costs of finding alternative employment for their resources. The manager's job and, therefore, a large chunk of the manager's human capital in the form of reputation, may be irretrievably lost on the downswing of a volatile income stream. Since the loss of the job can be an absorbing state (one that the manager cannot recover from), the manager has reason to prefer a smooth income series.

Unfortunately, from the managers' standpoint, there are limits on freedom to reduce the variability of the firm's income. Managers cannot iron out kinks in income already reported; their actions can only affect future reports. Altering production-investment decisions from their optimum levels has real cash-flow consequences for the firm. If the tax consequences of accounting choices alter the lifetime income of the firm, such decisions are best regarded as investment decisions. The effects of income shifts are usually spread over a number of future reporting periods, and managers can only estimate their pattern.

Managers cannot choose accounting methods at will. There is only a limited amount of flexibility in the accounting treatment of transactions, and they may have to obtain the consent of auditors to make a switch. Even if the auditors consent, any effect of accounting treatment on the current income will reverse in a later reporting period. Recall that the *Law of Conservation of Undiscounted Accounting Income* states that various accounting methods only shift income between the current and future reporting periods without altering the firm's total income over its lifetime. Feltham and Ohlson transform it into the *Law of Conservation of Discounted Residual Income*: the discounted current value of the residual income (accounting income–cost of equity capital) is insensitive to alternative accounting treatments.[6]

Managers are not certain about future results obtained in the absence of a smoothing decision. Furthermore, the firm's future income is uncertain, and managers do not know if the effect of current smoothing actions on the future income will actually increase the volatility of the income stream. They cannot sit down with a graph of the firm's income stream for the next ten years and iron out the peaks and valleys.

To make the earnings record look smooth, a manager could consider several type of actions, though none guarantee the intended effect. First, the manager could try to make the current income equal to last year's, possibly with some growth factored in. (But what if the last year's income was much lower than the previous year's income?) Second, the manager could try to make the current income closer to the average or weighted average for the past few years. (But what if next year's income is likely to be much lower than the current income? Would it be better to lower the expectations of next year's income gradually by lowering the current income to a certain extent, so next year's drop does not appear to be too steep?) The manager will have to make some assumptions about how far into the past the investors look at the accounting data and how far into the future the financial analysts probe in forming their expectations about the future. This process, unfortunately, is poorly understood.

Determination of Entitlements

Income measures the entitlement of the shareholders and helps determine the entitlement of the top managers. In addition, income-like measures, devised to determine the entitlements of the middle- and lower-level managers, play a crucial role in the control systems of firms.

Corporate net income is a weak motivating device for individual middle-level managers because their contribution to the overall income of the firm is small. For each middle manager, top managers devise an income-like measure to which compensation is linked. Each division of the firm can be thought of as a subfirm. The boss of the division head occupies the position of the sole shareholder and creditors in this subfirm. This single "owner" can exercise close control over how divisional income is measured.

Managers of relatively large divisions of the firm might be evaluated as investment, profit, and cost centers, depending on the extent to which they make resource contracts on their own. For example, when division managers make their own capital decisions, income of their units is measured in relation to the funds invested in them. If capital decisions are outside their control, but they control product market and other factor decisions, the units might be treated as a profit center. Absence of control over product market transactions may result in cost centers, where the cost of a given output becomes a negative measure of income for evaluation of the unit. Smaller units in an organization may have income-like measures specified in physical units.

Divisional income streams are aggregated to arrive at a corporate figure after elimination of double counting due to interdivisional transactions. Corporate income is the rope whose strands are threaded through the performance evaluation and control system at *all* managerial levels of the firm. The income number is the culmination of this managerial control process. The process of measuring at all levels is as important for the smooth operation of the firm's contracts as is the final number it produces. Although the chief executive officer wants broad discretion in the selection of accounting methods to determine the corporate income, the CEO might be reluctant to grant similar discretion to the divisional managers.

The government's share, in the form of income, excise, sales, value added, and property taxes, is also determined on the basis of the accounting system. Income plays a role only in determining income taxes, and the criteria for reporting revenue and expense for tax purposes are often different from the criteria used for financial reporting. This raises an interesting question: What is the economic explanation for these differences? The government, like the shareholders, has a residual interest in most firms. Indeed, it is often the largest single holder of such an interest. However, unlike the shareholders, the government does not make a precommitment of resources to the firm. These and other aspects of government involvement in accounting systems are discussed in Chapter 12.

A common system of accounting records and transactions analysis underlies the accounting for tax reporting as well as financial reporting. Most of their differences arise at higher levels of aggregation. This common system obviates the additional cost of maintaining and auditing a separate set of basic accounting records for each purpose.

Management of Income

The "first-best" mapping of physical resource income into dollars is rarely observed because the contractual system of the firm induces managers to depart from this neutral reporting. Furthermore, investors and other agents, expecting managers to engage in manipulation, would not necessarily accept the income reported as the result of such "first-best" mapping. Our understanding of how humans form expectations about natural events, the actions of others, and the expectations of others is still quite primitive. This weakness has frustrated many efforts to gain insights into the management of income by managers.

What do we understand by smoothness and smoothing of income? Managers' *attempts to smooth* income do not necessarily yield a statistically *smoother time series*. Indeed, such efforts can yield the opposite effect. In the following discussion we refer to corporate income, but most of it is equally applicable to income-like measures used at any level of managerial hierarchy.

Statistical Measures of Smoothness

There are many ways of measuring the smoothness of income series. Variability (about a constant mean, about a trend line, or about an exponentially smoothed mean) is a frequently used inverse measure of smoothness. First- and higher-order serial correlations provide another class of smoothness measures. The predictability of series from past data is the third class of measures.

The appeal of these measures is largely intuitive. Series that take extreme values can be said to be smooth in some well-specified sense. However, it is easy to construct counter-examples so that the statistics violate the intuition. For example, if series with low variability around a constant mean are to be regarded as smooth, a process that strictly follows a steep upward linear trend is less smooth than a constant mean process with a small independent error term (see Figure 5.1). The predictability of a series depends on the prediction model used and on the number of degrees of freedom one is willing to sacrifice in identifying the process from past data.

Income Processes: Smoothness versus Smoothing

Attempts to smooth time series of income are not always successful. The annual income of firms includes a significant *random walk* component.[7] In a random walk, current observation is the best bet for predicting the next observation. In such cases, manipulating the current observation to bring it closer to the preceding observation also increases the expected difference between the current and the following observation. So smoothing in the current period can be attained only by increasing the chance of a bigger change in the next period. It is in this sense that income smoothing and the so-called "big bath" are two sides of the same coin. We return to the big bath in the next section.

A manager can smooth income only one observation at a time, and cannot go back and change the past income already in the public domain. This restriction, combined with the random walk component of income and the *Law of Conservation of Undiscounted Accounting Income*, can cause a paradoxical situation. Managers may smooth income every period, and yet the smoothed time series so generated may be less smooth than the original series would have been.

Income Smoothing versus the "Big Bath" Hypotheses

The discretionary treatment of accounting items to decrease income in an otherwise poor year is called a *big bath* or *housecleaning*. What motives may sustain such behavior? Manager may believe that one very poor performance report is not as harmful as several mildly poor performance reports. Taking a big bath creates the opposite effect on subsequent performance reports. In January 1996, *The Wall Street Journal* reported that U.S. corporations were taking a big bath under the label of "restructuring charges" in order to set up healthy earnings growth in subsequent years.[8]

Several favorable performance reports could follow a big bath and more than compensate for its initial negative effect. Managers can choose the timing of the big bath so that it can be blamed on a poor year for the industry as a whole or on some disaster for the individual firm. The big bath can then readily be explained

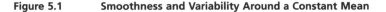

Figure 5.1   **Smoothness and Variability Around a Constant Mean**

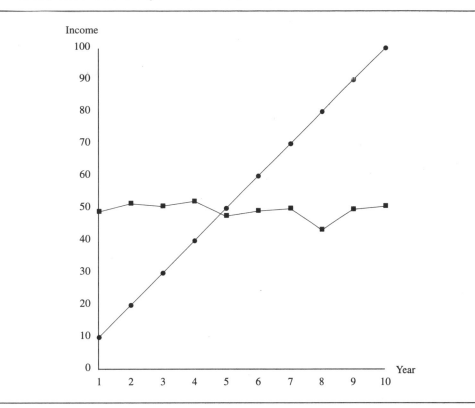

to outsiders as a consequence of factors outside management's control. The installation of a new management team is an attractive time to take the big bath, so that it can be blamed on the outgoing management. Finally, if the managerial compensation consists of a flat salary plus a nonnegative bonus based on the income of the firm, the manager can increase total compensation by loading the expenses into a single year when the firm's income is below the point that entitles the manager to a bonus. In other words, the convexity of the compensation schedule induces the big bath.

Income smoothing and the big bath complement each other in one sense, and contradict in another. If the raw, unsmoothed income follows a random walk, the variance of the cumulative sum of smoothing adjustments increases over time, and the probability that this adjustment will exceed the bounds of accounting discretion also increases with time. When the breaking point is reached, managers are forced to get back to the original path of the random walk by taking a big bath. In this sense, income smoothing of the random walk *causes* occasional big baths. A big bath is frequently accompanied by a change in management and the smoothing–big-bath cycle may repeat itself. Management may present smooth, moderately rising income for the years between the big baths. Thus, the smoothing motive is implicit in the big bath action, and the big bath is the likely consequence of smoothing in a random walk environment.

Management takes a big bath when it can avoid being blamed for it, thus excluding the loss of welfare involved in the large negative deviation and capturing the gain in welfare due to smaller period-to-period variations. If management can avoid the blame by appropriately timing the big bath, it can increase its welfare by the judicious use of smoothing and housecleaning actions within the framework of a broader policy of income management. If the tenure of a management team lasts the length of the interval between consecutive big bath actions, the loss of welfare caused by it is not imposed on the incoming management. From the point of view of the incoming management, it is best to clean house immediately after taking charge.

Instruments of Income Management

Instruments of income management can be divided into five classes: discretionary accounting treatment of transactions, selection of accounting principles, adjustment of accounting estimates, transfer prices, and substantive economic decisions. Let us look at each of these classes.

The accounting treatment of certain transactions, such as the repair and overhaul of equipment, the timing of recording a sale, and the write-down of inventories and equipment, is chosen by management. An outside observer cannot readily detect when such discretion is used with the intention to manage income.

Generally accepted accounting principles allow many transactions to be given one of two or more alternative accounting treatments. For example, choices can be made in accounting for inventory (LIFO, FIFO, average cost), depreciation (straight-line, accelerated), oil and gas exploration costs (full cost and successful efforts), and long-term contracts (completed-contract, percentage-of-completion). The initial choices and the changes in accounting principles are observable to outsiders. Most of the empirical work on income management concerns this type of instrument. However, as we have already discussed, accounting principles are not flexible instruments for income management: They cannot be put to repeated use, and the income shift effected through accounting methods tends to catch up with the manager over time.

Adjusting accounting estimates gives more flexibility to management. The allowance for bad debt, the economic life for depreciation, and the discount rate for pension obligations are some of the traditional instruments managers have used for many years. Massive restructuring charges, a relatively recent phenomena, also fall into this category for now, although they deserve a category of their own.

Firms that operate in multiple tax jurisdictions subject to progressive taxation have reason not only to transfer income from high-tax to low-tax jurisdictions, but also to smooth income within each tax jurisdiction. Transfer prices for goods and services exchanges among the subsidiaries of the firm provide an attractive instrument for this purpose.

Substantive economic decisions such as advertising, cash payments to pension plans, executive compensation, research and development, acquisition and divestiture of business segments, and the sale of property or investments may be motivated by considerations of their effects on short-run income. To find out whether and to what extent these decisions are affected by considerations of managing income, the "normal" decision of each type must be explicitly modeled and compared to the data. The difficulty of such modeling has been a major obstacle to obtaining unambiguous evidence on hypotheses about income management.

Although most individual research studies focus on only one or two of these instruments of income management, firms use many of these instruments at once. For example, most publicly held corporations in Japan work under the "main bank" system, in which they maintain a close relationship with their bank. These banks not only lend to highly leverage the firm, but also may hold substantial equity in the firm. They not only influence the dividend policy of their clients, but they also limit their discretionary decisions to manage their earnings through real transactions or accounting changes.[9]

Summary of Empirical Findings

The results of empirical investigation into income management have been weak and often inconsistent. A sampling of this literature is summarized below.

1. Gordon, Horwitz, and Myers examined the income series of the U.S. Steel Corp., using an exponential smoothing model, and concluded that the firm did not use the investment tax credit accounting as an instrument to smooth income.[10]

2. Archibald, Copeland, Copeland and Licastro, and White did not find evidence of income-smoothing.[11]

3. Cushing examined 666 instances of reported accounting changes for the period 1955–66 and found that material changes in accounting principles tended to smooth earnings.[12]

4. Dascher and Malcom found that discretionary smoothing variables were used in the chemical industry.[13]

5. Beidleman examined five variables and found that compensation, pension, research and development, and sales and advertising expenses are used as smoothing variables. Earnings remitted from the subsidiaries and plant retirements were not used in this manner.[14]

6. Moore found that management changes often coincided with income-reducing discretionary accounting decisions.[15]

7. Horwitz and Kolodny found that smaller companies tended to reduce their research and development outlays in response to FASB *Statement No. 2*, which

requires immediate expensing of such amounts.[16] Dukes, Dyckman, and Elliot found no evidence of such reaction among larger firms.[17]

8. Haselkorn found that the issuance of APB Opinion No. 8, specifying rules for expensing of pension costs, did not reduce the variability of pension expense.[18]

9. Sunder found no difference between short-run income response to new investments by the manager- and owner-run firms.[19]

10. Liberty and Zimmerman examined whether firms deliberately depressed reported income when labor negotiations were on-going[20] and did not find evidence supporting this hypothesis. (See also DeAngelo and DeAngelo.[21])

11. DeAngelo provided evidence that dissident shareholders take an immediate "bath" following a proxy contest to lay blame on prior management.[22]

12. DeAngelo examined whether managers systematically understated income prior to a management buyout. Evidence was not supportive.[23]

13. Jones provided evidence that managers implemented income-decreasing accruals during import relief investigations by the U.S. International Trade Commission (ITC).[24]

14. Boynton, Dobbins, and Plesko provided evidence that firms affected by the alternative minimum tax (AMT) book income provision undertook income-decreasing accruals in 1987.[25]

15. Cahan offered evidence that managers responded to antitrust investigations by adjusting their discretionary accruals.[26]

16. Pourciau provided evidence that when there are nonroutine executive changes, incoming executives managed accruals in a way that reduced income in the year of the change and increased income in the following year.[27]

On the whole, evidence in favor of the income-smoothing hypothesis is weak and inconsistent. This is not surprising, for four reasons.

1. Data are lacking to test a hypothesis about the relationship between two unobservables—raw or premanagement income and the managed component. Their surrogates, obtained mostly from their observable sum (the reported income) are not reliable enough.

2. Managers use many instruments (e.g., accounting methods, accounting estimates, production–investment–sales transactions, transfer pricing, tax planning) to manage income. Virtually all empirical studies of income management focus on one instrument, or type of instrument at a time.

3. As we have argued, income smoothing and the "big bath" are two sides of the same coin of income management, and we should expect them to coexist. Smoothing is too narrow an interpretation of income management.

4. If managers left obvious tracks of their income management activity in publicly available data, their contracts would be modified to discourage them from doing so. It is not surprising that they cover their tracks reasonably well.

Summary

Income to shareholders, being a residual, carries information valuable to all agents who participate in a firm or have an interest in doing so. Besides defining the entitlement of the shareholders, income to shareholders is often used to motivate managers by making their compensation dependent on it. This income also carries valuable clues to the future viability of the contract set and, therefore, plays an important role in agents' planning and renegotiation of the contracts.

Managers have special access to information about income and seek to manage income using instruments such as discretionary accounting treatment of transaction, choice of accounting principles, and substantive economic decisions. The use of substantive economic decisions to manage income helps to make the relationship between accounting and economic reality a reflexive one. When considerations of the appearance of accounting reports influence the objects that are reported upon, the reporting system can no longer be evaluated in terms of its representational faithfulness to those objects.

The smoothing and big bath hypotheses of accounting have received much attention from researchers. A premise of these efforts is that the income actually reported by firms gets corrupted by the self-serving actions of managers and, if we could define and identify this corruption, we could arrive at a more representationally faithful approximation of "economic income." The meaning and significance of *representational faithfulness* are doubtful in view of a reflexive relationship between accounting and its environment.

The contract model of the firm suggests that accounting is a system for producing mutually observable data for the purpose of settling exchanges and conflicts. Perhaps we could assess the value of alternative definitions of accounting income by focusing on how efficiently each measure serves that function, and not worry about its representational faithfulness per se to economic or any other concepts, especially if the latter are not defined in operational terms.

Notes

[1] J. R. Hicks, *Value and Capital*, 2d ed. (London: Oxford at the Clarendon Press, 1946), p. 172.

[2] S. S. Lim and Shyam Sunder, "Efficiency of Asset Valuation Rules Under Price Movement and Measurement Errors," *Accounting Review*, Vol. 66 (October 1991), pp. 669–693; Shyam Sunder and G. Waymire, "Marginal Gains in Accuracy of Valuation from Increasingly Specific Price Indexes: Empirical Evidence for the U.S. Economy," *Journal of Accounting Research*, Vol. 21, No. 2 (Autumn 1983), pp. 565–580; and "Accuracy of Exchange Valuation Rules: Additivity and Unbiased Estimation," *Journal of Accounting Research* (Spring 1984), pp. 396–405.

[3] Myron J. Gordon, "Postulates, Principles and Research in Accounting," *Accounting Review* (April 1964), pp. 251–263.

[4] John M. Keynes, *The General Theory of Employment, Interest and Money* (New York: Harcourt, Brace & Co., 1936), Chapter 12.

[5] Gordon, op. cit.

[6] Gerald Feltham and James Ohlson, "Valuation and Clean Surplus Accounting for Operating and Financial Activities," *Contemporary Accounting Research*, Vol. 11, No. 2 (Spring 1995), pp. 689–731.

[7] Sok-Hyon Kang, Li Zhang, and William Baber, "The Size and Economic Determinants of Random Walk Component of

Earnings," Carnegie Mellon University Working Paper (May 1996).

[8]Randall Smith and Steven Lipin, "Are Companies Using Restructuring Costs to Fudge the Figures?" *The Wall Street Journal*, January 30, 1996, p. A1.

[9]Takayoshi Okabe, "The Dividend Stabilization and Accounting Choices of Japanese Firms," Kobe University Working Paper, May 1995.

[10]M. J. Gordon, B. N. Horwitz and P. T. Meyers, "Accounting Measurements and Normal Growth of the Firm," *Research in Accounting Measurement*, ed. Ijiri and Nielsen Jaedicke (American Accounting Association, 1996), pp. 221–231.

[11]T. R. Archibald, "The Return to Straight Line Depreciation: An Analysis of a Change in Accounting Method," *Journal of Accounting Research*, Vol. 5 (Supplement 1967), pp. 164–180; R. M. Copeland, "Income Smoothing," *Empirical Research in Accounting: Selected Studies, 1968, Supplement to the Journal of Accounting Research*, Vol. 6 (1968), pp. 101–116; R. M. Copeland and R. D. Licastro, "A Note on Income Smoothing," *The Accounting Review* (July 1968), pp. 540–546; and C. E. White, "Discretionary Accounting Decisions and Income Normalization," *Journal of Accounting Research*, Vol. 8 (Autumn 1970), pp. 260–273.

[12]Barry E. Cushing, "An Empirical Study of Changes in Accounting Policy," *Journal of Accounting Research*, Vol. 7 (Autumn 1969), pp. 196–203.

[13]P. E. Dasher and R. E. Malcom, "A Note on Income Smoothing in the Chemical Industry," *Journal of Accounting Research*, Vol. 8 (Autumn 1970), pp. 253–259.

[14]Carl R. Beidleman, "Income Smoothing: The Role of Management," *The Accounting Review*, Vol. 48, No. 4 (October 1973), pp. 653–667.

[15]Michael L. Moore, "Management Changes and Discretionary Accounting Decisions," *Journal of Accounting Research*, Vol. 11, No. 1 (Spring 1973), pp. 100–107.

[16]Bertrand N. Horwitz and Richard Kolodny, "The Economic Effects of Involuntary Uniformity in Financial Reporting of R&D Expenditures," *Studies on Economic Consequences of Financial and Managerial Accounting: Effects on Corporate Incentives and Decisions*, Supplement to *Journal of Accounting Research*, Vol. 18 (1980), pp. 38–74.

[17]Ronald E. Dukes, Thomas R. Dyckman, and John A. Elliott, "Accounting for Research and Development Expenditures,"

Studies on Economic Consequences of Financial and Managerial Accounting: Effects on Corporate Incentives and Decisions, Supplement to *Journal of Accounting Research*, Vol. 18 (1980), pp. 1–37.

[18]Michael Haselkorn, "Effect of APB Opinion 8 on Variability of Pension Expense," Ph.D. Dissertation, University of Chicago (1979).

[19]Shyam Sunder, "Corporate Capital Investment, Accounting Methods and Earnings: A Test of the Control Hypothesis," *Journal of Finance*, Vol. 35, No. 2 (May 1980), pp. 553–565.

[20]Susan E. Liberty and Jerold L. Zimmerman, "Labor Union Contract Negotiations and Accounting Choices," *Accounting Review*, Vol. 61, No. 4 (October 1986), pp. 692–712.

[21]Harry DeAngelo and Linda E. DeAngelo, "Union Negotiations and Corporate Policy: A Study of Labor Concessions in the Domestic Steel Industry During the 1980s," *Journal of Financial Economics*, Vol. 30, No. 1 (November 1991), pp. 3–43.

[22]Linda DeAngelo, "Managerial Competition, Information Costs, and Corporate Governance: The Use of Accounting Performance Measures in Proxy Contests," *Journal of Accounting and Economics*, Vol. 10, No. 1 (January 1988), pp. 3–31.

[23]Linda DeAngelo, "Accounting Numbers as Market Valuation Substitutes: A Study of Management Buyouts of Public Stockholders," *Accounting Review*, Vol. 61, No. 3 (July 1986), pp. 400–420.

[24]Jennifer J. Jones, "Earnings Management During Import Relief Investigations," *Journal of Accounting Research*, Vol. 29, No. 2 (Autumn 1991), pp. 193–228.

[25]Charles E. Boynton, Paul S. Dobbins, and George A. Plesko, "Earnings Management and the Corporate Alternative Minimum Tax," *Journal of Accounting Research*, Vol. 30 (Supplement 1992), pp. 131–153.

[26]Steven F. Cahan, "The Effect of Antitrust Investigations on Discretionary Accruals: A Refined Test of the Political-Cost Hypothesis," *Accounting Review*, Vol. 67, No. 1 (January 1992), pp. 77–95.

[27]Susan Pourciau, "Earnings Management and Nonroutine Executive Changes," *Journal of Accounting and Economics*, Vol. 16, Nos. 1–3 (Jan–Apr–Jul 1993), pp. 317–336.

Additional Reading

Albrecht, W. S., L. L. Lookabill, and J. C. McKeown. "The Time-Series Properties of Annual Earnings." *Journal of Accounting Research* (Autumn 1977), pp. 226–244.

Ball, R., and R. L. Watts. "Some Time Series Properties of Accounting Income." *Journal of Finance* (June 1972), pp. 663–681.

Balsam, S., I. Haw, and S. B. Lillien. "Mandated Accounting Changes and Managerial Discretion." *Journal of Accounting and Economics*, Vol. 20 (July 1995), pp. 3–30.

Bartov, Eli. "The Timing of Asset Sales and Earnings Manipulation." *Accounting Review*, Vol. 68 (October 1993), pp. 840–855.

DeChow, Patricia M., and Richard G. Sloan. "Executive Incentives and the Horizon Problem." *Journal of Accounting and Economics*, Vol. 14 (1991), pp. 51–89.

DeChow, Patricia M., R. G. Sloan, and A. P. Sweeny. "Detecting Earnings Management." *Accounting Review*, Vol. 70 (April 1995), pp. 193–226.

DeFond, Mark L, and Jiambalvo James. "Debt Covenant Violation and Manipulation of Accruals." *Journal of Accounting & Economics*, Vol. 17, Nos. 1, 2 (January 1994), pp. 145–176.

Dye, Ron. "Earnings Management in an Overlapping Generations Model." *Journal of Accounting Research*, Vol. 26 (Spring 1988), 195–235.

Gaver, Jennifer, J., Kenneth M. Gaver, and Jeffrey R. Austin. "Additional Evidence on Bonus Plan and Income Management." *Journal of Accounting and Economics*, Vol. 19 (1995), pp. 3–28.

Gonedes, Nicholas J. "Income Smoothing Behavior Under Selected Stochastic Processes." *Journal of Business*, Vol. 45, No. 4 (October 1972), pp. 570–584.

Hand, J. "Did Firms Undertake Debt-Equity Swaps for an Accounting Paper Profit or True Financial Gains?" *Accounting Review*, Vol. 64 (October 1989), pp. 587–623.

Healy, Paul M. "The Effect of Bonus Schemes on Accounting Decisions." *Journal of Accounting and Economics*, Vol. 7 (April 1985), pp. 85–107.

Healy, Paul M., and Krishna G. Palepu. "Effectiveness of Accounting-Based Dividend Covenants." *Journal of Accounting and Economics*, Vol. 12, Nos. 1–3 (January 1990), pp. 97–123.

Hines, Ruth D. "Why Won't the FASB Conceptual Framework Work?" Working Paper, Macquarie University, 1987.

Holthausen, Robert W., David F. Larcker, and Richard G. Sloan. "Annual Bonus Schemes and the Manipulation of Earnings." *Journal of Accounting and Economics*, Vol. 19 (1995), pp. 29–74.

Kang, Sok-Hyon, and K. Sivaramakrishnan. "Issues in Testing Earnings Management and an Instrumental Variable Approach." *Journal of Accounting Research*, Vol. 33, No. 2 (Autumn 1995), pp. 353–368.

Lambert, Richard A. "Income Smoothing as Rational Equilibrium Behavior." *Accounting Review*, Vol. 59, No. 4 (October 1984), pp. 604–618.

Matsunaga, Steven R. "The Effects of Financial Reporting Costs on the Use of Employee Stock Options." *Accounting Review*, Vol. 70, No. 1 (January 1995), pp. 1–26.

McNichols, Maureen, and G. P. Wilson. "Evidence of Earnings Management from the Provision for Bad Debts." *Journal of Accounting Research*, Vol. 26 (Supplement 1988), pp. 1–31.

Neill, John D, Susan G. Pourciau, and Thomas F. Schaefer. "Accounting Method Choice and IPO Valuation." *Accounting Horizons*, Vol. 9, No. 3 (September 1995), pp. 68–80.

Ronen, Joshua, and S. Sadan. *Smoothing Income Numbers: Objective, Means and Implications*. Reading, Mass.: Addison-Wesley Publishing Co., 1981.

Sivaramakrishnan, K. "Information Asymmetry, Participation and Long-Term Contracts." *Management Science*, Vol. 40 (October 1994), 1228–1244.

Suh, Y. "Communication and Income Smoothing Through Accounting Method Choice." *Management Science*, Vol. 36 (1990), 704–723.

Sunder, Shyam. "Accuracy of Exchange Valuation Rules." *Journal of Accounting Research*, Vol. 16, No. 2 (Autumn 1978) pp. 341–367.

Sunder, Shyam. "Measurement of Smoothness of Accounting Series," University of Chicago Working Paper, August 1975.

Sweeney, A. P. "Debt-Covenant Violations and Managers' Accounting Responses." *Journal of Accounting and Economics*, Vol. 17 (1994), pp. 281–308.

Trueman, B. and S. Titman. "An Explanation for Accounting Income Smoothing." *Journal of Accounting Research*, Vol. 26 (Supplement 1988), pp. 127–139.

Watts, R. L., and R. W. Leftwich. "The Time Series of Annual Accounting Earnings." *Journal of Accounting Research* (Autumn 1977), pp. 253–271.

6

Investors and Accounting

● ●

A long interval of time often separates investors' commitment of resources to the firm and the receipt of their inducements. Although other agents may wait for days or weeks, investors typically wait for years. Moreover, equity investors are entitled only to what remains after the resources due to all other agents have been set aside. This arrangement renders shareholders' welfare highly sensitive to any malfunction in accounting and control. When some agents either fail to contribute the contracted resources, or take more resources than are due to them, the investors end up bearing much of the loss. Contribution and inducement measurement and the contract fulfillment aspects of accounting and control are therefore crucial in protecting investors' interests. How do accounting and control affect the welfare of various types of investors, and how do investors protect their interests?

Description of the Investor Class

In the following discussion, we will limit the scope to holders of common equity and debt securities. What characteristics of these investors determine their participation in a firm's accounting and control?

The Lack of Active Participation

Most individual shareholders of a large corporation do not have an effective voice in corporate decisions unless they cooperate among themselves. Such cooperation, in the form of proxy fights, occurs only infrequently. Equity investors' ability to participate directly in managerial decisions of the firm is largely confined to yes/no votes on resolutions framed by hired managers. In the absence of an organized proxy fight, resolutions placed before the shareholders by managers rarely go down to defeat. Most small shareholders have little information about, and understanding of, the issues that lie behind the resolutions. A page or two in explanation of each resolution, written by the managers themselves, is all that the shareholders receive. The financial press does not cover the details unless a proxy fight is on for a large firm.

The lack of active involvement in, and relative ignorance of, corporate affairs on the part of the shareholders is hardly accidental. It is exactly what the shareholders want and expect when they purchase the stock of a firm. Most shareholders have no desire to spend time or effort personally monitoring the performance of managers and other agents. They rely on auditors, regulators, and law enforcement authorities to use the system of accounting standards, corporate charters, and laws to protect shareholder interests. They pay for this protection through audit fees and taxes. They trade the loss of direct control of the firm against the corresponding gains in the form of diversification of their investment portfolio across firms, saving in personal effort and freedom from the need for investment expertise. They do little more than cash the dividend checks, glance at the pretty pictures and perhaps a few numbers in the annual report, and fill out the proxy card by marking x in a few boxes. They also reserve the right to sue if they believe that their fiduciary trust in the managers and auditors has been betrayed.

It would be inappropriate to conclude from this discussion that the return on equity investment in professionally managed firms should be lower than that in owner-managed firms. Following Berle and Means, a number of empirical studies of comparative returns on two types of corporations yielded ambiguous results.[1] If returns were higher to equity investment in corporations where a few large investors actively participated in its management, smaller investors would shift their investments to such firms. Such a shift has two consequences. First, the large shareholders, who contribute personal effort in managing the corporation, would extract extra returns for themselves in the form of pay or perquisites to prevent the smaller shareholders from taking a free ride on their efforts. This tends to equate the return to smaller shareholders across the two types of corporations. Second, economies of scale associated with certain technologies, say, the manufacture of large aircraft, may require firms of such large size that no single investor or group of investors has enough wealth to acquire an effective voice in its management. Equity investors in such industries may be able to earn a higher rate of return because owner-operated firms cannot compete in this segment. These two factors, considered together, narrow the difference between the rates of return on equity investment in the owner-managed and professionally managed firms.

Transferability of Contract

Rights and obligations associated with shares of stock are designed so that they can be transferred easily at minimal cost (usually at no more than 1–2 percent of value). When future prospects of the firm change, small transaction costs make it possible for the market price of the shares to adjust rapidly to reflect such change.

Equity markets are liquid because of information symmetry between the buyers and sellers of such rights. If the cost of obtaining information for the non-participating agents were significantly higher than for the existing shareholders, the former would be informationally disadvantaged, leading to wider bid–ask spreads (the difference between the highest price a buyer is willing to pay and the lowest price a seller is willing to accept) and, therefore, to a less liquid equity market. Because information available to both the participating and the nonparticipating shareholders is identical, they reap the benefits of a liquid market. In contrast, asymmetry of information about privately held firms causes the transaction costs associated with initial public offerings to be high.

Heterogeneity of Preferences

The existence of a liquid market for equity claims resolves the problem of heterogeneity of preferences among shareholders. As long as no one acquires a large block of stock, other participating agents need not pay attention to the risk and time preferences of individual stockholders. A well-functioning market summarizes all they need to know about the shareholder preferences in a single statistic: the market price. In a well-functioning market, the maximization of the market price is equivalent to maximizing the shareholders' wealth and it provides an unambiguous index of the preferences of a heterogeneous body of investors for managers and other participating agents.

Information and Speed of Price Adjustments

The market price of equity claims adjusts rapidly to changes in their prospects. The change in price is accompanied by a change in wealth. How this wealth is shared between existing and prospective shareholders depends on who gets the information first. During the interval when the price moves from the old to the new equilibrium level, informed investors have an opportunity to benefit from the change. Contractual arrangements are drawn to ensure that the release of such information, whenever it is within the control of managers, is equitable. Trading on the basis of inside information, accounting or any other, is illegal, not only for managers, but also for others who may have privileged access to it.

Information Intermediaries

The rapid adjustment of prices to information about changes in the future prospects of equity claims implies that such information is continually sought by at least some market participants. The effects of new events on the claims' value have to be evaluated and acted upon in a matter of days or hours, sometimes even in minutes. This activity is costly and needs expertise.

Other things being equal, it is better for risk-averse investors to spread their investments over several firms. However, the information costs of actively managing investments increase with the number of firms monitored. The costs of processing information and the benefits of diversification give rise to intermediaries who specialize in gathering and interpreting information. Information intermediaries sell either the digested information directly, or rights in a portfolio of investments managed on the basis of such information. Financial analysts belong to the former group; financial intermediaries, such as banks, mutual funds, and pension funds belong to the latter.

The growing presence of information intermediaries in the stock markets changes the picture of diffuse equity ownership that we have painted in the previous section. A large block of stock in the hands of an information intermediary, however, does not have the same effect as it would in the hands of a single large shareholder, because such intermediaries rarely seek to participate in operating control of the firm, and are often legally barred from exercising such control.

Since the quality and quantity of the portfolio managers' efforts are not directly observable, their contracts are designed to make their compensation dependent on investment results. These managers have an interest in managing portfolios to serve their own best interests. The performance of portfolios is less than perfectly correlated with the unobserved quality and quantity of the portfolio manager's effort. Moreover, the decision horizon of portfolio managers is shorter than that of the owners who benefit from the portfolio. As a result, portfolio managers rely on the short-term measures of corporate performance in their investment decisions. The reaction of corporate managers to such behavior by institutional investors is to alter their own production-investment and accounting decisions with a view to "manage" the annual as well as the quarterly reports.

The net result of institutionalized portfolio management is to shorten the decision horizon of corporate managers. Corporate managers can counteract this tendency by modifying their own compensation packages so a greater part of their personal wealth remains invested in the firm. Only those managers who feel confident about the future of the firm they manage can afford to send such a signal to the outsiders. Less competent and less optimistic managers can hardly afford to mimic such a strategy and convince the investors to put their trust in the future of the firm.

Since financial analysts sell information, they demand disclosure of accounting and other information. The greater the disclosure, the higher the value of their salable interpretive services. Individual investors want financial information to be easily understandable, but financial analysts can dissect complicated reports with their specialized skills and resources. Complex financial statements render the individual investor more dependent on the services of expert analysts. Thus, financial analysts help channel and focus the demand for more financial information, making the market for equity claims more liquid. By pressing for more detailed and complicated financial statements and disclosures, they shift resources from other investors to themselves. This resource transfer is the cost investors bear for the benefits of liquidity.

On the other hand, financial intermediaries who manage investment portfolios rarely demand public disclosures of financial and other data. They are more passive toward public financial reporting. When their investment in a firm is large enough, they can usually get the information they want by asking the firm directly. They have little incentive to press for public disclosure.

Creditors

Unlike shareholders, creditors do not make a permanent commitment of capital to the firm. Term, security, and diffusion are three characteristics of creditors that define their relationship to the accounting and control of their debtors.

Short-term creditors are interested largely in current assets and current liabilities and in the short-term ability of the firm to pay them. Until the early part of this century, when long-term loans were not yet common, much of the external audit effort was centered on verifying current assets and liabilities, and the auditors paid little attention to fixed assets.

On the other hand, long-term creditors place greater reliance on accounting and control, especially with respect to long-term assets, because the valuation of such assets is a weak link in accounting. Secured creditors have less interest in the operation of accounting and control because their interests are protected by the debt covenant.

Information intermediaries play a more important role when bonds are held by a large number of small investors. Large creditors have enough leverage with the debtor firm to demand and obtain the information they want directly. They rarely show much interest in the standard-setting activities of the FASB or the SEC.

Covenants accompanying debt instruments place restrictions on a firm's ability to pay dividends, to buy treasury stock, to issue new debt or retire old debt, or to allow certain accounting ratios to take values outside specified ranges. For example, the current ratio may be restricted from below and the debt-equity ratio from above. Debt covenants rarely use anything other than generally accepted accounting principles (GAAP) to specify such constraints, in spite of the possibility that the managers or shareholders may seek relief from such constraints by changing the methods of accounting. The multiplicity of accounting practices included in GAAP allows managers the flexibility to avoid violating debt covenants.

Why don't the creditors write debt covenants to tighten accounting constraints by insisting that the methods of accounting used at the time the covenant is signed remain applicable throughout the term of the covenant? One problem with such a "fixed" GAAP arrangement is that the creditor must incur the additional costs of outside auditors to monitor and enforce special accounting provisions of the covenant. A second possible explanation lies in the role accounting plays in the measurement of all inputs and entitlements of agents involved in the firm. Accounting changes may be induced by a variety of changes in the firm's environment as various agents make adjustments to protect their interests. By ruling out all changes in the accounting methods used for the enforcement of covenants, the creditor would also rule out any beneficial changes that may be implemented. It may be economical for creditors to cast their lot with other agents in relying on

GAAP to preserve the integrity of the accounting and control, instead of trying to set up a separate, parallel accounting apparatus specific to each debt covenant. If every agent tried to specify a special accounting system with the firm, the high cost and low credibility of multiple systems might render them even less attractive than relying on a floating GAAP.

Investor Attitudes and Preferences

It is important for investors to learn about contract performance by other agents. Investors weigh the information received from managers on the basis of its reliability and informativeness.

Reporting on Contract Performance

From an investor's point of view, a firm's accounting and control must ensure that the resources drawn by various agents from the firm's pool do not exceed what they are entitled to. The accounting system controls resource flows. A degree of costly redundancy is deliberately built into the double-entry bookkeeping to make it difficult for individuals to defraud the firm. Internal and external audits and the system review help implement this function.

Information on contract performance is important not only to the current but also to the prospective shareholders. The symmetric provision of such information to both existing and potential shareholders promotes liquidity in the market for shares of the firm. This liquidity is valued by shareholders, not only because one day they might wish to sell their shares, but also because the liquidity permits accurate and reliable valuation of the shares they might use as collateral in their other transactions.

Incentives to Managers

Inducing managers to contribute their optimum input and ensuring that they draw no more than their due are important and closely related functions of accounting and control. The financial reporting part of the accounting system is intended to control the top managers. The top managers have the responsibility for designing the incentives and controls for middle- and lower-level managers.

The relevance and reliability of data that can be provided by an accounting system are bounded from above by the considerations of cost and managerial incentives. The data most relevant to valuation of a firm's stock are also more subjective and costly to verify. Accordingly, their use has to be balanced against the possibility of deception by managers who provide the data. Asking managers to report data that cannot be independently verified at a reasonable cost adds nothing to the welfare of investors, because the response of the managers would be self-serving and investors would not trust it. This is exactly what seems to have happened to the unverified and often unverifiable data disclosed by oil and gas firms under the reserve-recognition accounting methods proposed by the SEC. In 1978, *Accounting Series Release No. 253* required firms to disclose estimated underground reserves of oil and gas.[2] The extreme subjectivity of such estimates rendered such data almost useless. In 1981, after a few years of experimentation, the SEC withdrew the proposal.

Aggregation Adds Information

More detailed financial reports are not necessarily more useful to investors. Using the theorem on greater value of information from a finer system, it has been argued that, in the absence of computational costs or information overload, more detailed data are more valuable.[3] However, it is inappropriate to apply Blackwell's theorem if the aggregation function for all levels of detail is not available to the decision maker. The free, universal availability of an aggregation function is not typical in accounting contexts. A single-page balance sheet can be more valuable to an investor than a hundred-page printout of all the account balances, not merely because of the computational costs but also because a considerable amount of detailed information must be *added* to these data in order to arrive at the aggregated balance sheet. The added information is contained in the aggregation function.

To illustrate, in the process of aggregation, accountants add their knowledge and judgment about similarities and dissimilarities of various accounts. To write a single line in the aggregated balance sheet (say, Inventories—$1 million), it is not sufficient to have a detailed list of each of the firm's resources. One must also know the characteristics of all the resources and be able to decide which items from the detailed list could be usefully aggregated into a single line item labeled *inventory* on the balance sheet. This task cannot be performed by a lay person. An accounting expert brings special knowledge of aggregation functions and adds this information to the disaggregated data in order to arrive at the aggregated balance sheet. As an example, most investors could not find much use for a computer printout of each item that General Motors owns, even if they had free access to a supercomputer and computational software.

Accounting Choice Mechanisms for Investors

Investors influence a firm's accounting decisions at four different stages: organization of the firm, trading in capital markets, voting on resolutions, and through sociopolitical institutions.

Organization of the Firm

In selecting a form of organization for a firm, its promoters also commit themselves to certain accounting features. In the United States, if the firm's stock is distributed publicly, the accounting requirements of federal security laws govern its contract set. These laws and financial reporting standards present shareholders and other agents with a contractual template or outline in which the details are filled in by the participants. Standardization restricts the agents' flexibility in designing the accounting and control to suit the specific needs of the firm. It also saves search and negotiating costs for the participants. The better fit of a custom-made contract set is not necessarily worth the additional cost.

Investors often insist on, and sometimes succeed in, altering certain financial reporting practices of the firm when it issues its securities. They often demand that the firm hire a reputed audit firm before they will buy or trade its securities. Primary issues are usually sold to investment bankers or large investors who have concentrated buying power. It is easier for such investors to negotiate effectively with the firm's managers.

When shares of stock pass through the secondary market, from investment bankers to a diffuse body of smaller shareholders, the ability of shareholders to exercise influence on accounting matters is attenuated and transformed. The shareholders have two instruments for making their preferences about the firm's accounting choices known to the managers: voting on resolutions placed before them and trading the stock of the firm in the tertiary market.

Voting and Proxies

Voting allows only a yes/no choice to the shareholders, with little participation in framing the agenda. It is occasionally possible for the shareholders to initiate a resolution and put it to a vote. Such resolutions rarely pass. Typical resolutions put to a vote of the shareholders deal with the appointment of the board of directors and auditors, modifications in managerial compensation, and changes in the charter of the firm. Rarely do they deal with accounting matters. The relative unimportance of the voting mechanism for accounting issues suggests that the shareholders have, at best, only limited ability or interest in changing the accounting system of the firm in which they hold an interest. Given the shareholders' vulnerability to fraud, this lack of interest may be surprising. In reality, shareholders have other, more effective, alternatives. In addition to using legal remedies, they vote with their feet, so to speak, in the stock market.

Trading in Capital Markets

A share of stock represents a bundle of contractual rights and obligations. Accounting is a part of this system of contracts. Investors can freely choose from a variety of contracts available in the market. The value of a share of stock derives, ultimately, from the dividends, and the size of dividends depends on how carefully the entitlements of various agents are determined and distributed. Other things being equal, investors would pay less for the stock of a firm that uses ineffective internal controls, internal audit, outside audit, and disclosure of accounting policies.

The influence of shareholders on accounting systems may be compared to the influence of car buyers on car designs. Neither the shareholder nor the car buyer takes a direct role in design, yet they influence it profoundly by their right to buy or not to buy the final bundle of products and services offered to them. The common stock of limited liability firms in the United States is more widely held than in any other country. It is tempting to speculate that this breadth of stock holdings and the liquidity of the stock market may be caused by the financial reporting and disclosure required of publicly held firms in the United States.

Current shareholders benefit from changing the accounting system of a firm if the result is a higher share price. Investor decisions on accounting are essentially "reactionary." They adjust their portfolios in response to decisions made by managers and auditors. Accounting control is a technical matter; direct input from investors is not feasible. Yet the anticipation of their preferences has a profound effect on the design of accounting and control systems. Managers' and auditors' anticipation of investor response affects their decisions on accounting, even though investors do not participate in the process directly.

Several accounting events support this view. We discussed the LIFO example in Chapter 4. In 1964, the Accounting Principles Board proposed that the investment tax credit be accounted for by using the deferral method instead of the then-prevalent flow-through method. They faced unified opposition from many managers and auditors, and ultimately had to back down. The possibility of negative investor response, though unsupported by data, was given as the basis of that opposition. Kaplan and Roll later found evidence that investor response was not negative.[4]

Sociopolitical Institutions

Legislatures, regulatory agencies, and the courts sometimes make or induce changes in accounting standards and in the institutions that set accounting standards. Such changes, usually triggered by major scandals or financial disasters, affect broad classes of firms. When some agents behave differently from what other agents expect of them, and the latter have no economic or legal remedy to make the former conform, the contract set falls apart. The disintegration of major firms, or of many small firms within a short period of time, suggests that the existing legal framework does not provide a stable basis for contracting in the prevailing economic environment and needs to be changed. The stock market crash of 1929 led to the passage of federal security laws and the creation of the SEC. These laws required that the annual financial reports of all publicly held firms in the United States be independently audited before publication. Since then, rules issued by the SEC have been a major force in shaping the accounting systems of publicly held corporations in the United States.

Similarly, the discovery of widespread use of bribes and unaccounted-for money led the U.S. Congress to pass the Foreign Corrupt Practices Act in 1977. The title of this statute is partially misleading. Its significant provisions relate not to briberies abroad but to the legal responsibility of corporate managers to maintain an effective system of internal controls to preserve their firm's resources against misappropriation. Prior to 1977, there were no explicit legal provisions to ensure that publicly held corporations protect the interests of their shareholders through appropriate design of their accounting and control.

Compared to stock prices, the response of sociopolitical systems to demands for change is slow. When changes do occur, they tend to be broader in scope. Changes through the market mechanism occur frequently and in smaller steps. In Chapters 11 and 12, we return to ask: To what extent should the shaping of the accounting and control be left to the markets versus the governmental and regulatory system?

Consequences of Accounting Policy for Investors

Although current shareholders pay the cost of accounting, financial reports are shared with the public. Professional investment analysts may even have better access to this information. A closer look at this arrangement reveals that it is not all unfavorable to the shareholders.

Accounting Information as Public Goods

Published financial reports are public goods. It costs no more to produce the financial reports for two people than for one, and it is difficult to keep those who do not pay for them from taking a free ride on the efforts of those who do. It has been argued that in the current system current shareholders pay the entire cost of financial reports, even though the benefits are shared with potential shareholders. Gonedes and Dopuch have argued that the resultant underproduction of information and misallocation of resources by corporations could be corrected if the right to accounting information were "unbundled" from the right to residual wealth, freeing the corporation to sell the information separately to those willing to pay for it.[5]

The availability of reliable information to all agents facilitates the smooth and orderly operation of a system of contracts. Assurance that they have or will receive the resources due to them from the firm is important. Without such information, an agent will refuse to participate. The information available to each agent acts as a constraint on others to induce them to meet the obligations they have accepted. The shareholders, being completely precommitted with respect to their capital, are not in direct touch with the day-to-day operations of the firm, and are too diffuse to act cohesively, to issue directives, or to negotiate directly. Therefore, they are especially vulnerable to the misappropriation of resources by other agents. The integrity of accounting and control is more important to them. All other participating agents are either in direct touch with the operations of the firm, or form a group cohesive enough to negotiate effectively with the firm and to have information about their entitlements available to them, outside published financial statements.

No stable system of contracts that denies information about the firm to the suppliers of equity capital seems feasible. Even if it were feasible, it would not be more efficient than the current system based on public disclosure. As we discussed earlier, the availability of information about a firm facilitates the operation of the markets for resources that flow into and out of the firm. Outsiders (agents who do not currently participate in the firm) are not the only ones who benefit from the liquidity of factor markets. Participating agents who wish to vacate their contractual slots in the firm to seek alternative opportunities also benefit. They can sell their current contractual slot or transport their reputation and human capital to more attractive employment someplace else. Further, participating agents who are not directly involved in the transaction also benefit from their ability to find a prompt replacement for the vacated slot when a participant leaves. Unfilled contractual slots hurt all participating agents (unless, of course, they are redundant). Thus, "free" distribution of information is important to the dynamic stability of the firm in order to keep it intact, in spite of the movement of some or even all of the participating individuals.

A further shortcoming of a private information system is that even if everyone were to buy information, agents would not know that everybody else is also informed. This lack of "common knowledge" in a private purchase system of information would induce strategic behavior, more conflicts, and less efficient renegotiation of corporate contracts.

In capital markets, accounting plays a role akin to the role of advertising in product markets. An automobile dealer who places an advertisement in a newspaper "gives away" information to prospective customers and competitors. The dealer's justification for paying the advertising costs lies in the belief that his or her own benefits outweigh the cost of advertising. Public disclosure of accounting information may also be viewed as advertisements to attract new participants to join the firm. The economic viability of such a "free" distribution system rests on the excess of benefits over costs to the current participants.

Production of Information By Intermediaries

When information intermediaries such as financial analysts and investment agents process information, who pays the cost, and what, if any, are the benefits to those who pay? Early empirical results on the ability of capital markets to rapidly adjust prices to incorporate newly available information produced a euphoria that lead some to declare that the days of financial analysts were numbered. Financial analysts who earn their living by reading patterns in the past history of stock prices, or those who keep a close watch on the economic prospects of specific firms and industries, have not only survived the revolution in the theory of finance, they are flourishing on Wall Street. Who pays their wages and why?

An analyst who finds out about or infers an event that affects the price of a firm, before other analysts, has the ability to earn abnormal returns in a shorter period of time than it usually takes for others to acquire the knowledge, and for the price to adjust to the new equilibrium level. This abnormal return is absorbed by the cost of the analysts' effort to discover and interpret the information. Since there are few barriers to entering this field, it seems reasonable to conclude that large economic rents, positive or negative, could not persist in the business of financial analysis.

An investor, who trades at random and without the benefit of advance information about economic events, expects to lose a small amount on transactions with an analyst, and the analyst expects to gain on the transaction. In equilibrium, the investor's expected loss is just enough to make him or her indifferent between continuing the current investment practice and buying the services of an analyst.

If nobody did the research, prices would have no relationship to economic events and, therefore, the capital market would fail to serve its resource allocation function in society. Even a small investor benefits from the ability of the market to adjust rapidly to new information because greater liquidity narrows the bid-ask spread and permits the investor to make transactions at reduced cost.

The release of financial information by corporate managers to financial analysts in the form of interviews, informal estimates of sales and earnings, and so on are sometimes criticized for favoring information intermediaries over smaller shareholders. Similar criticism is made of the newer financial accounting standards and disclosure requirements, which have made it easier for financial analysts to obtain detailed information, and at the same time, made the financial statements less comprehensible to nonexperts. Open entry to financial analysis makes it unlikely that analysts earn economic rents from this privileged access. The adverse terms of trade that an uninformed investor faces against an informed one must be balanced against the benefits of liquidity that accrue to all market participants in a well-informed market.

Summary

As a class of agents, investors occupy a special place in the firm. They precommit resources to the firm and agree to the passage of a relatively long, even indefinite, interval of time before receiving their share of resources from the firm. The resource entitlement of shareholders, as class, is defined as a residual and not as a function of their contribution. This arrangement makes investors vulnerable to unforeseen events and to the misappropriation of resources by other agents. When anything goes wrong with the implementation of contracts, investors end up bearing a large part of the loss. This vulnerability of investors to the malfunctioning of the contractual system is compensated by giving them special rights to elect the board of directors and to control the audit process.

The diffuse nature of equity ownership in public corporations renders it infeasible for investors to participate directly in making accounting and auditing decisions. They do, however, exert substantial influence on these decisions through capital market trading, information intermediaries, and socioeconomic institutions.

Investors' attitudes toward the accounting and control and other aspects of the firm are summed up in the price they are willing to pay to acquire equity rights in the firm. Other agents have no such single, readily accessible variable that can be used as an index of their preferences. It is hardly surprising, then, that the relationship between accounting and investors has been the subject of the most intensive empirical inquiry during the quarter-century following the ready availability of computers and stock price and accounting numbers in computer readable form. The next chapter takes a closer look at the relationship between accounting and the stock market.

Notes

[1] A. A. Berle and G. C. Means, *The Modern Corporation and Private Property* (New York: MacMillan Co., 1932); D. R. Kamerschen, "The Influence of Ownership and Control on Profit Rates," *The American Economic Review*, Vol. 58, No. 3 (June 1968), pp. 432–447; R. J. Monsen, J. Chiu, and D. Cooley, "The Effect of Separation of Ownership and Control on the Performance of the Large Firm," *Quarterly Journal of Economics*, Vol. 82 (August 1968), pp. 435–451; and M. Stano, "Monopoly Power, Ownership Control and Corporate Performance," *The Bell Journal of Economics*, Vol. 7, No. 2 (Autumn 1976), pp. 672–679.

[2] Securities and Exchange Commission, *Accounting Series Release No. 253*, "Adoption of Requirements for Financial Accounting and Reporting Practices for Oil and Gas Producing Activities," 1978.

[3] D. Blackwell, "Equivalent Comparison of Experiments," *Annals of Mathematical Statistics*, Vol. 24 (1953), pp. 265–272.

[4] Robert S. Kaplan and Richard Roll, "Investor Evaluation of Accounting Information: Some Empirical Evidence," *Journal of Business* (April 1972), pp. 225–257.

[5] Nicholas J. Gonedes and Nicholas Dopuch, "Capital Market Equilibrium, Information Production, and Selecting Accounting Techniques: Theoretical Framework and Review of Empirical Work," Studies on Financial Accounting Objectives: Supplement to the *Journal of Accounting Research*, Vol. 12 (1974), pp. 48–129.

Additional Reading

Alford, Andrew, Jennifer Jones, Richard Leftwich, and Mark Zmijewski. "The Relative Informativeness of Accounting Disclosures in Different Countries." *Journal of Accounting Research*, Vol. 31 (Supplement 1993), pp. 183–223.

Atkins, Derek R. "Diversification and Control." Working Paper #884, University of British Columbia, 1982.

Boatsman, James R., Bruce K. Behn, and Dennis K. Patz. "A Test of the Use of Geographical Segment Disclosures." *Journal of Accounting Research*, Vol. 31 (Supplement 1993), pp. 46–74.

Bushman, Robert M., and Raffi J. Indjejikian. "Voluntary Disclosures and Trading Behavior of Corporate Insiders." *Journal of Accounting Research*, Vol. 33, No. 2 (Autumn 1995), pp. 293–316.

Daley, Lane A., John S. Hughes, and Judy D. Rayburn. "The Impact of Earnings Announcements on the Permanent Price Effects of Block Trades." *Journal of Accounting Research*, Vol. 33, No. 2 (Autumn 1995), pp. 317–334.

Demski, Joel S., and Gerald A. Feltham. "Market Response to Financial Reports." *Journal of Accounting and Economics*, Vol. 17 (1994), pp. 3–40.

Easton, Peter, Trevor Harris, and James A. Ohlson. "Aggregate Accounting Earnings can Explain Most of Security Returns: The Case of Long Return Intervals." *Journal of Accounting and Economics*, Vol. 15, Nos. 2–3 (June–September 1992), pp. 119–142.

Frankel, Richard, Maureen McNichols, and G. Peter Wilson. "Discretionary Disclosure and External Financing." *Accounting Review*, Vol. 70, No. 1 (January 1995), pp. 135–150.

Frost, Carol, and Grace Pownall. "Accounting Disclosure Practices in the United States and the United Kingdom." *Journal of Accounting Research*, Vol. 32, No. 1 (Spring 1994), pp. 75–102.

Gonedes, Nicholas J. "Information Production and Capital Market Equilibrium." *Journal of Finance*, Vol. 30, No. 3 (June 1975), pp. 841–864.

Hand, John R. M. "A Test of the Extended Functional Fixation Hypothesis." *Accounting Review*, Vol. 65, No. 4 (October 1990), pp. 740–763.

Hand, John R. M. "Resolving LIFO Uncertainty: A Theoretical and Empirical Reexamination of 1974-75 LIFO Adoptions and Nonadoptions." *Journal of Accounting Research*, Vol. 31, No. 1 (Spring 1993), pp. 21–49.

Harris, Trevor S., and James A. Ohlson. "Accounting Disclosures and Market's Valuation of Oil and Gas Properties: Evaluation of Market Efficiency and Functional Fixation." *Accounting Review*, Vol. 65, No. 4 (October 1990), pp. 764–780.

Holthausen, Robert W. "Evidence on the Effect of Bond Covenants and Management Compensation Contracts on the Choice of Accounting Techniques: The Case of the Depreciation Switch-Back." *Journal of Accounting and Economics*, Vol. 3, No. 1 (March 1981), pp. 73–109.

Kang, Sok-Hyon. "A Conceptual Framework for the Stock Price Effects of LIFO Tax Benefits." *Journal of Accounting Research*, Vol. 31, No. 1 (Spring 1993), pp. 50–61.

Kang, Sok-Hyon, John O'Brien, and K. Sivaramakrishnan. "Analysts' Earnings Forecasts: Evidence on the Forecasting Process." *Journal of Accounting Research*, Vol. 32, No. 1 (Spring 1994), pp. 103–112.

Kim, Oliver, and Robert E. Verrecchia. "Market Liquidity and Volume around Earnings Announcements." *Journal of Accounting and Economics*, Vol. 17 (1994), pp. 41–67.

Krasznik, Ron, and Baruch Lev. "To Warn or Not to Warn: Management Disclosures in the Face of an Earnings Surprise." *Accounting Review*, Vol. 70, No. 1 (January 1995), pp. 113–134.

Leftwich, Richard. "Evidence on the Impact of Mandatory Changes in Accounting Principles on Corporate Loan Agreements." *Journal of Accounting and Economics*, Vol. 3, No. 1 (March 1981), pp. 3–36.

Lev, Baruch, and S. Ramu Thiagarajan. "Fundamental Information Analysis." *Journal of Accounting Research*, Vol. 31 (Autumn, 1993), pp. 190–215.

McNichols, Maureen, Brett Trueman. "Public Disclosure, Private Information Collection, and Short-term Trading." *Journal of Accounting and Economics*, Vol. 17 (1994), pp. 69–94.

Palmer, J. "The Profit Performance Effects of the Separation of Ownership from Control in Large U.S. Industrial Corporations." *The Bell Journal of Economics and Management Science*, Vol. 4, No. 1 (Spring 1973), pp. 293–303.

Patell, James M., and Mark Wolfson. "The Intraday Speed of Adjustment of Stock Prices to Earnings and Dividend Announcements." *Journal of Financial Economics* (June 1984), pp. 223–254.

Schultz, Joseph J. Jr., Douglas A. Johnson, Deigan Morris, and Sverre Dyrnes. "An Investigation of the Reporting of Questionable Acts in an International Setting." *Journal of Accounting Research*, Vol. 31 (Supplement 1993), pp. 75–103.

Sivakumar, Kumar N., and Gregory Waymire. "The Information Content of Earnings in a Discretionary Reporting Environment: Evidence from NYSE Industrials, 1905–10." *Journal of Accounting Research*, Vol. 31, No. 1 (Spring, 1993), pp. 62–91.

Skinner, Douglas J. "Why Firms Voluntarily Disclose Bad News?" *Journal of Accounting Research*, Vol. 32, No. 1 (Spring 1994), pp. 38–60.

Sunder, Shyam. "Corporate Capital Investment, Accounting Methods and Earnings: A Test of the Control Hypothesis." *Journal of Finance*, Vol. 35, No. 2 (May 1980), pp. 553–565.

Sunder, Shyam. "Market for Information: Experimental Evidence." *Econometrica*, Vol. 60, No. 3 (May 1992), 667–695.

Warfield, Terry D., John J. Wild, and Kenneth L. Wild. "Managerial Ownership, Accounting Choices, and Informativeness of Earnings." *Journal of Accounting and Economics*, Vol. 20, No. 1 (July 1995), pp. 61–92.

$'7'$

Accounting and the Stock Market

• •

Let us review how the functions of accounting interface with shareholders of the firm. Shareholders' contributions to the firm, usually in cash or real assets, are identified and recorded in the accounting system before the firm issues stock. The entitlement of the shareholders is determined by accounting records in the form of real capital and, for the purposes of preparing financial statements, converted into units of money through the application of valuation rules. The contractual performance of shareholders does not have to be reported to other participating agents because shareholders' obligations to the firm are fulfilled as soon as they pay for their shares. To help increase the liquidity of markets for equity claims, the accounting system provides credible and verifiable facts about the past operations of the firm, with special emphasis on the shareholders' interests. Reliable information about the firm attracts prospective investors who might buy shares from the current shareholders willing to vacate their positions in the firm. Public disclosure eliminates information asymmetry between the current and potential shareholders.

The accounting system of a firm and its surrounding markets operate in a symbiotic relationship. How do they depend on and influence each other? This chapter explores this question.

The Limited Role for Valuation Rules

Shareholders are entitled to the residual real or physical capital of the firm. Valuation rules translate this entitlement into units of money, say dollars. All valuation rules are imperfect and vulnerable to manipulation. Fortunately, the choice of a valuation rule affects only one of the five functions of accounting. The data provided for the functioning of equity markets are based largely on valuation rules. The other four functions of accounting (measurement of inputs, determination of entitlements, contract performance, and provision of the common knowledge base) are largely independent of the valuation rules chosen to prepare financial statements. Valuation rules play no role in measuring inputs of agents because these are measured in physical units, nor do they determine the entitlement of any agent except, partly, the top managers.

The Role of Information Intermediaries

The market for equity claims consists of three segments. In the primary market, authorized shares of stock are sold by the firm, usually to a syndicate of investment bankers for a negotiated price or on a best-efforts basis for a fixed fee. The sale of stock to smaller investors by the primary buyers in the secondary market occurs shortly after the primary sale. These buyers often trade the stock among themselves in tertiary markets via organized exchanges or in special computer networks, designed for dealers (e.g., NASDAQ) or for institutional investors (e.g., INSTINET). Most of the trading volume occurs in this tertiary market. However, the firm itself is directly involved only in the primary market transactions (except for dividend reinvestment plans and occasional treasury stock operations). Transactions in the secondary and tertiary markets change the list of shareholders of the firm, but do not affect the number of shares outstanding, or cash, or any other assets of the firm.

Although some stock may be sold directly by the firm to large investors, much of the demand for stock in the primary market is derived demand. Investment bankers are intermediaries who buy the stock with the intention of reselling it to other investors. As buyers, they negotiate with the issuer of securities about disclosures, financial statements, auditors, exchange listings, and so on. Then they sell the potential investors on the stock's attractive prospects. Investment bankers' profit margins, the difference between the two prices, are the compensation for creating an effective search and negotiating mechanism between a single informed seller and a large body of buyers.

Investment bankers may also have an incentive to collude with issuing firms and to sell stock to buyers at inflated prices. However, investors protect themselves by relying on the good reputation of the investment banker and the auditor. This investor behavior limits the profitability of such collusive strategies in an environment of repeated transactions.

It is not unusual for investment bankers to insist, at the time a firm attempts its first stock offering, that the firm engage a reputable firm of auditors to verify its financial statements and registration forms, even though any licensed CPA is legally qualified to do this job. This practice has been criticized by smaller audit firms because they lose their fast-growing, most successful clients to larger audit firms in this process. From the shareholders' point of view, larger audit firms, with better-known reputations to protect, provide a more credible assurance of the client's accounting and control. Further, the larger pool of wealth controlled by the partners of such firms and their insurance carriers provides a more promising recourse if an audit report turns out to be false.

Questions About Accounting and the Stock Market

Let us use the following six questions to frame our discussion of the relationship between accounting and the stock market:

1. Is it possible to make money in the stock market by analyzing publicly available accounting data?
2. Is it possible to make money in the stock market by gaining access to accounting data before they become publicly available?
3. Does the choice of accounting principles or of methods of disclosure affect the behavior of the stock market?
4. Does the behavior of the stock market affect the accounting and control?
5. What changes would take place in the stock market in the absence of accounting?
6. What changes would take place in accounting in the absence of the stock market?

Money from Accounting Numbers

The stock market rewards the discovery and use of information. If the trading value of information is less than the cost of gathering and processing it, the information remains unutilized. All publicly available information cannot be utilized for generating private profits for trading any more than *all* gold can profitably be extracted from sea water or riverbeds.

Information that meets this test (private trading value exceeds the cost) will be driven by competition among analysts to be processed as early as possible, until the marginal cost of faster processing approaches its expected marginal private trading value. If competition in the market for processing information were perfect, each type of information would take only as long to be utilized for trading purposes as the time it takes to process it, without the cost of processing exceeding its trading value.

Trading to profit from information tends to eliminate the opportunities for making such profit. The amount of time or the number of transactions that it takes to eliminate opportunities for making a profit depend on the liquidity of the market. When the expected profit is greater than the cost of trading, opportunities persist only as long as the price moves sufficiently to make the gross profit equal to, or less than, the transaction cost. In a market with large transaction volume, it would take a larger trading volume, but only a short period of time, to dissipate such opportunities. In shallow markets, dissipation can occur with only a small volume, but possibly over a longer interval of time.

The characteristics of market response to information follow from its competitive nature and apply to information from accounting as well as other sources. It is difficult to find information that is publicly available and whose profit potential has escaped the attention of other investors and analysts. However, it is not impossible, because someone has to be the first to make each discovery, and the relationship between the stock market and economic data and events is not fully understood.

Looking for publicly available accounting data that will help make money in the market is like prospecting for gold: easily accessible stream beds have already been searched, and going further up into the hills requires commitment and effort with no assurance of success. There is enough gold hidden in that corporate balance sheet to support a few hardy prospectors. A large nugget may occasionally be found, but there simply isn't enough to precipitate a gold rush.

Academic reports about discovery of accounting numbers that can serve as the basis of profitable trading strategies are like new treatments for cancer reported in the medical journals every month. Both are results of careful analysis of special cases, and have less than perfect reliability. Such academic findings have to be followed up by a study of their practical feasibility in a world of frictions and transactions costs. Not surprisingly, only a small number of such ideas are ever put into practice (say, by opening a mutual fund to exploit such information), and even fewer actually succeed when they are employed. Commitment of a substantial amount of time and money and the chance of failure usually separate a research finding reported in an academic journal and getting rich from this finding. Researchers tend to undercount the false alarms sounded in the past, and underestimate the amount of time it *should* take for research findings to enter into practice. Practitioners cannot take all research at face value until they try out new ideas with small amounts of money. Those few ideas for making money from accounting numbers that do survive this long process and get into practice undermine their own validity through the competitive process. Trading in markets can transfer money but cannot print it.

If market prices adjust instantaneously to publicly available information, allowing no opportunity to recover the costs of the effort and time spent gathering and processing it, such efforts would not persist. The hypotheses of instantaneous adjustment of price to new information lead paradoxically to the conclusion that such an adjustment cannot occur due to the absence of private incentives to gather information. This conclusion, in turn, provides private incentives for search.

There can be no economic equilibrium in the market for information if prices adjust instantaneously to information.[1] Relatively small but finite adjustment periods eliminate the apparent paradox that arose out of the early empirical studies of the stock market, which failed to detect price reaction to various types of publicly available information at the time of announcement. These findings led to some overzealous conclusions about the market reflecting all available information at all times and about financial analysis being a waste of effort. As it turned out, early empirical studies were conducted using monthly return data, and the price adjustments that took mere hours or days to complete were drowned out in the noise of monthly returns. More recent studies, using daily and hourly data, show consistent price reaction to various types of information at the time they first become available. Volume studies support the hypothesis of small but finite adjustment periods.

Money from Advance Access to Accounting Numbers

What is meant by access to accounting data in advance of its availability to the public? It could refer to data that, having been gathered or compiled through the accounting system, are kept in the custody of managers for subsequent public release. During the interim, these data are used by managers for internal planning and negotiation and execution of contracts with various agents. Their use for the purpose of trading in the equity market is prohibited. Would it be possible to formulate profitable trading strategies on the basis of such undisclosed data?

Given all the fuss about insider trading and disclosure laws, the answer must surely be affirmative. There is some evidence from commodity futures markets, for example. The U.S. Department of Commerce and the Department of Agriculture gather survey data that are kept confidential until formally released. At the time of release, these data have a measurable impact on the relevant markets. There are documented cases of profits made from occasional leakage of these data through the employees of these departments. However, it is difficult to gather data to provide an empirical answer to this question in stock markets. One would have to gather reliable data on when information is produced inside the firm. It is difficult to know for sure if managers use data for personal profit after it becomes available to them, because such acts are illegal and would not be done openly.

Researchers have generally based their tests of the profitability of trading strategies on the hypothetical assumption that accounting data become available for portfolio selection a specified number of days, weeks, or months prior to public release. The "information content" studies measure the contemporaneous correlation between accounting numbers and changes in the stock price that occur during the period from which the accounting data are taken.[2] The hypothetical assumption about the availability of such data rules out causal inferences about accounting and the stock market. All that can be concluded is that accounting numbers seem to contain some of the same kinds of information that determine the value of stock in the market place. The assumption that this information reaches the market through the accounting system must be avoided, however, because it is difficult to measure the price changes associated with the identifiable public release of accounting data.

The Ball and Brown study, the earliest and the best known of this genre, does not directly address the question of whether the knowledge of a firm's income, twelve months in advance, would help make a profit in the market.[3] Nobody actually knows that number at the beginning of the fiscal year when the investment portfolios of their study are selected. Interpretation of the performance of portfolios formed on the basis of information that does not exist at the time of their formation is highly ambiguous. Empirical evidence to support an answer cannot be provided until a study is conducted using actual, rather than hypothetical, advance access to accounting information.

The Effect of Accounting Methods on the Stock Market

The market value of a share of stock is derived from investor expectations of the level and uncertainty of future dividends (or, alternatively, cash flows or earnings). Expectations of individual traders are aggregated by the market mechanism. Market value depends on investors' own beliefs about future dividends, as well as their beliefs about the beliefs of other investors. Accounting can influence both types of beliefs.

At the simplest level, accounting generates a time series of financial reports that serve as an important input into future projections. These projections become the basis of valuation that investors attribute to the firm, and therefore their trading decisions. The past data constitute the foundation of beliefs and expectations about the future. When accounting changes the observed data, it affects the projections and the stock prices. The process of belief and expectation formation is, perhaps, the most poorly understood part of economics. Various attempts have been made (e.g., the rational expectations hypothesis) to place some reasonable bounds on the admissible expectation formation processes. But our understanding of the process remains poor. Since expectations are rarely observed directly in the field, attempts have been made to study expectations formation processes in economically rich laboratory settings. These studies reveal it to be far more complex and variable than the ad hoc assumptions (e.g., the mean of past observations) routinely made in a great deal of research. This lack of our understanding of expectations most likely accounts for the great deal of variability that exists in econometric studies of the stock market consequences of changes in accounting for depreciation, inventory, oil and gas properties, research and development outlays, and many others. The fundamental problem is that the econometrician can control only for observable conditions. Unobservable expectations, so crucial to the valuation process, may vary greatly and be left out of the research designs.

Second, future dividends depend on the current physical resources of a firm, its contracts, and how well they are managed to produce wealth. Individual investor beliefs about the future (dividends, cash flows, or earnings) depend on what they learn about current physical resources and contract management from accounting or other sources of information. Internal accounting and control preserves the physical resources of the firm by ensuring that agents receive no more than what they are entitled to from the firm's resource pool. This function of accounting, important to the market value of the firm's stock, has not received much attention from accounting researchers. It is buried in the details of procedures that are used to create and maintain accounting and records, and is obscured by the limelight that financial reporting attracts.

Third, preserving the resources of a firm is important but hardly sufficient to generate future dividends. Managers must be motivated to utilize resources in a manner consistent with the contracts of the firm. This motivation is provided through design of the compensation, promotion, and job termination environment. Changes in accounting systems often alter managerial incentives and induce behavior more or less consistent with the goals of investors and other agents. It has been shown that the issuance of FASB *Statement No. 8* on foreign currency translation led to changes in the way managers handled foreign exchange transactions[4] Similar arguments have been made with respect to the *Statement No. 2* requirement to expense research and development outlays.[5]

Fourth, a firm's contract set induces interdependency among agents. Managers' compensation may depend on the stock price, and the stock price depends on managers' actions. We can think of patterns of decision making by managers and stock valuation by investors that fit each other so well that neither side has a reason to deviate from the pattern. If their contract is changed, these patterns of decision making may have to change to another pair that is in mutual equilibrium. Each accounting system linking the firm to the stock market corresponds to an equilibrium set of investment/dividend decisions by the managers and to competitive prices determined by the investors.[6] Altering the accounting system changes the stock price, not because the market is fooled by the alteration, but because the firm's production-investment decisions under the new contract are different.

Finally, accounting systems also differ on how well they distinguish poor managers from better ones. When firms choose among alternative accounting systems, the better managers can self-select themselves into the group of firms using conservative accounting methods. By doing so, they can signal to shareholders the quality of their own abilities, something that cannot be matched by less-skilled managers.[7] By narrowing the range of accounting practices firms can choose from, the standardization of accounting also reduces the opportunities for the better managers to stand out amidst the crowd of mediocrity.

Changes in accounting policies are especially troublesome. Even public disclosure of accounting policies cannot completely ensure that all investors know that everybody has learned about the change. Accounting changes can cause the market price to change by virtue of their effect on the common knowledge aspects of information, even when they have no effect on the private information of any participant in the market.

The Effect of the Stock Market on Accounting

Empirical evidence on the effect of the stock market on accounting has not been sought with the vigor that has been applied to seeking the influence accounting might have on the stock market. The first efforts to standardize accounting methods used by unregulated publicly held firms in the United States originated in the stock exchange regulations governing the reporting requirements for listed firms. However, the attraction of brokerage commissions rendered the exchange officials' devotion to enforce these regulations less than exemplary, especially for well-established firms.

(The) R.J. Reynolds Tobacco Company did not publish an annual report until 1947 (for the year 1946) which included a standard form income statement, a management review of the previous year, and the outlook for the coming year. Up until that time the company had merely sent its shareholders once a year a two-page document entitled "Financial Statement" which set forth only a condensed statement and balance sheet for the year in question; in retrospect, it is shocking to recall the primitive status of financial reporting in a period as recent as the 1940s. In fact, this particular company, which had long been listed on the Big Board, did not reveal its gross revenues in its income statement until 1937. Because this concession followed the 10-K requirement by a year or so, it would seem a reasonable conjecture that statutory compulsion was the lever that reluctantly induced the change of policy.[8]

Regulations are more effective in influencing the accounting of new applicants for listing on the New York Stock Exchange. It is not unusual to find smaller firms, when they go public for the first time, being persuaded by their investment bankers to change their accounting methods as well as their outside auditors.

Surveys of corporate managers consistently reveal stock market reaction as a major concern in making or not making accounting changes. For example, when Granof and Short asked managers why they did not adopt LIFO during years of inflation, one of the frequently given responses was the fear of negative stock market reaction to lower LIFO earnings.[9] The significance of stock market response to accounting methods was widely discussed during the debate on accounting for the costs of exploration for oil and gas. How important the alleged stock market effect actually turned out to be in the final decisions made by lobbying firms, the SEC and the FASB remains clouded after many investigations.[10]

Accounting Without the Stock Market

The accounting of closely held commercial firms is different from that of publicly held firms. Few formal comparative studies of accounting systems of firms listed and unlisted on the stock market are available. It is feasible, though not easy, to conduct a comparative study of accounting in private and public firms of similar size and in similar industries, and draw conclusions about what accounting might be like in the absence of the stock market. We should not be surprised to find less detail in financial statements, less disclosure, comparatively smaller expenditures on external audit, and greater diversity in the accounting practices of such firms.

One could argue that matching for size and industry is insufficient. There must be other economic differences that could explain why one firm *chooses to be* publicly held and another is not. An event-study could be focused on firms that were taken private but maintained public debt. Going public or private and adopting an appropriate accounting system is a joint decision of the firm, and such a study may reveal if the equilibrium combinations of organizational forms and accounting systems exhibit joint variations.

The Stock Market Without Accounting

The simple, and to many people the obvious, answer is that the stock market could not exist without accounting. Such people find it astounding that so many people spent a quarter-century answering the question: "Do financial reports have information content?" Perhaps the answer is not so obvious. What would the stock market be like without accounting? Let us look again at how accounting and control interact with existing and potential investors.

Accounting measures the input of investors. The records of an individual investor's input are kept by the company registrar. This part of accounting and control also determines how the total entitlement of shareholders (in the form of cash, kind, or stock dividends) is distributed among individual investors. Without proper accounting and control, investors will have little faith that they will receive their share of the dividends declared by the directors and will refuse to buy the stock of such a firm. This aspect of accounting and control is necessary for the very existence of the stock market.

Because shareholders' wealth is a residual, it is sensitive to any leakage of resources from the firm. Changes in accounting rules raise the possibility of weaker control over managers' behavior. The weaker the internal controls, the higher is the risk borne by the firm's shareholders and the greater is the cost of transactions of the stock. Similarly, weaker disclosure and a less reliable system of financial reporting increase the transaction cost, reduce liquidity, and thus hurt both existing and potential shareholders by reducing their return on investment in the firm.

Given the legal problems of trading stocks in firms without an accounting system, research on the relationship of accounting and the stock market has been centered on measuring market price changes correlated with small changes in accounting systems. Major accounting events could have an observable effect on the stock price. But the effect of most accounting changes is small, and it is unlikely to be detected in volatile stock markets buffeted by so many forces. Conducting studies of small, incremental changes in accounting amounts to testing the importance of bricks to a building by taking out one brick at a time. Predictably, most studies on the correlation between accounting and stock market events do not find that accounting changes affect stock prices, in spite of the traditional publication bias against negative results.

Designing a research project to observe a stock market without accounting systems is infeasible, but thought experiments and comparisons with other markets for various types of claims are possible. One might speculate that in the absence of accounting, stocks will become more like other gambling claims, such as tickets bought at the race course. But even race courses use at least a rudimentary system of accounting, auditing, and public reporting of the pedigree and historical performance data about the horses, jockeys, and owners. These data provide mutually observable variables to define and settle the bets on the race course. Likewise, it is practically impossible to enforce a contract, "I bet five dollars on horse X," unless the correspondence between the label X and a specific four-legged beast is mutually agreed upon, and a mechanism exists to collect the five dollars and to resolve disputes on this matter.

Accounting and control provides mutually observable variables in terms of which the shareholders' (and many others') contract is defined and made enforceable. In the absence of such a system, diffuse ownership of equity claims is not only inefficient, but also impossible. Claims that in an efficient market the accounting function is essentially limited to providing information about market risk and to explaining abnormal, firm-specific returns miss the whole point of what accounting and control does in a firm.

Problems of Inference

The empirical measurement of the relationship between the stock market and accounting is rendered difficult by several problems of inference and data. These may be described as "the needle in a haystack," the "expectations," and the "self-selection" problems.

The Needle in a Haystack Problem

When the size of the accounting effect on stock price is small, it is difficult to detect in a noisy market. It is possible to estimate the chances of discovering an accounting effect of a specified size in the stock market. There is only a 50 percent chance that an accounting event with a stock price effect as large as 6 percent over twelve months can be successfully detected at a 5 percent level of significance.[11]

There are few accounting events for which one could argue, on a priori grounds, that their effect on the market value is large enough to allow a reasonable chance of detection through analysis of stock prices. It is hardly surprising that the results of most such studies report no stock price effects. One cannot conclude that there is no needle in a haystack by examining the haystack from an airplane.

What can we do? Before collecting data, it is prudent to estimate the approximate size of the market value effect one intends to look for and the size of the sample necessary in order to have an acceptable chance of discovering such an effect, if it exists. Such back-of-the-envelope analysis can save much effort and disappointment later.

The Expectations Problem

Markets tend to anticipate future events to the extent that such information is available and to incorporate it into prices. This characteristic has been the major rationale for using market value as an input to the process of making accounting policy. However, this property also turns out to be a major obstacle in measuring the value consequences of accounting policy for the value of the shares. This is the expectations problem. The consequences of the expectations problem are discussed first at the level of choices made by individual firms, and then at the social level of standard setting and rule making.

A classical firm is motivated to change its accounting methods if it sees an opportunity to increase its value to its owners. As the firm's environment changes, the management may switch from accounting method A to accounting method B in order to increase its value by x dollars. In a rational market where participants observe these environmental changes, the accounting changes will not come as a complete surprise. Even if the market does not know the identity of the specific firms that make the changes, it will be able to assess the probability that any given firm will make this accounting change in a given period. Let π be the probability of change in accounting method. In a rational market, the expected gain from a change in accounting method from A to B (which is x) will be incorporated into the market value of the firm before the market has any information about the identity of specific firms that make the change. Upon announcement of the change, the full effect of the accounting change on market value, x, will be observed. However, the price change observed at the time of announcement will be only $x(1 - \pi)$, because $\pi \times x$ has already been incorporated into the price.

Note that the higher the probability of change, π, the smaller the observed fraction of the total market effect. However, there is a consolation prize. The high value also means that from a given universe of N firms, a large expected sample size $\pi \times N$ will be available. Conversely, small sample sizes are associated with larger fractions of the total market value effect being observable at the time of announcement.[12] The larger the collectible sample size, the smaller is the fraction of the total market value effect that can be observed at the time of announcement. The ability of a competitive market to anticipate the future thus makes the task of measuring market value effects more difficult.[13]

This problem is often addressed by using a control sample of firms that do not make the change and examining the difference between the two samples. The control sample research design eliminates the expectations problem, but only at the cost of introducing a new one—self-selection. We return to the self-selection problem in the next section.

At the social level of standard setting and rule making, the ability of the market to anticipate the future creates an even more serious problem. Suppose that a standard-setting agency, the FASB, made the following announcement:

> We propose that effective January 1, all firms should use accounting method A instead of method B. We think such a change will increase the market value of the equity of firms. But just to be sure, we have commissioned a research study to assess the effect of the proposed change in market value. If this effect is found to be negative, we shall withdraw this proposal.

Suppose that the effect of such an accounting change on a firm's cash flow is a negative number x. Consider what will happen in a rational market. Prices will decline by x, and the market will conclude that the FASB will withdraw the proposal. Thus, the decline in price does not occur, which in turn implies that the FASB will not withdraw the proposal. This implies that the market price will go down by x, and so on. In a noiseless market, which acts rationally to anticipate the future, it is not clear what the equilibrium point of this process is. A careful consideration of the rational expectations in security markets complicates the interpretation of empirical results, and especially their use for making policy.[14]

The Self-Selection Problem

In a true experiment, the researcher randomly assigns each subject or firm to a treatment. For example, to examine the effectiveness of a new drug for cholesterol control, a medical researcher may randomly assign patients to be treated by the new drug, an old drug, or a placebo. In a quasi-experiment, on the other hand, the researcher looks at the attributes of the subjects and classifies them. For example, the researcher may separate those heart disease patients who smoke from those who don't. Patients in this case are not randomly assigned by the researcher to smoking–nonsmoking treatments; they self-select *themselves* into those samples. If the condition of the smoking patients is found to be worse, one cannot necessarily conclude that smoking is the cause. Such inference is easier in the case of a true experiment.

Self-selection is perhaps the most difficult problem facing those who try to measure the stock market effects of accounting decisions. The quasi-experimental designs of such research are based on the assumption that there are no systematic differences between the two samples that are relevant to the accounting event being tested. In other words, we assume that firms have been randomly assigned to the test and control samples. This assumption is hard to defend. If accounting decisions were made suddenly, unexpectedly, and for no systematic reason, we can reasonably talk about measuring their effects on the stock price. If they are known in advance, the stock market must discount them in advance. If there are economic variables that can explain these decisions, any stock market effects must be associated with these variables and not with the accounting decisions per se.

This argument significantly complicates the measurement of stock price effects of accounting events. Much stock market research is conducted within the economic paradigm—agents act rationally to enhance their welfare within the constraints of their environment, and accounting decisions are seen as part of such actions. All stock price effects can properly be attributed to exogenous variables and not to endogenous variables. If accounting choices are endogenous to the system, no stock price effects can logically be attributed to such actions. Following this argument, the inference drawn from a stock price study becomes a function of how the researcher chooses to define the boundaries of the economic system. To the extent these boundaries are drawn arbitrarily, the inference drawn about the cause of the effect on the stock price becomes arbitrary also.

Summary

Because of the residual claimant status of shareholders, the stock market is one of the more important factor markets that interact with accounting in publicly held firms. The financial reporting and public disclosure aspects of accounting are particularly important for shareholders. Financial reporting includes assurances on the proper functioning of internal controls, because the shareholders' resource entitlement is in the form of physical capital and it is not easily verified by them directly. Many aspects of this intimate link between accounting and the stock market remain empirically undocumented because of our lack of knowledge of how investors form expectations to value firms, the low signal-to-noise ratio, the anticipatory nature of competitive markets, and the self-selection problem of quasi-experiments. As a practical matter, the most fruitful avenue for research is to understand how accounting data can be used for estimating the value of firms' securities.

The role of the managerial market in accounting has already been discussed in Chapters 4 and 5. We now turn our attention to external auditing, one of the important factors that publicly held firms must acquire and pay for.

Notes

[1] See Sanford J. Grossman and J. E. Stiglitz, "On the Impossibility of Informationally Efficient Markets," *American Economic Review*, Vol. 70, No. 3 (June 1980), pp. 393–408; Shyam Sunder, "Market for Information: Some Experimental Evidence," *Econometrica*, Vol. 60, No. 3 (May 1992), pp. 667–695; Shyam Sunder, "Asset Market Experiments: A Review," in John Kagel and Alvin Roth, eds., *Handbook of Experimental Economics* (Princeton, N.J.: Princeton University Press, 1995), pp. 445–500.

[2] See Baruch Lev and James A. Ohlson, "Market-Based Empirical Research in Accounting: A Review, Interpretation and Extension," *Studies in Current Research Methodologies in Accounting: A Critical Evaluation. Journal of Accounting Research*, Vol. 20 (Supplement 1982), pp. 249–322; and Ray Ball and George J. Foster, "Corporate Financial Reporting: A Methodological Review of Empirical Research," *Studies in Current Research Methodologies in Accounting: A Critical Evaluation. Journal of Accounting Research*, Vol. 20 (Supplement 1982), pp. 161–234, for surveys.

[3] Ray Ball and Phillip Brown, "An Empirical Evaluation of Accounting Income Numbers," *Journal of Accounting Research*, Vol. 6 (Autumn 1968), pp. 159–177.

[4] Philip Revsin, "Bitter Exchange: New Accounting Rules Make Multinationals Alter Their Strategies," *The Wall Street Journal* (8 December 1976), p. 1; Raj Aggrawal, "FASB No. 8 and Reported Results of Multinational Operations: Hazards for Managers and Investors," *Journal of Accounting, Auditing and Finance* (Spring 1978), pp.

197–216; John Shank, Jesse Dillard, and Robert Murdock, *Assessing the Economic Impact of FASB-8* (New York: Financial Executives Research Foundation, 1979).

[5] B. Horwitz and R. Kolodny, "The Economic Effects of Involuntary Uniformity in the Financial Reporting of R&D Expenditures," *Journal of Accounting Research*, Vol. 18 (Supplement 1980), pp. 38–74; John Elliot, Gordon Richardson, Thomas Dyckman, and Roland Dukes, "The Impact of SFAS No. 2 on Firm Expenditures on Research and Development: Replications and Extensions," *Journal of Accounting Research*, Vol. 22, No. 1 (Spring 1984), pp. 85–102.

[6] C. S. Kanodia, "Effects of Shareholder Information on Corporate Decisions and Capital Market Equilibrium," *Econometrica*, Vol. 48, No. 4 (May 1980), pp. 923–953.

[7] P. Hughes and E. Schwartz, "The LIFO/FIFO Choice: An Asymmetric Information Approach," *Journal of Accounting Research*, Vol. 26 (Supplement 1988), pp. 41–58; and C. Levine, "Conservatism, Contracts and Information Revelation," Doctoral Dissertation, Carnegie Mellon University (1996).

[8] Douglas A. Hayes, "Ethical Standards in Financial Reporting: A Critical Review," in *Corporate Financial Reporting*, ed. John C. Burton (New York: American Institute of CPAs, 1972).

[9] M. H. Granof, and Daniel Short, "Inventory Choice: Some Additional Evidence," *Journal of Accounting, Auditing and Finance*, Vol. 7 (Spring 1984), pp. 323–333.

[10]D. W. Collins and W. T. Dent, "The Proposed Elimination of Full Cost Accounting in the Extractive Petroleum Industry: An Empirical Assessment of the Market Consequences," *Journal of Accounting and Economics*, Vol. 1, No. 1 (March 1979), pp. 3–44; T. R. Dyckman and A. J. Smith, "Financial Accounting and Reporting by Oil and Gas Producing Companies: A Study of Information Effects," *Journal of Accounting and Economics*, Vol. 1, No. 1 (March 1979), pp. 45–74; Baruch Lev, "The Impact of Accounting Regulation on the Stock Market: The Case of Oil and Gas Companies," *Accounting Review*, Vol. 59, No. 1 (July 1979), pp. 485–503; George Foster, "Accounting Policy Decisions and Capital Market Research," *Journal of Accounting and Economics*, Vol. 2, No. 1 (March 1980), pp. 29–62.

[11]The residual variance in the regression of monthly stock returns on the regression of market returns is about 0.007. If residuals from a sample of N firms were accumulated over T periods, the variance of the test statistic would be 0.007 T/N. For $N = 100$ and $T = 12$, the standard deviation is about 0.03. This assumes a normal distribution and two-tailed test. Chances of detecting smaller effects, from smaller portfolios and with fat-tailed distributions, become even more remote.

[12]The t-statistic of the observed effect is therefore proportional to $x(1 - \pi)/(\pi \times N)$.

[13]Shyam Sunder, "Research in Accounting and Reporting Policy," in Daniel L. Jensen, ed., *Accounting Dissertations: Research Design and Implementation* (Columbus: Ohio State University, 1982).

[14]Shyam Sunder, "Why Event Studies in an Efficient Market Cannot Provide Systematic Guidance for Revision of Accounting Standards and Disclosure Policy," *Contemporary Accounting Research*, Vol. 60 (1989), pp. 667–695.

Additional Reading

Abdel-Khalik, A. R., and James McKeown. "Understanding Accounting Change in an Efficient Market: Analysis of Variance Issues." *Accounting Review*, Vol. 62 (July 1987), pp. 597–600.

Aggarwal, Raj. "Accounting Changes, Management Belief in Efficient Market and the New Foreign Currency Translation Standards." Working Paper presented at the Annual Meetings of the American Accounting Association at Toronto, 1984.

Amershi, Amin H., and Shyam Sunder. "Failure of the Stock Prices to Discipline Managers in a Rational Expectations Economy." *Journal of Accounting Research*, Vol. 25, No. 2 (Autumn 1987), pp. 177–195.

Archibald, T. Ross. "Stock Market Reaction to the Depreciation Switch-Back." *Accounting Review*, Vol. 47 (January 1972), pp. 22–30.

Ball, Ray. "Changes in Accounting Techniques and Stock Prices." *Empirical Research in Accounting: Selected Studies, 1972*, Supplement to *Journal of Accounting Research*, Vol. 10 (1974), pp. 1–44.

Ball, Ray. "The Earnings-Price Anomaly." *Journal of Accounting and Economics*, Vol. 15, Nos. 2–3 (June–September 1992), pp. 319–346.

Beaver, William H. "The Information Content of Annual Earnings Announcements." *Journal of Accounting Research*, Vol. 6 (Supplement 1968), pp. 67–92.

Benston, George J. "Published Corporate Accounting Data and Stock Prices." *Empirical Research in Accounting: Selected Studies, 1967*, Supplement to *Journal of Accounting Research*, Vol. 5 (1967), pp. 1–54.

Datar, Srikant, Gerald Feltham, and John Hughes. "The Role of Audits and Audit Quality in Valuing New Issues." *Journal of Accounting and Economics*, Vol. 14 (March 1991), pp. 3–49.

Feltham, Gerald, John Hughes, and Dan Simunic. "Empirical Assessment of the Impact of Auditor Quality on the Valuation of New Issues." *Journal of Accounting and Economics*, Vol. 14, No. 4 (December 1991), pp. 375–400.

Friedman, Daniel, and Shyam Sunder. *Experimental Methods: A Primer for Economists*. Cambridge, U.K., and New York: Cambridge University Press, 1994.

Greig, Anthony C. "Fundamental Analysis and Subsequent Stock Returns." *Journal of Accounting and Economics*, Vol. 15, Nos. 2–3 (June–September 1992), pp. 413–442.

Holthausen, Robert W., and David F. Larcker. "The Prediction of Stock Returns Using Financial Statement Information." *Journal of Accounting and Economics*, Vol. 15, Nos. 2–3 (June–September 1992), pp. 373–411.

Marimon, Ramon, and Shyam Sunder. "Expectations and Learning Under Alternative Monetary Regimes: An Experimental Approach." *Economic Theory*, Vol. 4, (1994), pp. 131–162.

Marimon, Ramon, and Shyam Sunder. "Indeterminacy of Equilibria in a Hyperinflationary World: Experimental Evidence." *Econometrica*, Vol. 61, No. 5, (1993), 1073–1108.

Mayer-Sommer, Alan P. "Understanding and Acceptance of the Efficient Markets Hypothesis and Its Accounting Implications." *Accounting Review*, Vol. 59, No. 1 (January 1979), pp. 88–118.

Ou, Jane A., and Stephen H. Penman. "Financial Statement Analysis and the Prediction of Stock Returns." *Journal of Accounting and Economics*, Vol. 11 (1989), pp. 295–330.

Ou, Jane A., and Stephen Penman. "Accounting Measurement, Price-Earnings Ratios, and the Information Content of Security Prices." *Journal of Accounting Research*, Vol. 27 (Supplement 1989), pp. 111–152.

Spear, Stephen E., Shyam Sunder, and Ramon Marimon. "Expectationally-driven Market Volatility: An Experimental Study." *Journal of Economic Theory*, Vol. 61, No. 1 (1993), 74–103.

Sunder, Shyam. "Stock Price and Risk Related to Accounting Changes in Inventory Evaluation." *Accounting Review* (April 1975). Abstracted in *The C.F.A. Digest*, Vol. 5, No. 3 (Summer 1975).

Sunder, Shyam. "Relationship Between Accounting Changes and Stock Prices: Problems of Measurement and Some Empirical Evidence." In *Empirical Studies in Accounting: Selected Studies, 1973,* Supplement to the *Journal of Accounting Research*.

'8'

Auditors and the Firm

• •

Auditors contribute their services to the firm in exchange for a fee. Therefore, we can think of auditors as agents who seek their own goals through participation in the organization. There is, however, a difference. Resource contributions of other agents enter into an organization's production function, while auditors' contributions are necessary only when the organization takes specific forms. The audit function in a proprietor-run grocery store is quite different from that in a chain store, even though the production function of the two is similar. Auditors play an important role in defining, operating, and enforcing the contract set of the firm.

A managerial or performance audit of publicly held firms can expand the scope of an audit beyond the accuracy and fairness of accounting reports. In private-good organizations it is possible to design contracts for the managers in such a way that the operational and internal audit functions can be entrusted to the managers themselves. For reasons we discuss in Chapter 13, it is not efficient to entrust operational audits to the supervision of managers in public-good organizations. In this chapter we concentrate attention on external auditing.

Neither the measurement and reporting of the auditor's resource contribution to the firm nor the determination of the audit fee can be entrusted to the accounting system of the firm. The auditors' primary contribution to the firm is verification of the system. The determination of their entitlement on the basis of the firm's accounting system would create a moral hazard. Therefore, monitoring their input is carried out at a higher level, through peer reviews within the auditing community, enforcement actions by the Securities and Exchange Commission (SEC) and, ultimately, through the courts. We return to the regulation of auditing in a later section of this chapter and in Chapter 12.

Audit fees are negotiated between an auditor and a committee of the nonmanager members of the board of directors, outside the accounting system. The firm's accounting system records, but does not determine, the audit fees.

The input of auditors is not monitored by other agents in the client firm. In exchange for a negotiated audit fee, auditors accept certain responsibilities for the veracity of financial statements and disclosures. The auditors' obligation is determined and enforced by law and not by the contracts specifically negotiated for the firm. Thus, auditors have a vital interest in the laws that detail how much responsibility they bear for the accuracy of financial statements. Allocating the fees received from the client among profit, verification efforts, and the development and application of audit technology is the range of auditor decision making.

Auditors form partnerships to marshall sufficient audit resources to meet the demands of their larger clients. The structure of the audit firm can be understood by modeling it as a set of contracts among individual agents and by examining the problems of measuring resource inputs, entitlements, and the performance evaluation of auditors and their staffs. Alchian and Demsetz provide an interesting economic analysis of professional partnerships as a form of business organization.[1] We touch on some issues of audit firm organization in a later section of this chapter. For simplicity, and to retain the focus of this book on the client firm, we treat the auditor as an individual and not as a multiagent organization. We start by analyzing the economic functions of the audit in the firm, followed by an analysis of the various decisions that auditors make.

The Function of the Audit in the Firm

Why hire an auditor? If firms were technological black boxes consuming inputs and producing outputs by a fixed and specified production technology, the involvement of auditors, who contribute no tangible goods or services to the black box, would be parasitic. Perhaps our socioeconomic–political system has inflicted the dead-weight loss of auditing on itself. After all, many aspects of external auditing in the United States and elsewhere are governed by laws and regulations issued by governmental agencies.

Perhaps, but not likely. External auditing not only predates the U.S. socioeconomic–political system, it is coextensive in other societies. Many forms of auditing (e.g., internal auditing and quality control) exist without any significant government role.[2] It is incorrect to think of all external auditing as a creature of government regulation. On the contrary, such regulation arises as a societal response to the public-good aspects of external auditing. Abandoning the mechanistic model of the firm, we seek to understand how auditing as a service can add to the size of the organization's pie of resources.

When two agents act without sharing all information, and their acts affect each other, they are usually unable to generate as large a "resource pie" as they could if the information had been shared. This larger pie is called the "first-best" solution. The shortfall relative to the first-best solution is referred to as *agency cost*. Agency cost arises under uncertainty, not because agents act suboptimally relative to their information, preferences, and opportunities, but simply because two separate, rational individuals, working independently in the best way they can, still cannot achieve a total output as large as could be attained if all resources, actions, and information were endowed in a single individual. Agency costs are truly the cost of organizing. The economic role of auditing is to reduce agency costs.

Why could two or more individuals not act as one, and eliminate the agency cost? To act as one, their preferences must be combined to eliminate a clash of interests. The elimination of ego is a precondition for sharing information in such a manner that each agent, and the group as a whole, acts as if it had all the information. With less-than-perfect elimination of ego, the sharing of information cannot be perfect either. Residual selfish motives leave open the possibility that the "information" shared by the individuals is incomplete or even incorrect. We cannot overestimate the difficulties of completely eliminating agency costs. Small, kinship-based groups can achieve this substantial elimination of ego under environments hostile to the group as a whole. To this day, many specialist firms at the nerve center of that bastion of commercial culture, the New York Stock Exchange, are run by kinship groups.

There are two hurdles to engaging an auditor. First, the reduction in agency cost must be at least as large as the compensation necessary to persuade the auditor to do the work. Only when agency costs become large, due to the difficulties of direct mutual monitoring (e.g., in shareholder-manager, borrower-lender, or corporate-divisional executive agencies), is an auditor engaged.

The second problem is that the introduction of a third agent into a two-person agency not only alters the relationship between the first two, but gives rise to two new relationships and the associated agency costs that did not exist before. In a shareholder-auditor-manager system, the shareholder does not know what the auditor actually discovered or how diligent the investigation and preparation of the audit report were. Everything is possible: a cursory audit, less than truthful reporting, and auditor-manager collusion. To justify the addition of an auditor to the contract set, shareholders must believe that the expected losses from these possibilities, plus the audit fees, are less than the expected benefits of the audit report. Both managers and auditors have an information advantage over the shareholders. In addition, managers have an information advantage over the auditors, while auditors have the advantage of their accounting expertise. The resulting three-agent contract set must promise better prospects to each of them, compared to what they could get alone or by forming smaller coalitions.

However, people cannot be fooled all the time. Shareholders protect themselves against manager-auditor collusion by engaging large, reputable audit firms who can provide a degree of insurance through their deep pockets. DeAngelo argues that audit firm size and the quality of audit services are related to each other.[3] The responsibility for monitoring against auditor-manager collusion is thus transferred from the shareholder to the internal quality control of the audit firm, to the audit profession, and to the regulatory and judicial systems, while the economic cost is added to the price of the audit services. Publicly held firms almost universally require an external audit. When audit fees rise, or when agency costs between managers and investors decline, we should expect that marginal public firms will pass into private ownership.

Auditor Decisions

Each type of auditor decision can be analyzed from the economic perspective of finding the desirable course of action, after examining the costs and benefits of various options. While economic self-interest has always been assumed to be the primary motivation of investors, it has not been customary to think of auditors in that manner. We review the structure of the various decisions that auditors make from an economic perspective in order to integrate the auditor into the contract theory of accounting as an economic agent. Starting with short-run decisions, the following discussion is ordered by the time span over which these decisions are made or are effective. Cushing and Loebbecke and the Public Oversight Board provide other classifications of auditor decisions.[4] Mautz and Sharaf conduct a broad survey of auditing.[5]

Allocation of Resources in an Audit Assignment

Auditors are inclined to spend as little money as possible on the audit and maximize their net remuneration, but reduced audit effort also exposes them to greater risk of material misstatements in the audited reports, and therefore diminishes their welfare. They must devise an audit resource allocation plan that achieves a balance between profit and risk, after considering the past performance of the firm and its managers, the cost of various audit resources, and the effectiveness of each resource in reducing the audit risk.

Auditors also have to decide how much of each resource is to be used to observe and evaluate the internal controls, analytical review, and the direct tests of transactions and balances. The cost-effective ways of reducing audit risk must be identified. Formally, the problem could be stated as one of minimizing cost, subject to resource and risk constraints, or of minimizing risk, subject to a cost constraint. The theoretical optimum allocation of resources among audit tasks is reached when the marginal cost of reducing audit risk is equal to the marginal benefit across all instruments of risk reduction in the auditors' arsenal. Beginning in the 1950s, Cyert, Davidson, Trueblood, and others developed the tools of statistical decision theory to identify the most effective opportunities for the application of audit effort.[6] Statistical sampling represents a landmark innovation in auditing technology.

Virtually all the decisions auditors make in allocating their resources have to be based on their subjective judgments and beliefs about the client and its business. Objective probability distributions are scarce. Much of auditors' training and experience can be seen as the opportunity to accumulate experiential frequencies and subjective probability distributions. Learning probability calculus does not come naturally to most people, and auditor errors in handling such information can be costly. Consequently, auditors face the challenge of training their staff either to develop their intuition to correctly handle probabilistic data or to use mechanical decision aids. Ashton, Felix, Jamal, Joyce, Kinney, Libby, Mock, Waller, and many others have conducted a fruitful research program to assist auditors in this respect.[7]

Audit Opinions

After the examination, the auditor might recommend that the managers alter some accounting numbers, methods, or disclosures, implicitly threatening an adverse opinion if these recommendations are not accepted. In pressing the manager to alter financial statements, the auditor risks losing a client. A firm always has the option to fire its auditors instead of acceding to their demands for changes in financial statements and disclosures. Corporate audit committees, consisting largely of outside directors, are supposed to mediate the auditor relationships to minimize the chances of such breakdowns.

When the client declines to comply, the auditor weighs the potential loss of business against the chances of audit failure, with its consequent cost of litigation and settlement, and losses of reputation and bargaining leverage with other clients. Cash costs can be significant. *The Wall Street Journal* reported that during the fall of 1984, a single U.S. audit firm reached out-of-court settlements in three unrelated cases involving payments of $65 million owed to various parties who claimed to have been injured by faulty audits.[8]

Auditors needed malpractice insurance because, until the early 1990s, their firms were organized as partnerships and their personal wealth was not protected by the limited liability provisions that apply to corporations. The professional environment turned litigious in the 1980s, and insurance premiums rose sharply, doubling in some years.[9] Due to increased litigation, auditors' legal costs have also gone up. This cost inflation influences both stages of auditors' decisions—evidence gathering and opinion rendering—in the direction of defensive auditing.

In negotiating with the client, auditors evaluate the consequences of a range of options (from unqualified opinion to denial of opinion). Opinions may be qualified with respect to the consistency of accounting methods, the scope of audit examination, or the uncertainty associated with major, unresolved contingencies. At the end of the negotiating process, auditors choose an opinion that suits them best, considering the chances of its various consequences.

Pricing Services and Bidding for Clients

Audit firms compete with one another on price, quality, location, and special services. As in other professional services, the cultivation of personal relationships is an important instrument of marketing. Because clients do not monitor the number of hours their auditors spend on the assignment, the hourly billing rate is not a meaningful measure of price. The total price of the audit assignment—the cost of buying the audit certificate—is the relevant price variable. In his study of the pricing of audit services, Simunic found that the audit fee is roughly proportional to the square root of the assets of the firm within an industry.[10] However, it is difficult to compare the size of firms across industries by a single measure because the audit effort needed for a bank and a manufacturer, both with one billion dollars in assets, is quite different.

Simunic and Dopuch also examined pricing policies in the audit industry and concluded that the audit industry is price-competitive.[11] Audit firms also compete on the basis of the quality of services offered. The reputation of an audit firm, built over the years through careful quality control, is probably the most important measure of the quality of services it provides. Activities that build reputation (e.g., information seminars and distribution of literature and media advertising) cost money, and the audit firm expects to earn rents on its investment in its reputation. For example, in his pricing study, Simunic found that Price Waterhouse & Co., one of the oldest audit firms in the United States, was able to charge higher fees than its competitors on similar audit engagements.[12] Whether selling higher quality service at higher prices is more profitable depends on the price elasticity of demand with respect to quality. Econometric estimates of the price elasticity of demand are not available.

Audit firms also compete by providing a variety of special services to their clients, such as the advice of industry specialists on accounting policy, tax planning, the design of internal controls, and so on. Auditors save marketing costs when they also sell advisory services to their audit clients. Do auditors pocket the entire savings, or do they share it with the clients who buy both kinds of services from them? In his study of consulting services sold by auditors, Simunic found that the clients who buy such services from their auditors pay more, not less. The evidence suggests that audit firms earn rent on their reputations.[13]

When firms switch outside auditors or engage them for the first time, they invite bids from various audit firms. In bidding for a new engagement, auditors evaluate potential revenues over several years, because large publicly held firms do not change auditors frequently. A change of auditors alarms the investors. The cost of changing auditors confers some advantage on the existing auditor, who can extract extra fees. When new bids are invited, auditors have an incentive to "low ball" in order to get the assignment, and then raise fees in later years.[14]

There is, however, another side to the story. Lack of familiarity with the client and its control system raises the cost of an audit during the first year of engagement. Aware of the up-front costs that auditors incur in familiarizing themselves with the firm, clients may be willing to pay a higher audit fee during the first year of engagement and then expect a lower fee in subsequent years. Given the transaction costs of initial engagement on both sides, the auditor and the client face each other in a bilateral monopoly. Neither side can quit without having to abandon its initial investment. Whether this leads to the initial price being too low or too high relative to competitive equilibrium cannot be determined without measuring the characteristics of demand and supply and competitive conditions in the market for audit services.

Competitiveness in the audit market is another important consideration in bidding. Only a few auditors command enough resources in the United States and abroad to audit the larger corporations. Some firms specialize by concentrating their practice in certain industries or cities, thus reducing the number of effective competitors.

Just as audit firms have opportunities to build reputations, so do their clients. A client firm pays an extra fee to buy into the reputation of a good auditor, and an audit firm pays by accepting a lower fee from a firm that has developed a reputation for good financial management and integrity. Soundly managed clients impose less risk on the auditor, who can afford to issue an opinion with fewer hours of examination. In a competitive setting, at least a part of this saving in audit costs is passed on to the client. On the flip side, auditors screen client firms for poor business and manager risks. The auditors' involvement in management recruitment raises troubling questions about their independence, but it does facilitate screening out poor risks.

Audit Policies, Training, Quality Control, and Self-Regulation

An audit firm, itself being a set of contracts, requires a system to ensure smooth cooperation among its participating agents. These contracts must induce the audit partners and the staff to choose actions consistent with what others expect of them. These contracts take the form of audit and compensation policy, training, and internal quality control in the audit firm.

Cushing and Loebbecke provide extensive evidence in their comparative study that audit firms design procedures and guidelines to inform their staff about what they are expected to do under different circumstances.[15] The staff is trained in the use of these procedures. Many audit firms use statistical sampling and computer-based statistical techniques such as linear regression because their use can help increase the consistency of audit judgments even if they do not increase efficiency. Consistency is a useful defense in a court of law against charges of negligence or poor judgment.

Audit firms also conduct internal audits and quality control reviews. Auditors periodically scrutinize the work of their partners for conformity to the firm's policies. Clients cannot monitor auditor input. Auditors have to monitor themselves to ensure that one partner does not benefit by doing substandard work at the expense of the firm as a whole.

In addition to individual and firm-specific components, auditor reputation also has an industry-wide component. Since the mid-1970s, the SEC Practice Section of the American Institute of CPAs (AICPA) and the Public Oversight Board, created by the auditing industry, have undertaken a program of "external audit" of procedures used by firms that audit publicly held firms.[16] This costly program, called peer review, limits the incentives for a firm to get a free ride on the reputation of the audit profession as a whole. Critics of the self-regulatory program see the Public Oversight Board as institutionalized mutual back-scratching.

The Technology of Audit

There have been two major developments in the technology of auditing since the 1950s. The first is the application of statistical methods of sampling, estimation, and search in auditing by Cyert, Trueblood, Davidson, and their colleagues.[17] Audit firms have devoted substantial effort to developing statistical techniques, writing and testing software, integrating these new procedures into more traditional methods, and training their staff. In making these decisions, auditors trade off the cost of audit technology against the increased audit efficiency, the reduction in cross-sectional variation, and greater legal protection.

The second major change concerns the audit of computer-based accounting systems, electronic data processing (EDP) auditing. Pen- and paper-based accounting systems are fast disappearing, even in small businesses, limiting the applicability of the traditional techniques of audit. When a transaction is authorized and recorded electronically, the absence of paper radically changes the nature of the auditor's task. Computerized accounting offers new opportunities for both mistakes and fraud. A major part of the effort to develop EDP auditing is directed at these problems.

Institutional Structure of the Audit Profession

The institutional structure for setting standards influences the choice of standards. Auditors have sought to maintain a significant influence over the structure, as well as the personnel, of these institutions.

The Development of Audit Standards

Although the promise of examination "in accordance with the generally accepted auditing standards (GAAS)" started appearing in audit certificates in 1941, work on the development of auditing standards did not start until 1947. This work has been carried out by professional auditors, and few others participate.

The U.S. courts do not accept a proof of compliance with the auditing standards as conclusive evidence that the auditors have met their responsibility. In the Continental Vending case, the auditors were found to have met the auditing standards. However, this defense was insufficient, and an audit manager and two partners of the defendant firm were found guilty.[18]

The AICPA launched a major effort to develop auditing standards after this judgment. Though adherence to auditing standards does not constitute a complete defense for auditors against a charge of negligence, they still have an incentive to seek standardization of auditing across audit firms to reduce cross-sectional variability. It is safer for auditors to follow a standard, and attribute any inadequacies to the generally accepted practice and, therefore, to the entire profession. Modification of extant standards seems more appropriate than punishing the auditor. There is safety in numbers.

When Price Waterhouse & Co. failed to discover the fraud perpetrated by Phillip Coster, an ex convict working as the president of McKesson & Robbins under a false name, they had never sought to verify the inventory. Nor had they attempted the direct confirmation of the receivables. Their defense that physical verification of inventory and direct-mail confirmation of receivables were not the prevailing practice in the mid-thirties saved the day for Price Waterhouse.

This case was followed by basic changes in U.S. audit practice. The Special Committee on Audit Procedure, established by the AICPA after the McKesson & Robbins hearings, recommended that auditors physically observe the inventory count and directly confirm the receivables as part of normal audit procedures. Further, they should report in the certificate if either of these tests were omitted. It required that the auditors' testing be based on a review of the internal control system of the firm. These recommendations extended audits in the United States beyond the books of the firm to establishing the actual existence of assets and liabilities shown on the balance sheet. Six decades later, in the mid-nineties, the first step of an audit program is a review of the internal control system, which largely determines the direction and extent of subsequent steps.

It is conceivable that auditors could use practice standards to enlarge their share of the corporate pie. Given the cost and time it takes to enter the partner ranks, existing partners could extract economic rents from raising the demand for audit services by insisting that the amount of work they need to perform in order to issue audit certificates must be greater than that currently performed. This could happen if there were no substitutes for audit services, and if standards could be used as an effective device to collude. Competition among auditors ensures that even if they write collusive standards intended to raise the demand for their services, individuals continue to have incentives to cut corners. Given the difficulty of monitoring such behavior, collusive standards by a cartel of auditors are not effective.

The internal controls and internal audit of a firm are partial substitutes for an outside audit. For one multinational corporation, external audit hours decreased from 65,000 to 40,000 over a period of five years (1978–83), while the number of internal audit hours increased from 25,000 to 70,000 over the same period. The cost-effectiveness of an internal audit places an upper limit on how far the external auditors can use standards as a device to increase the demand for their services.

Standardization of auditing procedures cuts the costs of training auditors and collegial monitoring of the quality of the work. Training the staff to develop their personal judgment, and exercising control on the quality of the subjective judgments they make, is more expensive than developing standards.

Standardization of the audit also carries some risks and additional costs. First, auditors accustomed to standardized procedures are less likely to recognize innovations in fraud and concealment. Even if they recognize such incidents, their standard operating rules may not allow them enough flexibility to pursue the clues of wrongdoing they may find. Second, it is more costly to adjust standardized practice to match a changing environment and technology. The introduction of computers has altered the environment of auditing and the way auditors do their work. It is not difficult to see the pitfalls of commitment to audit standards just when flexibility is needed to keep pace with the revolution in information technology. The revolution brings new opportunities for the cops as well as the robbers.

The Development of Accounting Standards

Most efforts to standardize accounting practice in the United States have originated from the AICPA and its predecessor body, the American Institute of Accountants. Zeff and Chatfield chronicle the history of accountants' participation and initiatives, starting with the joint bulletin with the Federal Reserve Bank in 1917, the Committee on Cooperation with the Stock Exchange in 1930, the Committee on Accounting Procedures in 1939, the Accounting Principles Board in 1959, and the Financial Accounting Standards Board in 1973.[19] Standardization of accounting methods reduces an auditor's risks. Unlike auditing standards, accounting standards afford a significant protection from third-party lawsuits to an auditor who stays within the boundaries.

When auditors disagree with the accounting method or disclosure used by managers, it is easier for them to read the rule book to the manager than to argue on the basis of their *judgment*. Many standards issued by the FASB originate from auditors' demands for explicit and situation-specific rules.

The FASB's *Statement No. 44* issued in 1980 is a good example.[20] Trucking licenses to operate on interstate freight routes, carried on the balance sheets of trucking firms as intangible assets at their amortized purchase price, became largely worthless when the industry was deregulated. Trucking firms that had substantial intangible assets of this type were reluctant to write them off against their current income. Managers of these firms argued that these assets represented the goodwill they had earned on the routes. Instead of resisting the client pressure on the basis of a general standard for treatment of intangibles contained in APB *Opinion No. 17*, auditors found it more convenient to press the FASB for an industry-specific ruling to require immediate write-off of these trucking licenses. The FASB complied.

Could the managers of other industries be blamed for demanding to see industry-specific rules from their auditors before agreeing to their recommendations? Auditors may have to return frequently to the board for more specific rulings. In using the process of standardization to win battles against recalcitrant clients, the auditors may lose the war for maintaining the role of judgment in financial reporting.

Accounting standards affect the risk borne by the auditor. General price-level adjustments (GPLA), for example, can be made by mechanically applying the government's price indexes to historical cost numbers. Current cost methods, on the other hand, require estimation and judgment on the part of the accountant and the auditor, and expose them to risk. They have generally sided with GPLA proposals during times of high inflation.

Who Sets the Standards?

The audit-standard-setting institution in the United States is a committee of the AICPA (Auditing Standards Board or ASB), consisting of part-time, unpaid volunteers supported by a full-time staff. A similar structure is used in Canada. Since investor interests are protected by common law that transcends auditing standards, such standardization has been left almost entirely to the auditors themselves. In their report, the Special Committee on Standard Setting established by the Canadian Institute of Chartered Accountants stated:

> Accounting standards have considerably higher public profile than auditing standards and the need for outside involvement is correspondingly greater. We do not see a need for . . . direct involvement of nonauditors in technical preparation of auditing standards. From a practical standpoint, it is difficult for nonauditors to sustain an interest in, or be capable of contributing to, the highly technical discussion that takes place among auditors developing standards of professional audit practice. Auditing standards, generally speaking, are developed by auditors for auditors.[21]

The National Commission of Fraudulent Financial Reporting recommended the participation of nonauditors in setting standards. The AICPA opposed the proposal, and few outsiders have clamored to climb aboard.

The audit-standard-setting body is large enough to allow representation of a variety of experience and points of view within the profession. The voluntary, part-time nature of the membership allows many members of these bodies to represent the interests of their own firms and clients, without burdening them with the responsibility of taking unbiased positions. Differences among members can be thrashed out through bargaining and negotiation. The level of generality at which standards are written, and the differences in the audits of small and large firms, have been two of the recurrent issues before the ASB.

The control of accounting standards has gradually slipped out of the hands of U.S. auditors. The Committee on Accounting Procedure and the Accounting Principles Board were committees of the AICPA, as is the case with Canada's Accounting Standards Committee. The FASB was set up as an independent body in 1973, with a provision that a clear majority of its seven members should have been auditors in public practice. Over the years, the formal requirement that a majority of its members be auditors was dropped, and the representation of auditors on the FASB declined from five to three. In the mid-nineties, auditors continue to be the single largest group represented among the members of the board, its Advisory

Committee, staff, and financial supporters. In early 1996, the Financial Executives Institute proposed that the membership of the FASB be cut from seven to five, with a vote of four to approve a new standard. They also asked for two seats on the board, which will give corporate executives an effective veto power over its decisions. Audit firms and corporate executives respond to discussion memoranda and exposure drafts issued by the FASB, participate in their hearings, and remain the most influential groups in setting accounting standards.

The Auditors' Responsibility for Detection of Fraud

Fraud is an attempt to directly withdraw more resources from the firm's pool than one is entitled to. Managers can also commit fraud by misleading other participants about their entitlements. For example, some division managers of TRW, Inc. falsely inflated the cost of certain components supplied to the U.S. Department of Defense in order to make the divisional performance look better than it was.[22] Such fraud can be carried out through fictitious transactions, transactions without economic substance, or the deliberate misapplication of accounting methods to actual transactions in order to produce misleading results.

The public believes that auditors are responsible for the detection of fraud. Indeed, they see it as *the* reason why they are willing to pay for the audit. The SEC has listed the detection of fraud as an important objective of the audit, saying in *Accounting Series Release (ASR) No. 19* and again in *ASR No. 153*, that "the discovery of gross overstatements in the accounts is a major purpose of . . . an audit even though it may be conceded that it might not disclose every minor defalcation." In the 1980s, courts held auditors responsible for their failure to detect fraud if it could be proven that they failed to exercise due professional care.

Responsibility for fraud detection presents auditors with a difficult economic problem to be resolved at the social, not the individual, level. Either a complete denial or a complete acceptance of such responsibility would quickly put auditors out of business. Nobody would have reason to hire them in the former case, and nobody would be willing to be hired to do the audit in the latter. The higher the level of their responsibility, the greater is the value placed on their services by other agents, and the greater is the risk they must bear. There is no contractable measure for defining this level of responsibility, nor are these values and risk functions known. As the following historical summary indicates, auditors have been engaged in a continual and difficult balancing act to define their responsibility during much of this century. Gode presents an interesting economic analysis of the auditor liability problem.[23]

In the early days of auditing, the detection of fraud was a chief objective of the independent audit. In the 1920s, it was recognized that normal audit procedures will not necessarily disclose defalcations nor every understatement of assets concealed in the records of operations or by manipulation of accounts. During the 1930s, the auditor was expected to be concerned with management's accountability for the company's assets and to guard against fraud-induced material misstatements in the financial statements. In the 1950s, auditors asserted that the ordinary examination performed in order to render an opinion on the company's financial statements was not designed, and should not be relied upon, to disclose defalcation, although it was often discovered. By 1960, the auditors' position on fraud detection acquired a stronger negative tone. The ordinary examination was still not designed to uncover defalcation or similar irregularities. If the auditors failed to comply with generally accepted auditing standards (GAAS) during their examination, they had to share the blame if the fraud was later exposed.

In 1974, the AICPA appointed the Commission on Auditors' Responsibilities in an attempt to close the gap that existed between the auditors and the public's expectations of them. The Commission, in its 1978 report, recommended that the independent auditor was to be held responsible for detecting those frauds that could be detected through the exercise of normal professional skill and care. After the collapse of the savings and loan industry, and the related audit failures, the National Commission on Fraudulent Financial Reporting suggested in 1987 that auditors should provide reasonable, but not absolute, assurance that financial statements are free from material misstatements. It is difficult to be precise without resorting to extremes.

Competition, Entry, and Discipline

If audit services were an ordinary commodity, market competition could attain a socially efficient solution subject to the standard legal regime of commercial law. However, audit services have a special characteristic: their quality cannot be monitored by other agents at the time of delivery. Even after delivery, it is difficult to monitor their quality because the frequency of audit failure is low. Auditors' reputation becomes all important. Open competition allows unscrupulous and incompetent auditors to prey on the reputation of the industry as a whole, with only a small probability of being exposed within a reasonable period of time. The regulation of entry, licensing, quality, and discipline by professional and governmental organizations is intended to remedy these weaknesses of free competition in the market for audit services. It is not always successful. Auditors actively participate in all phases of such regulation and often dominate, and even capture, the regulatory mechanism to serve their own ends. An analysis of the government's role in the regulatory mechanism of the auditing profession is taken up in Chapter 12.

The conditions of entry into the public accounting profession are effectively regulated through the design of the Uniform CPA Examination, which all aspiring entrants must pass. State Boards of Accountancy set the standards for training and experience necessary to receive the license to practice as a CPA. With only a few exceptions (such as "snowbird repellents" in Florida that try to keep out the seasonal inflow of professionals during the winter), the control of entry into the CPA profession has not been used as an effective barrier to entry. The cost of meeting the necessary college and experience requirements of entry to public accounting is lower than that of medicine, law, and dentistry. Unlike other professions, only a small proportion of qualified CPAs enter public practice, and an even smaller proportion stay there for their careers. All this suggests that the qualification standards for the certification and licensing of CPAs have not been an effective barrier to entry to the profession. In the 1970s, the AICPA floated a proposal to make a five-year professional graduate degree a prerequisite to entry. This effort coincided with the broadening of antitrust laws to include professional groups by the Federal Trade Commission, the U.S. Department of Justice, and the federal courts, and has made only limited headway.

CPAs have a major stake in monitoring the quality of audit done by others, both inside as well as outside their firm. Audit failures receive wide publicity and inflict a loss of reputation not only on the erring individuals, but on their partners and professional colleagues outside their firm as well. Punishment of errant CPAs alone is not an efficient disciplining device. CPAs have developed an elaborate system of peer review to monitor and identify weaknesses in audit practices *before* they lead to audit failure and to help their colleagues rectify such deficiencies.

As with other kinds of insurance, a policyholder of malpractice insurance does not bear the entire cost of mistakes or negligence. A substantial part of the cost is passed on to other auditors when insurers raise the premiums for the entire industry in response to higher malpractice awards against a few. This economic externality motivates auditors to band together to seek a common solution to the problem of audit quality by their peers.

The peer review system works at both the firm and the industry level. Each CPA firm that audits publicly held firms is required to maintain and operate a system whereby partners review the work of their colleagues to identify weaknesses, to continually train their personnel, and to supervise their work effectively. To ensure that each firm actually does so, the SEC Practice Section of the AICPA arranges triennial peer reviews of firms by the staff of other firms. Firms that receive qualified peer review reports are required to make up their deficiencies and are helped in this effort to improve the quality of their audit services. The Public Oversight Board oversees the peer review system in order to protect the credibility of the system in the eyes of the public.

The system of peer review in auditing is supposed to raise the quality of audit services by limiting quality competition among auditors. It could also be criticized that it encourages CPA firms to cartelize the industry, especially because the demand for a certain quantity of audit services originates in the federal security laws. Given the peculiar characteristics of audit service as an economic good, the first-best competitive solution in the audit market is not attainable. The existence of a profession-wide component of auditor reputation requires a profession-wide mechanism for quality control to prevent market failure. The prohibition of such cooperation among auditors, and attempts to enforce conditions of perfect competition among individual auditors, may well lead to an even less efficient result in the form of a market for lemons, a market in which firms will compete to provide the lowest possible quality of service.

When certain provisions of the AICPA's *Code of Ethics* were declared anti-competitive, and therefore unlawful, in the mid-1970s, audit firms began to advertise and to aggressively market their audit and nonaudit services to their current and potential clients. The introduction of express competition in the audit market, combined with the pre-existing competitive market for nonaudit services, has had the interesting side effect of growth in advisory services and the weakening of auditors' independence.

The problem is that the auditing service produces a byproduct for the auditor—information about the client's need for nonaudit services and a relationship of trust between the auditor and client personnel. The auditors may point out to the client the latter's need for, say, a new computer or software system, and the attendant cost savings on the basis of information acquired in the course of an audit. This knowledge is an economic externality and it gives a competitive edge to the audit firm in providing nonaudit services to its clients. Many audit firms have developed the capacity to provide such services to exploit their position.

As long as the audit market was protected from express competition, audit revenues remained high enough to mute the motivation to profit from the sale of nonaudit services to audit clients. The removal of competitive restraints in the audit market has also weakened any pre-existing qualms about exploiting this externality. The result is a decline in both audit revenues and the apparent profitability of the audit services, coupled with rising nonaudit revenues and their apparent profitability.

Assessing the real profitability of each service would require a system of transfer prices between the audit and the advisory divisions of the audit firm. The advisory services division would have to pay the audit division for the information about the client, and the reduction in the cost of marketing the advisory services. Likewise, the audit division would have to pay the advisory services division for the saving in audit cost and risk due to informational advantage provided by the advisory services. The difficulty of determining appropriate transfer prices in an imperfect market precludes most firms from properly reckoning the profitability of each type of service. Audit firms aggressively compete in pricing their audit services with the hope of recouping their losses by providing nonaudit services to their clients.

There is a second source of trade-off between competition and independence in the audit industry. Larger audit firms, receiving only a small fraction of the total revenue from any single client, can be more independent of the client. However, given the total amount of audit work that needs to be done in the economy, larger size means fewer audit firms, and therefore less competition. In any given economy, there exists a set of efficient combinations of number and size of audit firms. During the 1980s, U.S. audit firms grew in size by forming international alliances without significantly reducing the number. But there is a limit to how far this process can be carried out.

The effect of enhanced competition in the audit market has been to weaken the independence of outside auditors. Economic forces have linked the provision of audit and nonaudit services and their prices, and undermined the intent of the security laws to ensure that the financial reports of publicly held firms be certified by outside parties who have no fiduciary interest in the firm. Whether the loss of independence is worth the gain in efficiency from competition is not known.

Summary

Much of the professional literature of the auditing profession remains garbed in the jargon of professional judgment, fairness, and ethics. Such language serves the purpose of peer review, quality control, and the coordination internal to the profession. Professional often show discomfort with the economic analysis of the decisions of auditors and the structure of the profession. Cost–benefit considerations and utility maximization were seen as the very antithesis of ethical professional judgment, which was said to govern the conduct of auditors. Without denying the usefulness of the ethical/judgment approach in operating a social system, this chapter has attempted to show that modeling auditors as economic agents can help us understand many aspects of their behavior and institutions. Understanding the behavior of individual auditors when they act by intuition requires methods and tools of cognitive psychology.

Notes

[1]A. A. Alchian and H. Demsetz, "Production, Information Costs and Economic Organization," *American Economic Review*, Vol. 62, No. 5 (December 1972), pp. 777–795.

[2]See Richard Brown, *A History of Accounting and Accountants* (Edinburgh, Scotland: T. C. and E. C. Jack, 1905); R. K. Mautz and Hussein A. Sharaf, *The Philosophy of Auditing* (Sarasota, Fla.: American Accounting Association, 1961); and Michael Chatfield, *A History of Accounting Thought* (Huntington, N.Y.: Robert E. Krieger Publishing Co., 1977).

[3]Linda E. DeAngelo, "Auditor Size and Audit Quality," *Journal of Accounting and Economics*, Vol. 3, No. 3, (December 1981b), pp. 183–199.

[4]Barry E. Cushing and James K. Loebbecke, *Comparison of Audit Methodologies of Large Audit Firms*, Accounting Research Study No. 26 (Sarasota, Fla.: American Accounting Association, 1986); Public Oversight Board, *Audit Quality: The Profession's Program* (New York: 1984).

[5]Mautz and Sharaf, op. cit.

[6]Richard M. Cyert, "Test Checking and the Poisson Distribution," *Accounting Review*, Vol. 32 (July 1957); Cyert and Robert M. Trueblood, "Statistical Sampling Applied to Aging of Accounts Receivable," *Journal of Accountancy* (March 1954), pp. 293–298; Cyert and Trueblood, *Sampling Techniques in Accounting* (Englewood Cliffs, N.J.: Prentice-Hall, 1957); and Cyert and H. Justin Davidson, *Sampling for Accounting Information* (Englewood Cliffs, N.J.: Prentice-Hall, 1962).

[7]See, for example, Robert Ashton and Allison Ashton, *Judgment and Decision Making Research in Accounting and Auditing* (New York: Cambridge University Press, 1992); William L. Felix, "Evidence on Alternative Means of Assessing Prior Probability Distributions for Audit Decision Making," *Accounting Review*, Vol. 50 (October 1976), pp. 800–807; Robert Libby, *Accounting and Human Information Processing* (Englewood Cliffs, N.J.: Prentice-Hall, 1981); Edward Joyce and Gary Biddle, "Are Auditors' Judgments Sufficiently Regressive?" *Journal of Accounting Research*, Vol. 19 (Autumn 1981), pp. 323–349; and William Waller, *Auditors' Probability Assessments*, University of Arizona Manuscript, 1990.

[8]"Insurers Tell Big Accounting Concerns Liability Rates May Rise, Sources Say," *The Wall Street Journal*, November 8, 1984, p. 4.

[9]Ibid.

[10]Dan Simunic, "The Pricing of Audit Services: Theory and Evidence," *Journal of Accounting Research*, Vol. 18 (Spring 1980), pp. 161–190.

[11]Dan Simunic and Nicholas Dopuch, "The Nature of Competition in the Auditing Profession: A Descriptive and Normative View," in John W. Buckley and J. Fred Weston, eds., *Regulation and the Accounting Profession* (Belmont, Calif.: Lifetime Learning, 1980).

[12]Simunic, op. cit.

[13]Dan Simunic, "Auditing, Consulting and Auditor Independence," *Journal of Accounting Research*, Vol. 22 (Autumn 1984).

[14]Linda DeAngelo, "Auditor Independence, 'Low Balling,' and Disclosure Regulation," *Journal of Accounting and Economics*, Vol. 3, No. 2 (August 1981a), pp. 113–127; and Jon S. Davis, *Auditor Bidding and Independence: A Laboratory Markets Investigation*, Doctoral dissertation, University of Arizona, 1987.

[15]Cushing and Loebbecke, op. cit.

[16]Public Oversight Board, *Audit Quality: The Profession's Program* (New York, 1984a); and Public Oversight Board, *Annual Report 1983–84* (New York, 1984b).

[17]Cyert, Trueblood, and Davidson, op. cit.

[18]*The United States v. Carl Simon et al.*, U.S. Dist. Ct. S.D.N.Y. Docket No. 66, Crim. 831 (1968).

[19]Chatfield, op. cit.; and Stephen A. Zeff, *Forging Accounting Principles in Five Countries: A History and an Analysis of Trends* (Champaign, Ill.: Stipes Publishing Company, 1971).

[20]Financial Accounting Standards Board. *Statement of Financial Accounting Standards, No. 44: Accounting for Intangible Assets of Motor Carriers* (Stamford, Conn.: FASB, 1980).

[21]Canadian Institute of Chartered Accountants, *Report of the Special Committee on Standard Setting* (Toronto: 1975).

[22]"TRW Tells Pentagon, Other Customers It Overcharged by Several Million Dollars," *The Wall Street Journal*, November 16, 1984, p. 6; and "TRW Cites Division-Level Employees in Overcharging for Jet Engine Parts," *The Wall Street Journal*, November 19, 1984, p. 6.

[23]Dhananjay K. Gode, "Auditor Liability," University of Rochester Working Paper, 1995.

Additional Reading

Abdel-Khalik, A. R., and Ira Solomon, eds. *Research Opportunities in Auditing: The Second Decade.* Sarasota, Fla.: American Accounting Association, 1989.

Amer, Tarek, Karl Hackenbrack, and Mark Nelson. "Context Dependence of Auditors' Interpretations of the SFAS No. 5 Probability Expressions." *Contemporary Accounting Research*, Vol. 12, No. 1 (Fall 1995), pp. 25–39.

Antle, Rick. "The Auditor as an Economic Agent." *Journal of Accounting Research* (Autumn 1982), Part II, pp. 503–527.

Ashton, Robert. "Effects of Justification and a Mechanical Aid on Judgment Performance." *Organizational Behavior and Human Decision Processes*, Vol. 52 (1992), pp. 292–306.

Atkinson, A. A., and William Scott. "Linear Incentive Contracts and the Production Effects of Auditing." Queens University Working Paper, 1977, #77-40.

The Audit Agenda. London: The Auditing Practices Board, December 1994.

Baber, William, E. Brooks, and W. Ricks. "An Empirical Investigation of the Market for Public Services in the Public Sector." *Journal of Accounting Research*, Vol. 25 (1987), pp. 293–305.

Baber, William E., Krishna R. Kumar, and Thomas Verghese. "Client Security Price Reactions to the Laventhol and Horwath Bankruptcy." *Journal of Accounting Research*, Vol. 33, No. 2 (Autumn 1995), pp. 385–396.

Bailey, Andrew D., Jr. *Statistical Auditing: Review, Concepts and Problems.* New York: Harcourt Brace Jovanovich, 1981.

Baiman, S., J. H. Evans III, and N. Nagarajan. "Collusion in Auditing." *Journal of Accounting Research*, Vol. 29 (1991), pp. 1–18.

Baiman, Stanley, John H. Evans, III, and James C. Noel. "Optimal Contracts with a Utility Maximizing Auditor." *Journal of Accounting Research*, Vol. 25 (1987), pp. 217–244.

Balachandran, B. V., and R. Ramakrishnan. "Internal Control and External Auditing for Incentive Compensation Schedules." *Journal of Accounting Research*, Vol. 24 (Supplement 1986), pp. 140–171.

Balvers, R., B. McDonald, and R. Miller. "Underpricing of New Issues and the Choice of Auditors as a Signal of Investment Banker Reputation." *Accounting Review*, Vol. 63 (1988), pp. 605–622.

Beatty, R. "Auditor Reputation and the Pricing of Initial Public Offerings." *Accounting Review*, Vol. 64 (1989), pp. 693–709.

Bedard, J. C., and S. F. Biggs. "Pattern Recognition, Hypothesis Generation, and Auditor Performance in an Analytical Task." *Accounting Review*, Vol. 63 (July 1991), pp. 622–642.

Bonner, Sara E. "Experience Effects in Auditing: The Role of Task-Specific Knowledge." *Accounting Review*, Vol. 65 (January 1990), pp. 72–92.

Briloff, Abraham J. "We Often Paint Fakes." *Vanderbilt Law Review*, Vol. 28, No. 1 (January 1975), pp. 165–200.

Burton, John C. "SEC Enforcement and Professional Accountants: Philosophy, Objectives and Approach." *Vanderbilt Law Review*, Vol. 28, No. 1 (January 1975), pp. 19–30.

Carcello, J., R. Hermanson, and N. McGrath. "Audit Quality Attributes: The Perception of Audit Partners, Preparers, and Financial Statement Users." *Auditing: A Journal of Practice and Theory*, Vol. 11 (1992), pp. 1–15.

The Commission on Auditors' Responsibilities. *Report, Conclusions and Recommendations*, New York: AICPA, 1978.

Craswell, Allen T., Jere R. Francis, and Stephen L. Taylor. "Auditors Brand Name Reputations and Industry Specializations." *Journal of Accounting and Economics*, Vol. 20, No. 3 (December 1995), pp. 297–322.

Danos, P., and J. Eichenseher. "Long Term Trend Toward Seller Concentration in the U.S. Audit Market." *Accounting Review*, Vol. 61 (1986), pp. 633–650.

Datar, S., Gerald A. Feltham, and John S. Hughes. "The Role of Audits and Audit Quality in Valuing New Issues." *Journal of Accounting and Economics*, Vol. 14, No. 1 (March 1991), pp. 3–50.

Davidson, R., and D. Neu. "A Note on the Association Between Audit Firm Size and Audit Quality." *Contemporary Accounting Research*, Vol. 9 (1993), pp. 479–488.

Davis, L., D. Ricchiute, and G. Trompeter. "Audit Effort, Audit Fees, and the Provision of Nonaudit Services to Audit Clients." *Accounting Review*, Vol. 68 (1993), pp. 135–150.

Defining the Roles of Accountants, Bankers and Regulators in the United States. A Study Group Report. Washington D.C.: Group of Thirty, 1994.

DeFond, Mark. "The Association between Changes in Client Firm Agency Costs and Auditor Switching." *Auditing: A Journal of Practice and Theory*, Vol. 11 (1992), pp. 16–31.

Demski, Joel S. *Managerial Uses of Accounting Information*. Boston: Kluwer Academic Publishers, 1994.

Dopuch, Nicholas, Ronald R. King, and Jeffrey W. Schatzberg. "An Experimental Investigation of Alternative Liability Regimes with an Auditing Perspective." *Journal of Accounting Research*, Vol. 32 (Supplement 1994), pp. 103–139.

Dye, Ron. "Auditing Standards, Legal Liability, and Auditor Wealth." *Journal of Political Economy*, Vol. 101 (1993), pp. 887–914.

Dye, Ron. "Incorporation and the Audit Market." *Journal of Accounting and Economics*, Vol. 19 (1995), pp. 75–114.

Elliott, Robert K., and J. J. Willingham. *Management Fraud: Detection and Deterrence*. New York: Petrocelli, 1980.

Evans III, J. H. "Economic Models of Auditing in Accountability Environments." Unpublished Ph.D. dissertation, GSIA, Carnegie-Mellon University, 1979.

Fiflis, T. J. "Current Problems of Accountant's Responsibilities to Third Parties." *Vanderbilt Law Review*, Vol. 28, No. 1, (January 1975), pp. 31–146.

Francis, Jere, and D. Simon. "A Test of Audit Pricing in the Small Client Segment of the U.S. Audit Market." *Accounting Review*, Vol. 62 (1987), pp. 145–157.

Francis, Jere, and E. Wilson. "Auditor Changes: A Joint Test of Theories Relating to Agency Costs and Auditor Differentiation." *Accounting Review*, Vol. 63 (1988), pp. 663–682.

Frederick, D., V. Heiman-Hoffman, and R. Libby. "Structure of Auditors' Knowledge of Financial Statement Errors." *Auditing: A Journal of Practice and Theory*, Vol. 13 (1994), pp. 1–21.

Gibbins, M., and K. Jamal. "Problem-Centered Research and Knowledge-Based Theory in Professional Accounting Setting." *Accounting, Organizations and Society*, Vol. 18, No. 5 (1993), pp. 451–466.

Gibbins, M., and J. D. Newton. "An Empirical Exploration of Complex Accountability in Public Accounting." *Journal of Accounting Research*, Vol. 32 (Autumn 1994), pp. 165–186.

Gigler, Frank, and Mark Penno. "Imperfect Competition in Audit Markets and Its Effect on the Demand for Audit-Related Services." *Accounting Review*, Vol. 70, No. 2 (April 1995), pp. 317–336.

Hackenbrack, Karl, and Mark W. Nelson. "Auditors' Incentives and Their Application of Financial Standards." *Accounting Review*, Vol. 71, No. 1 (January 1996), pp. 43–59.

Harrison, K. E., and L. A. Tomassini. "Judging the Probability of a Contingent Loss: An Empirical Study." *Contemporary Accounting Research*, Vol. 5 (1989), pp. 642–648.

Hayes, Douglas A. "Ethical Standards in Financial Reporting: A Critical Review." In John C. Burton, ed., *Corporate Financial Reporting*, New York: AICPA, 1972.

Jeter, Debra, and Pamela Erickson Shaw. "Solicitation and Auditor Reporting Decisions." *Accounting Review*, Vol. 70, No. 2 (April 1995), pp. 293–315.

Jiambalvo, J., and N. Wilner. "Auditor Evaluation of Contingent Claims." *Auditing: A Journal of Practice and Theory*, Vol. 4 (1985), pp. 1–11.

Johnson, Paul E., K. Jamal, and R. Glen Berryman. ""Effects of Framing on Auditor Decisions." *Organizational Behavior and Human Decision Processes*, Vol. 50 (1991), 363–391.

Kachelmeier, Stephen J., and W. F. Messier. "An Investigation of the Influence of a Nonstatistical Decision Aid on Auditor Sample Size Decisions." *Accounting Review*, Vol. 65 (1990), pp. 209–226.

Kanodia, Chandra S., and Arijit Mukherji. "Audit Pricing, Low Balling and Auditor Turnover: A Dynamic Analysis." *Accounting Review*, Vol. 69, No. 4 (October 1994), pp. 593–615.

Kennedy, Jane. "Debiasing the Curse of Knowledge in Audit Judgment." *Accounting Review*, Vol. 70, No. 2 (April 1995), pp. 249–73.

Kinney, W. R. "A Decision Theory Approach to Sampling Problem in Auditing." *Journal of Accounting Research*, Vol. 13 (Spring 1975), pp. 117–132.

Lys, Thomas, and Ross Watts. "Lawsuits Against Auditors." *Journal of Accounting Research*, Vol. 32 (Supplement 1994), pp. 65–93.

Magee, Robert P. "Employment Contracts and Accounting: The Auditor as an Economic Agent." Northwestern University Working Paper, 1976.

Magee, Robert P., and M. Tseng. "Audit Pricing and Independence." *Accounting Review*, Vol. 65, No. 1 (April 1990), pp. 315–336.

McMillan, J. J., and R. A. White. "Auditors' Belief Revisions and Evidence Search: The Effect of Hypothesis Frame, Confirmation Bias and Professional Skepticism." *Accounting Review* (July 1993), pp. 443–465.

Melumad, N., and L. Thoman. "On Auditors and Courts in an Adverse Selection Setting." *Journal of Accounting Research*, Vol. 28 (Spring 1990), pp. 77–120.

Mock, Theodore J., and J. L. Turner. "The Effect of Changes in Internal Controls on Audit Programs." In Thomas J. Burns, ed., *Behavioral Experiments in Accounting II*, Columbus: College of Administrative Science, Ohio State University, 1979.

Moore, J. "Implementation in Environments with Complete Information." *Advances in Economic Theory: Sixth World Congress*, ed. Jean-Jacques Laffont, Vol. 1, Chapter 5, pp. 182–282. Cambridge, England: Cambridge University Press, 1992.

Narayanan, V. G. "An Analysis of Auditor Liability Rules." *Journal of Accounting Research*, Vol. 32 (Supplement 1994), pp. 39–59.

Ng, D. S., and J. Stokenius. "Auditing: Incentives and Truthful Reporting." *Journal of Accounting Research*, Vol. 17 (Supplement 1979), pp. 1–24.

Noel, J. C. "Agency Costs and Demand and Supply of Auditing." Unpublished Ph.D. Dissertation, Ohio State University, 1981.

O'Keefe, T., R. King, and K. Gaver. "Audit Fees, Industry Specialization, and Compliance with GAAS Reporting Standards." *Auditing: A Journal of Practice and Theory*, Vol. 134 (1994), pp. 40–55.

Palmrose, Z. "Audit Fees and Auditor Size: Further Evidence." *Journal of Accounting Research*, Vol. 24 (1986), pp. 97–110.

Palmrose, Z. "An Analysis of Auditor Litigation and Audit Service Quality." *Accounting Review*, Vol. 63 (1988), pp. 55–73.

Patterson, Evelyn R. "Strategic Sample Size Choice in Auditing." *Journal of Accounting Research*, Vol. 31 (Autumn 1993), pp. 272–293.

Raghunandan, K., R. A. Grimlund, and A. Schepanski. "Auditor Evaluation of Loss Contingencies." *Contemporary Accounting Research*, Vol. 8 (Spring 1991), pp. 549–569.

Report of the National Commission on Fraudulent Financial Reporting. New York: American Institute of CPAs, 1987.

Simunic, Dan, and M. Stein. *Product Differentiation in Auditing: Auditor Choice in the Market for Unseasoned New Issues*. Vancouver: Certified General Accountants' Research Foundation, 1987.

Sunder, S. "Accuracy of Exchange Valuation Rules." *Journal of Accounting Research*, Vol. 16 (Autumn 1978), pp. 341–367.

Sunder, S., and G. Waymire. "Marginal Gains in Accuracy of Valuation from Increasingly Specific Price Indexes: Empirical Evidence for the U.S. Economy." *Journal of Accounting Research*, Vol. 21, No. 2 (Autumn 1983), pp. 565–580.

Tirole, J. "Collusion and the Theory of Organizations." *Advances in Economic Theory: Sixth World Congress*, ed. Jean-Jacques Laffont, Vol. 2, Chapter 3, pp. 151–206. Cambridge, England: Cambridge University Press, 1992.

Titman, S., and B. Trueman. "Information Quality and the Valuation of New Issues." *Journal of Accounting and Economics*, Vol. 8 (1986), pp. 159–172.

Wallace, Wanda. "Are Audit Fees Sufficiently Risk Adjusted?" *Advances in Accounting* (Supplement 1, 9, 1989), pp. 3–38.

Wright, W. F. "Properties of Judgments in a Financial Setting." *Organizational Behavior and Human Performance*, Vol. 23 (February 1979), pp. 73–85.

PART THREE

Macrotheory of Accounting and Control

‚9‚

Conventions
and Classification

●●●

Accounting has a specialized lexicon. Accountants themselves differ about conventions, postulates, principles, and doctrines. Nonaccountants hardly know what they mean. We have made a few references to these concepts and terms in modeling accounting and control systems as implementation and enforcement mechanisms for the firm's contract set (Part One), and in examining the role of managers, investors, and auditors as economic agents (Part Two). We can now examine the traditional accounting concepts and language in terms of the contract theory of accounting and control.

The contract model of accounting allows us to interpret the traditional, fundamental concepts of accounting by reference to other social science concepts. Specifically, each feature of accounting can be identified either as a convention or an economic choice. Some economic features of accounting have been mistaken as conventions, apparently because of their extraordinary temporal stability. The ability to distinguish conventions from economic features of accounting is important for the process of setting accounting standards.

Like all other bodies of rules and law, the rules and standards governing the preparation of financial statements and disclosures constitute a system of classification. An analysis of the general nature of systems of classification suggests that the oft-used accounting concepts of uniformity and comparability have weak theoretical support. Lacking substantive operational meaning, these accounting terms have become rhetorical devices for accounting debates.

Conventions

A *convention* is a coordinating device in games among two or more people. When coordination by direct communication is difficult, costly, or impossible, it may be socially advantageous to coordinate through such a convention. Hardin gives a detailed analysis of contracts by convention.[1] Consider, for example, the following two-person coordination game.[2]

		Column Player	
		Left	Right
Row Player	Top	2,2	1,1
	Bottom	1,1	2,2

Each player must choose one out of the two possible moves. In each cell, the first number is the payoff of the row player, the second number is the payoff of the column player. If the row player chooses top, the best thing for the column player is to choose left; if the column player chooses left, the best thing for the row player is to choose top. Since the choice of top row and left column are the best responses to each other, this cell constitutes a *Nash equilibrium* of this game. By similar argument, bottom right is also a Nash equilibrium; the top right and bottom left are not.

No player can improve his or her payoff by moving out of the Nash equilibrium cells if the opponent is playing that cell. However, in the absence of some implicit or explicit coordination between the players, there can be no assurance that they will achieve the high payoffs associated with the Nash equilibria. Both players would be better off if they adopted some convention to coordinate their moves.

Certain conditions must be satisfied for a pattern of behavior to be a convention. First, it must apply to recurrent situations and not to one-of-a-kind events. Second, a convention has to be common knowledge. Not only does everyone behave in a certain way, but everyone also expects and knows that others will behave in that manner. Third, it is in everyone's interest for one more person to conform to the convention. Finally, for a convention to be meaningful, there must exist an alternative pattern of behavior that is preferred by everyone, on the condition that everyone else conforms to that alternative.[3] Thus, driving on the right-hand side of the road could be regarded as a convention. The social or economic value of the convention arises not from the particular choice (e.g., driving on the left or right), but from the fewer collisions that coordination yields in this example.

Accounting Conventions

Most accounting textbooks and standards enumerate accounting conventions. The sense in which the term is used varies. Statements of fact, statements contrary to fact, conclusions from argument, assumptions, opinions, and wish lists all seem to find shelter under the umbrella of accounting conventions. Chambers provides an illuminating analysis of this and other problems associated with accounting conventions.[4]

Davidson, Stickney, and Weil take a broad view of conventions—as accounting methods without official sanctions.[5] The officially sanctioned accounting methods, in turn, are called *accounting principles*, thus setting up a mutually exclusive relationship between conventions and principles.

The Accounting Principles Board, on the other hand, took a narrower view of conventions. In 1971, they listed items that are frequently cited as conventions by other writers (e.g., accounting entity, going concern, time period, monetary unit, and exchange price) out of a larger set, called "basic features of financial accounting."[6] The board labeled all generally accepted accounting principles as conventions because "they become generally accepted by agreement (often tacit agreement) rather than formal derivation from a set of postulates or basic concepts. The principles have developed on the basis of experience, reason, custom, usage, and to a significant extent, practical necessity."[7] They essentially defined all accounting practice as conventional. However, in the list of "pervasive accounting principles," they included six "measurement principles" and three "modifying conventions": conservatism, emphasis on income, and application of judgment by the profession as a whole. The large volume of accounting literature on conventions leaves the reader surprisingly unenlightened.

The few clear and precise statements in the literature defining an accounting convention are easily lost in the clutter. The earliest statement is also one of the best. Gilman identified two characteristics of accounting propositions that constitute a convention: (1) they are based on general agreement and (2) they are more or less arbitrarily established.[8] Among all generally accepted propositions, only those that are arbitrarily determined qualify. The definition and some of the examples given in *Kohler's Dictionary* have a similar flavor: "The adoption of a particular convention may be a historical accident, but once adopted, a convention acquires value as a means of communication and cooperation."[9] The idea that convention is an arbitrary social choice—whose value lies in the mere fact of its general acceptance rather than in the particular choice made—captures its economic essence.

An accounting convention survives only because it happens to be in current use, is familiar and known to all agents, and change or abandonment imposes new search and adjustment costs on all agents. Once a change in convention has been made, and adjustment completed, no one is better or worse off than if the change had not been made, except for the cost of the adjustment itself. Therefore, agents have a stake in maintaining the status quo on conventions as long as the environment remains stable.

Conventions are differentiated from the "economic features" of accounting (discussed in the following section) only by agent preferences for specific options in the latter case, and not by the presence or absence of economic rationale. Yet the distinction is quite important for those who set the accounting standards. Once an accounting issue has been identified as a matter of convention, the standard setter can proceed expeditiously to select a standard to minimize the cost of adjustment because otherwise all options are equally desirable for all agents. If, on the other hand, an economic feature of accounting is involved, the standard setter would have to discover the economic consequences of each option for various agents before making a choice.

The bookkeeping practice of writing debits on the left and credits on the right-hand side of a sheet of paper is a convention in this sense. If the convention were reversed (debits on the right and credits on the left, as is the prevalent practice in some countries), the interests of all agents would remain unaffected, except for the cost of adjustment during the transition. If the convention were abandoned, the economic benefits of general agreement by convention would be lost, and the additional cost would be borne by various agents in the form of the extra effort needed to audit, read, and interpret financial statements and accounting books.

Listing the assets and liabilities in order of decreasing rather than increasing liquidity is another example of an accounting convention. Are there any agents whose interests would be affected by a change to increasing the order of liquidity? In introductory accounting, students must memorize these conventions, because they cannot arrive at these features of accounting by application of reason to some basic axioms.

Economic Features of Accounting

Features of accounting that are not conventions can be explained in terms of the economic interest of agents. Many of these features have social value (in addition to their private value) that arises from general agreement, and are often referred to as conventions in accounting texts and periodical literature. However, since economic interests drive the choice of these features of accounting, they must be seen as equilibrium outcomes and not as conventions.

The economic features of accounting can be understood on the basis of economic interests of agents; one does not have to memorize them. A persistent feature of accounting in time and space does not justify calling it a convention. Such a persistence suggests that the economic forces that led to the development of that feature are stable and extensive. Whether a feature of accounting is a convention or an economic feature can be determined by asking the following question: Aside from the cost of *adjusting* to the new system, will substitution of the feature by an alternative affect the interests of any agents in equilibrium? A convention will not.

Conservatism is a good example of an accounting feature that is often called a convention, but does not fit its economic definition. The Accounting Principles Board, in *Statement No. 4*, defined conservatism as preference for "possible errors in measurement in the direction of understatement rather than overstatement of net income and net assets."[10] *Kohler's Dictionary* defines it as "a guideline which chooses between acceptable accounting alternatives . . . so that the least favorable immediate effect on assets, income, and owner's equity is reported."[11] The presence of uncertainty and the downward bias of measured current-period income, assets, and owner's equity in the presence of uncertainty seem to be the essential aspects of conservatism.

We can identify the economic forces that drive accounting practices toward conservatism. Financial reporting takes place in an environment of *state* as well as *strategic uncertainty*. Investors do not know the real state of affairs in the firm, or whether the auditors have done their job conscientiously. Auditors do not know for sure if the managers have misled them. Managers do not know how shareholders will react to what they learn. In the absence of any constraints, bonus-motivated managers would rather not use conservative accounting practices. However, the cost of the gain in their welfare entails a greater risk of being sued by investors in the event their investment turns sour. Auditors would have fewer conflicts with management if financial reporting did not have to be conservative. However, they would have to bear a higher risk of being sued by the investors, and therefore would demand higher fees. The absence of conservatism allows greater discretion to the managers and therefore leads to lower investor confidence in the reports. Economic interests of various agents are not indifferent with respect to the choice of conservatism over neutral or aggressive reporting. Therefore, this feature of accounting is not a convention.

What are the economic forces incident on other features of accounting, variously described as conventions, assumptions, doctrines, and so on? At the risk of some repetition, let us examine a few.

Entity

An entity is simply a set of contracts. A subset of contracts (e.g., a subsidiary, a division, a factory, or a department of a firm) is also an entity. Suitable accounting and control is designed for entities at all levels of hierarchy. In a subsidiary of a corporation, for example, the boss of the head of the subsidiary exercises the powers of the sole "owner" of an independent firm and does not have to deal with a diffuse body of shareholders, as the head of a publicly held firm must do. Accordingly, the accounting and control of the subsidiary does not need to include many of the features typical of accounting systems of its own publicly held parent, even though they are both accounting entities in their own right. The definition of an *entity* determines the accounting and control appropriate for it. Since it has real economic consequences, the choice of entity is not arbitrary, and therefore is not a matter of convention.

Going Concern or Continuity

If we could trade any resource at any time at a well-defined price (i.e., if all factor markets were perfect and complete), there would be no need for a going concern assumption in preparing accounts. The valuation of partially used, long-lived assets could be ascertained without resorting to such an assumption. The valuation of the real capital of a firm, in terms of dollars, requires a decision to be made regarding resources whose use value and disposal values are uncertain and possibly unequal. The going concern or continuity assumption is the preference for use value over disposal value (use value being determined by the lower of historical cost and replacement cost).

In the absence of the continuity assumption, it would be open to the managers to choose between the use value and the disposal value of assets, carried over from one accounting period to another. Managers may prefer to exercise such choice on the basis of their own interests or whims. However, the auditors would find the managers' choices difficult to attest to, and this would result in investors having less confidence in financial statements. Another option is to require managers to use disposal values that, in many cases, would imply the immediate write-down of long-lived assets.

The use of the going concern assumption in accounting reduces managerial discretion in valuation and reduces investor uncertainty, or keeps managers from resorting to extreme conservatism. In either case, the assumption has important consequences for the welfare of agents and can be classified as an economic feature of accounting.

Period

The periodicity of many accounting activities arises for two reasons: the use of long-lived resources and the fixed cost of updating, closing, summarizing, and auditing books to prepare periodic reports. Resources that require continual investment and yield continual return over a long period of time came into wide use after the Industrial Revolution. The accounting period is the result of the trade-off between the higher cost of frequently prepared reports and the benefits of access to timely information. With computer technology, the bookkeeping cost of frequent reporting is no longer a major factor. However, the cost of the end-of-the-period adjustments that require managerial attention, and of the periodic audit that accompanies external periodic reports, is still substantial and limits the frequency of reports. Internal reporting has become more frequent with the introduction of computers, because auditing is not applicable to such reporting. When continuous audit technology is developed to keep pace with computerized accounting systems, the audit constraint, too, may be relaxed, and external reports may appear with greater frequency. In any case, the periodicity of accounting reports is an economic feature, and not a convention, because the choice of period affects the interests of various agents.

Valuation

Valuation is aggregation. It maps vectors of quantities and prices into a scalar money amount. Accounts and reports are prepared in dollars because prices are usually quoted in dollars, although theoretically, prices could be measured in terms of any other resource or combination of resources. To what extent is valuation an economic feature or convention?

When resources are few and their attributes are well-known to agents, valuation-free accounting systems can serve the needs of the organization. For example, stewardship accounts in medieval England did not use valuation. They were based on real resources, such as four cows, ten sheep, and so on. Even in a modern corporation, accounting operations within certain subunits are confined to quantities and are, therefore, valuation-free. At certain levels, inventory and production control systems and performance evaluation in plants are based on quantities, not on dollar values. Performance at these levels can be reckoned in terms of a small number of resources. As the number of different resource flows in a firm increases, it becomes difficult for agents to remain informed about the relevant attributes of these resources, and a list of the quantity of resources becomes less informative. In the absence of knowledge about the attributes of various resources, an agent can get greater use from aggregated numbers prepared by someone who is knowledgeable about these attributes. Therefore, the use of valuation is an economic feature of accounting systems. It is not a convention, and in simpler settings, even within large corporations, valuation is not used when it is not useful.

Accrual

Accrual is the practice of recording cash, as well as noncash resources, and obligations to parties other than the shareholders on the books of the firm. In pure cash-basis accounting, on the other hand, the only recorded resource is cash and the only recorded equity is the owners'. The accrual basis of accounting recognizes that a firm, through its system of contracts, is entitled to receive certain noncash economic resources from various agents. Accrual accounting also recognizes, in the form of liabilities, that under the firm's contracts resources are owed to agents. Shareholders are not the only claimants on a firm's resources. One consequence of recognizing these additional resource rights and obligations is that the rights of shareholders in the resource pool can be more than, equal to, or less than the cash resources of the firm. Under cash-basis accounting they are necessarily equal.

Cash-basis accounting is used for personal accounts or simple (proprietorship) business organizations. Modified forms of cash-basis accounting have survived in many governmental and not-for-profit organizations (see Chapter 13). In simple organizations, accounting serves the limited purposes of one agent, and the formal recording of noncash assets and outside obligations adds little information and a lot more bookkeeping if the proprietor is personally familiar with them. The real economic consequences of the choice between accrual and cash accounting make them an economic rather than a conventional feature of accounting.

Temporal Stability of Economic Features

Conventions come into usage by design or happenstance, and continue to be used by weight of tradition, since no one benefits from changing them. The economic features of accounting, on the other hand, are determined by interaction among interests of accounting agents, and changes in these interests generate pressure to alter such features. Changes in accounting can be traced back to the pressures generated by changes in the environment in which business operates. For example, an increase in the rate of inflation generates pressure to move away from historical cost accounting toward some form of current valuation. In the energy crisis of the mid-seventies, the U.S. government pressured oil companies to eliminate their differences in accounting for the costs of exploration.

The economic features of accounting may be classified on the basis of their temporal stability. The long-run stability of some features of accounting simply means that the forces that brought them into existence in the first place are relatively stable, and the equilibrium solution has not changed over the years. They should not be mistaken for conventions.

Double Entry

The double-entry system of accounting has been used for at least five hundred years, perhaps much longer. Two interpretations of double entry are causal and classificational. Under "causal" interpretation, the "double" part of double-entry accounting arises from simultaneous consideration given to the causes and effects of economic events and actions. The apparent perfection of the double-entry system arises from the match with our two-valued system of logic. It is not a matter of convention. It is possible that one day we may discover more causal links or switch our system of logic, in which case triple- or even quadruple-entry systems would be more appropriate.[12]

Under the "classificational" interpretation, the double-entry system classifies all resources of the business entity on the basis of two criteria: first, the form (cash, receivable, inventory, or plant, etc.), and second, the source (trade creditor, bank, preferred, or common stock owner, etc.). The addition of other criteria for classification of the entity's resources (for example, location, product line, etc.), would lead to a multiple-entry accounting system. Such classification of resources using multiple criteria is common in the internal accounting reports of firms, but not in external reports. The absence of multiple-entry systems of accounting suggests that, on the whole, the double-entry systems have been found to be most desirable in the prevailing environments. Advances in the technology of processing information may, however, change this.

Economic Resources

A precise definition of a firm's resource pool can exist only in concept, because this pool depends on expectations in its contract set. There is no guarantee that these expectations are identical across agents or that they will be realized. Among agents who manage the firm, expectations of individuals may diverge, even without deception or misrepresentation. The expectations of each agent about future events depend on the agent's current beliefs and information.

Many accounting controversies (for example, accounting for leases, research and development, goodwill, cost exploration for oil and gas, and pension costs) are rooted in this basic difficulty. Solving the problem of recognition of revenue, expenses, assets, and liabilities requires answers to: (1) Whose expectations are to form the basis of accounting? (2) What is to be the cutoff point in the indefinitely long series of future expected transactions? and (3) How uncertain the expectation of a transaction has to be to justify its exclusion from accounting?

A general theoretical answer to these questions is unlikely. Instead of trying to define the "true" economic resources of the firm, it is more fruitful to explore the consequences of various operationally definable accounting procedures. For example, it is easier to find how efficiently the firm's system of contracts can operate if all leases are capitalized (or expensed, for that matter) than to try to find the "true value" of the lease arrangement to the firm. In a similar vein, it would be more fruitful to discover and learn what would be the equilibrium consequences for a system of contracts if accounting were based on managers' versus investors' expectations.

Uniformity and Classification[13]

Uniformity is the holy grail of rule-making in accounting. Diversity of accounting practices invites criticism. It is an intuitively appealing idea that if only the accountants could be persuaded to treat like things alike and different things differently in their books, financial statements would accurately reflect the economic reality. Unfortunately, it is not that simple.

The problem is that no two events or transactions are exactly identical, nor totally different. If you look hard enough, you can find some similarity as well as some differences between virtually any two transactions. Transactions come in infinite variety, and the accountant must classify and aggregate them into a manageably small number of categories. Categorization of multi-attribute objects into a small number of categories could be based on one of two principles:

1. Treat any two transactions that have any differences differently.
2. Treat any two transactions that have any similarity to each other alike.

If we follow one of these principles, the other will necessarily be violated. This gives rise to a fundamental problem in defining and attaining uniformity and comparability in financial statements.

Applying the first criterion, if each transaction is different from others, it is treated differently. This will yield a thick accounting rule book, and each rule will be used but once. In effect, there will be no categorization and no aggregation. Some may call this a system without rules and uniformity, because no two transactions are treated alike. Others can, with equal justification, refer to the system as the ultimate in uniformity in the sense that two transactions must be exactly identical in order to qualify for the same treatment. The pursuance of uniformity carried far enough leads to complete diversity.

Paradoxically, applying the second criterion does not improve things. If any two transactions that have anything in common must be treated alike, all transactions will end up in a few, or even a single, category. This is not of much use either. This problem is common to all systems of rules and laws, as well as to other schemes of classification.

Consider the accounting treatment of leases before the FASB issued *Statement No. 13*. The accounting classification of leases in that period was sufficiently coarse to permit both short- and long-term leases to be treated as operating leases. Proponents of change thought that the differences among various lease transactions were sufficiently important to warrant the creation of two or more separate classes. Accounting for leases could be made more uniform, they argued, by refining the classification scheme so that each transaction is in a class by itself.

But such a proposal could not satisfy the second criterion: treating two transactions that have any similarity alike. For example, critics observed certain similarities between long-term buy-lease-back and borrow-and-buy transactions, and argued that these two types of transactions should be given identical accounting treatment. If we examined all possible features of a transaction, we would find some similarities in almost any pair. The identical treatment of all transactions is just as susceptible to criticism as a unique treatment of each transaction.

Now we can return to the term *uniformity* and try to examine what, if any, useful meaning can be assigned to it. If there is no way of making an accounting system more uniform, without making it less uniform at the same time, the term *uniform* does not help choose among accounting methods.

At a higher level of abstraction, uniformity has been a useful vehicle for conveying certain ideas. The term "liberty," for instance, has been a powerful moving force in history. It helped lay the foundations of many of the constitutional and legal rights we cherish in the modern democratic state. Yet the term is little used in legal proceedings because it does not help determine the guilt or innocence of a person. The law itself may be based on the concept of liberty, but legal proceedings are not. Perhaps it is best to use the concept of uniformity at higher levels of abstraction and to avoid using it at the operational level of accounting.

The uniformity of accounting also suggests reduction in the level of discretion available to individual managers or their auditors in determining how an event is recorded. If such discretion is taken away from managers, the argument goes, the application of accounting rules across firms will be more comparable. How detailed should the criteria be to determine the classification of transactions, and how much discretion to classify should managers and auditors have? No criteria can be detailed enough to eliminate all management discretion. The presence of discretion affects interfirm comparability of data, but not always adversely.[14] The cost and volume of accounting rules and regulations grows with their volume. The increased volume and complexity of regulations have their own consequences.

The greater the length and complexity of accounting rules, the greater the diversity in their interpretation by different managers and accountants, the larger the number of questions that arise about their meaning and intent, and the faster is the growth of written interpretations, clarifications, and guides for application of these rules. This happened to financial accounting rules in the sixties and the seventies, as a running count of the number of pages in the *Financial Accounting Standards* will confirm.

A more popular analogy is to the U.S. Internal Revenue Code. Whether the increased complexity of the code, with all its rules and interpretations, leads to a more uniform application of tax laws across individual and corporate taxpayers is a matter of serious debate. A case can be made that a less detailed specification of tax laws might actually be more equitable than the current tax code. Simplification of the tax code, using a flat tax, and elimination of various deductions is a recurrent theme in U.S. political campaigns. A more complex specification of rules allows for the discovery of more loopholes to avoid taxation. It also makes it more difficult to discover whether rules have been violated, and even if they are discovered, it is more difficult to prove tax evasion. It is not obvious if a more detailed specification of rules can narrow the discretion of management in the classification of accounts.

The accounting treatment of research and development (R & D) outlays is a case in point. Until the FASB issued *Statement No. 2* in 1974, capitalization of these outlays was left largely to the discretion of management. Practices varied across firms. Demands for uniformity led the FASB to search for rules that would reduce management discretion in capitalization decisions and closely approximate the economic nature of these events. It soon became evident that there was no way of satisfying both these requirements. The nature and circumstances of research and development outlays, and their results, vary so greatly that it is not feasible to lay down rules that will remove management discretion, without also weakening the link between the economic consequences of R & D outlays and their accounting treatment.

The FASB removed managers' discretion by requiring that these outlays be expensed. It achieved uniformity of form, but not substance. The underlying event that is supposed to be recorded is not the R & D expenditure alone, but also its economic consequences. Compulsory expensing of R & D outlays, irrespective of its results, creates a greater divergence between the underlying event and its accounting treatment than might be the case under a discretionary system. Two firms, each having spent $10 million on research, will have identical financial statements, irrespective of the development of a hot-selling product by one of the firms. Whether *Statement No. 2* has led to greater uniformity of financial statements in this fundamental sense is open to question.

Summary

The fundamental concepts of accounting can be interpreted in the language of social sciences. Specifically, the contract model of the firm and the classification theory provide a useful framework for examining the force and meaning of traditional accounting concepts, such as entity, valuation, accrual, and uniformity. This framework also helps us reduce the multiple and frequently overlapping and confusing categories, such as postulates, principles, doctrines, and features of accounting, into a simpler classification of conventions and economic features. Concepts such as uniformity and comparability are operationally vacuous for accountants' work.

Notes

[1] Russell Hardin, *Collective Action* (Baltimore, Md.: Johns Hopkins Press, 1982), chapters 10–13.

[2] Thomas C. Schelling, *The Strategy of Conflict* (Cambridge, Mass.: Harvard University Press, 1960).

[3] David K. Lewis, *Convention: A Philosophical Study* (Cambridge, Mass.: Harvard University Press, 1969), p. 78, formally defines conventions as follows: A regularity R in the behavior of members of a population P when they are agents in a recurrent situation S is a *convention* if and only if it is true that, and it is common knowledge in P that, in almost any instance of S among members of P, (1) almost everyone conforms to R; (2) almost everyone expects almost everyone else to conform to R; (3) almost everyone has approximately the same preferences regarding all possible combinations of actions; (4) almost everyone prefers that any one more (person) conform to R, on the condition that almost everyone conform to R; (5) almost everyone would prefer that any one more (person) conform to R', on condition that almost everyone conform to R', where R' is some possible regularity in the behavior of members of P in S, such that almost no one in almost any instance of S among members of P could conform both to R' and to R.

[4] R. J. Chambers, "Conventions, Doctrines, and Common Sense," *The Accountants' Journal* (February 1964), published by New Zealand Society of Accountants).

[5] S. Davidson, C. L. Stickney and R. L. Weil, *Financial Accounting: An Introduction to Concepts, Methods, and Uses*, 3d ed. (Chicago: Dryden Press, 1982).

[6] Accounting Principles Board, *Statement No. 4: Basic Concepts and Accounting Principles Underlying Financial Statements of Business Enterprises* (1970).

[7] Ibid., Paragraph 139.

[8] Stephen Gilman, *Accounting Concepts of Profit* (New York: The Ronald Press Company, 1939), p. 184.

[9] W. W. Cooper and Yuji Ijiri, eds., *Kohler's Dictionary For Accountants*, 6th ed. (Englewood Cliffs, N.J.: Prentice-Hall, 1983).

[10] Accounting Principles Board, op. cit. Paragraph 171.

[11] Cooper and Ijiri, op. cit.

[12] Yuji Ijiri, *Triple-Entry Bookkeeping and Income Momentum. Studies in Accounting Research #18* (Sarasota, Fla.: American Accounting Association, 1982).

[13] This section is based on Shyam Sunder, "Limits to Information," in K. R. Bindan, ed., *Accounting Research: Theoretical and Applied* (Tuscaloosa: University of Alabama Press, 1983).

[14] Ron Dye, "Strategic Accounting Choice and Effects of Alternative Financial Reporting Requirements," *Journal of Accounting Research*, Vol. 23, No. 2 (Autumn 1985), pp. 544–574; Ron Dye and Robert G. Verrecchia, "Discretion vs. Uniformity: Choices Among GAPP," *Accounting Review*, Vol. 70, No. 3 (July 1995), pp. 389–415; and Carolyn Levine, "Conservatism, Contracts and Information Revelation," Ph.D. Dissertation, Carnegie Mellon University (1996).

Additional Reading

Financial Accounting Standards Board. *Accounting for Research and Development Costs, Statement of Financial Accounting Standards No. 2*. Stamford, Conn.: FASB, 1974.

Financial Accounting Standards Board. *Accounting for Leases, Statement of Financial Standards No. 13*. Stamford, Conn.: FASB, 1976.

Ijiri, Yuji. *Theory of Accounting Measurement. Studies in Accounting Research #10*. Sarasota, Fla.: American Accounting Association, 1975.

Nash, John. "Equilibrium Points in n-Person Games." *Proceedings of the National Academy of Sciences*, Vol. 36 (1950), pp. 48–49.

⁄10⁄

Decision Criteria and Mechanisms

●●

Part Two covered independent pursuit of their own interests by individual agents. However, standards and conventions require social coordination. Individuals can buy their own houses independently, but the housing code for the city must be arrived at collectively. Whether we should use accounting standards, and what they should be, are collective decisions. Before analyzing standards in Chapter 11, let us discuss the criteria and methods for making such decisions. An important collective decision-making mechanism in society is called government. In Chapter 12 we discuss how government makes laws and regulations that govern the operation of proprietorships, partnerships, and private and public corporations.

Individual choice depends on the preferences of one person or homogenous group. Collective choice depends on the preferences of many (if we ignore dictatorial imposition). The latter has all the complications of individual choice, plus more. We start with the criteria and then go to the methods, and finally discuss the strengths and weaknesses of various ways of setting accounting standards.

Criteria for Social Choice

What we choose depends on what we look for and where and how far we search. What we look for, or the criterion for choice, is not unique.[1]

Technological Efficiency

In engineering and physical sciences, a criterion of choice is efficiency, which is the ratio of physical output to physical input of a process. Suppose you lose 10 percent of the weight of potatoes in hand peeling, and only 2 percent in machine peeling. Machine peeling, at 98 percent, is more efficient than hand peeling at 90 percent. Computerized bookkeeping is often technologically superior to manual bookkeeping in this sense. In the same sense, the application of statistical sampling to audits is superior to purely judgmental techniques in many situations.

Simple Economic Efficiency

The technologically efficient method for peeling potatoes is not necessarily the cheapest. Economic efficiency of a process is the ratio of the dollar value of its output to the dollar value of the inputs it needs. Convert all inputs into money and add them up. Do the same for the outputs, before taking the ratio of the two. If labor and potatoes are cheap and machines are expensive, hand peeling might turn out to be the efficient economic choice.

Technological efficiency affects, but does not determine, simple economic efficiency. If the dollar prices of inputs and outputs are chosen by the analyst, the latter is less objective, and is applicable to decisions made by individuals or homogeneous groups. Whether the owner of a grocery store replaces mechanical cash registers with a computerized checkout system is a matter of simple economic efficiency. The owner seeks the cheapest way to collect revenue. Whether an auditor chooses statistical methods over judgmental sampling can also be seen as a matter of simple economic efficiency. The auditor seeks the cheapest way to detect each error or each dollar of error.

Multiperson Economic Efficiency

How do we choose what is best for a group of two or more people when they do not agree among themselves? If the group were homogenous, we could use the simple economic efficiency criterion just described. If the goals of the members of the group are diametrically opposed—one side's gain is the other side's loss—no criterion of efficiency can be applied to the group. Members of most groups have overlapping interests, part common—part opposed. The common part induces a foundryman and a machinist to produce a component. The opposing part induces them to haggle on who gets how much of the sale price. How could the group make its choice?

Consider "better for some, worse for none" as a criterion of group choice. Compare two options at a time. If one is better for some but worse for none, discard the other option. Continue making pair-wise comparisons until none of the remaining options can be discarded. The set of remaining options is called the Pareto efficient set, and the criterion is called *Pareto efficiency*.

Unlike technological and simple economic criteria, this one rarely leads to a unique choice. Picking one of the Pareto efficient set over another necessarily sacrifices the interests of some members of the group for the benefit of others. One member of the set is no better than another by this criterion. This incompleteness of the Pareto criterion has led some to use cost–benefit criterion instead. Cost–benefit criterion compares options on the basis of their *aggregate* costs and benefits, without regard to the *distribution* of these costs and benefits among individuals. We discuss cost–benefit criterion for social decisions in a later section.

Cyert and Ijiri and Beaver and Demski argue that important accounting issues concern the interests of many people.[2] Budgeting, cost center, profit center, transfer price, inventory valuation, depreciation, and disclosure decisions affect many people. Each person can make a personal decision based on personal costs and benefits. However, these personal costs and benefits are affected by the decisions of others. To understand the consequences of accounting decisions, we need to consider this interdependency among individuals.

Two complicating factors can be added to each of these three criteria of efficiency (technological, simple economic, and Pareto). First, the consequences of many decisions are realized over a long period of time. Second, the consequences are often uncertain at the time the decision is made.

Multiperiod Problem

The efficiency of a decision, whether technological, simple economic, or Pareto, may vary over time. For example, the technological efficiency of a potato-peeling machine may decline with wear and tear, while the efficiency of hand peeling may improve with experience. One option is better in some periods, while another is better in others. How do we choose among them?

Since technological efficiency is defined in physical quantities of inputs and outputs, and not in terms of money, the multiperiod problem is usually resolved by simple or weighted averaging across periods. This amounts to treating all periods, early or late, alike.

Simple economic efficiency is reckoned in dollar costs and benefits. When the same option is not the best in all periods, each dollar amount is adjusted for the time value and the purchasing power of money, using one or more discount rates. A discount rate is the opportunity cost of money. The person making the decision can choose an option by comparing the net present value of each option, a single number.

In a multiperson context, it is possible, theoretically at least, to have each individual apply his or her personal discount rate to reduce the vector of period-by-period net benefits to the net present value of each option. These personal net present values could then be used to identify the Pareto efficient set as described. However, identifying this Pareto efficient set requires knowledge of various alternatives, their outcomes, and the preferences of individuals with respect to these outcomes.

In cost–benefit analysis, a common social, instead of a personal, rate of discount is used to aggregate multiperiod data. Determining an appropriate social rate of discount is even more difficult. It implies calculating the exchange rate in intergenerational transfers, and requires specification of the long-term goals and desires of the society.

Uncertainty Problem

The consequences of actions and choices are often uncertain. The longer the passage of time, the greater is the uncertainty. Let us start by considering uncertainty within a single period.

If one option is always better than others, no matter what happens, it is safe to pick that option. If option A has, say, two outcomes, a_1 and a_2 in state s_1 and s_2 respectively, and option B also has two corresponding outcomes, b_1 and b_2, then A is unambiguously preferred only if a_1 is greater than or equal to b_1 and a_2 is greater than or equal to b_2, and at least one of the two inequalities holds strictly. In many decisions this condition is not fulfilled because either (a_1, a_2) and (b_1, b_2) do not have such a relationship, or the two options divide the state space in noncomparable ways. How do we rank options in such cases?

In assessing technological efficiency, when one option does not dominate others in all states of the world, we resort to picking the option that has the higher expected efficiency. We may pick A over B if the former is better than average, but not always. We must supply not only the outcome under each state of the world, but also the probability of each state. In technological applications, it is sometimes possible, in concept if not in practice, to conduct experiments to determine the relative frequencies of various outcomes associated with an option. These relative frequencies are used as probabilities in weighting outcomes to calculate the mathematical expectation of the option.

The expected value criterion assumes that the desirability of options is linear in measured attributes. Under uncertainty, the expected utility—average desirability of each outcome associated with an option weighted by its probability—is currently a popular method of comparing options by simple economic efficiency. Use of a desirability or utility function allows for the possibility of a nonlinear relationship, but requires data about probabilities as well as the desirability of each outcome of each option.

It is rarely possible to obtain objective estimates of the relative frequencies of outcomes, making it necessary to rely on subjective probability assessments or the beliefs of the decision maker. The presence of uncertainty renders the efficiency of alternative courses of action a matter of belief, not fact. There is evidence that individual decisions made by intuition are not well-described by this expected utility criterion.

Before we discuss the implications of uncertainty for multiperson economic efficiency, one more consequence of uncertainty must be pointed out. Consider a grocery store owner who paid $1,000 in premium for fire insurance during the year. Fortunately, there was no fire. Was buying insurance a good decision? One might be tempted to respond that $1,000 was wasted because the store owner did not get anything of substance in return. Without the insurance policy, the owner would have had the same store, plus a higher balance in the bank. On the other hand, for a merchant whose store does burn down, an insurance premium is an excellent investment. It might yield a return of, say, 10,000 percent.

Because almost any option can turn out to be desirable in some circumstances, after-the-fact criterion cannot form a basis of choosing decisions in the presence of uncertainty, and it must be replaced by before-the-fact criterion, two examples of which are expected outcome and expected utility. Such criteria of efficiency are *expected* to yield more desirable outcomes on the average, but do not necessarily generate more desirable outcomes in every instance or even in a majority of instances. This leads to difficult problems of choice in multiperson economic settings.

The Pareto criterion of efficiency requires that the chosen option make at least someone better off without making anyone worse off. In the presence of uncertainty, the desirability of an option for each person can be assessed in terms of expectations before the fact, rather than in terms of actual events after the fact. Whose expectations or beliefs are to be used in applying the criterion? Except in the special case when all individuals have identical beliefs, there is no obvious interpretation of the Pareto criterion. Consider a few examples.

Let each person identify Pareto efficient options in terms of personal beliefs. If option A is identified to be superior to B by every individual on this basis, then A is socially preferred over B. However, this "super" Pareto criterion is even less complete than the Pareto criterion, and except in special rare cases, the diversity of individual beliefs renders most options noncomparable by this criterion.

A second possibility is to let each individual rank each option on the basis of his or her own beliefs *and* welfare. If option A is ranked higher than B by at least some individuals and not ranked lower by any, then A could be considered more efficient than B. Note that since each individual is using a simple economic criterion, the ranking of options will be reasonably complete. Multiperson ranking is still incomplete, but not as incomplete as the criterion mentioned in the preceding paragraph. This improvement in completeness is obtained only by discarding any information individuals may have about the effects of various options on the welfare of all other agents. This efficiency criterion wastes available information.

A third possibility is to assume that the information in the separate possession of all individuals is, by some process—possibly an appropriately designed institution such as a market—pooled and made available to all individuals. Therefore, everybody becomes as well-informed as they would be by an honest exchange of information. These homogeneous beliefs simplify the problem so that the Pareto criterion can be applied. Such arrangements for pooling information are not always possible, nor are they costless.

Selecting a criterion of efficiency is rendered difficult by considering uncertainty and time. Considering them both simultaneously invites even more complications.

Social Cost–Benefit Analysis

Social cost–benefit analysis sets aside the question of equity. The decision criterion is the difference between the sum of the incremental costs borne by all individuals and the sum of the incremental benefits across all individuals. Because summation across individuals is necessary to apply the criterion, the utility or desirability of the options is replaced by the monetary value of the options in the form of costs and benefits.

Which Costs and Which Benefits?

Setting the ethical question of equity aside, a second and equally difficult ethical problem plagues cost–benefit analysts: Which costs and which benefits must be included in evaluating options? Should we consider all costs and benefits? If not, which ones should be included? The scientific ethic favors measurability and objectivity. A scientist is likely to include only the costs and benefits that can be objectively measured. The social ethic drives one to include costs and benefits that are regarded as socially admissible and to ignore those that are not. If a new accounting standard reduces the possibility of fraud, and gains from fraud are regarded as socially inadmissible, a social cost–benefit analysis of the proposal can be conducted by ignoring the loss to defrauders and reckoning the benefits to the victim. The business or private ethic, on the other hand, requires that the costs one has to pay and the benefits one can capture be included in the cost–benefit analysis, and the others be ignored.

Which costs and benefits are included in analysis is a fundamental ethical choice. Therefore, the results of cost–benefit analysis depend on the ethical perspective used. Some business decisions may generate controversy when exposed and examined in a broader social context. For example, the fuel tanks of Pinto cars produced by Ford Motor Company were found to cause fire and injury in automobile collisions. In designing its Pinto model, Ford Motor Company tested the fuel tanks and decided, under business ethics, that the benefits of that design (lower costs) exceeded the costs (potential liability of Ford to customers). Since social ethics do not permit trading lives for money, at least not explicitly, Ford could not present this decision rationale before the jury in a court of law. A business or private cost–benefit ethic, hardly a secret, may face social condemnation in the public domain.

This discrepancy between the private business ethic and the social ethic also plagues discussions of what auditors and accountants do. The AICPA and other similar professional bodies, in carefully and jealously guarding their rights to set standards in their professions, proclaim that they do so for the public good. Businesspeople, when they fail to disclose data to their shareholders, claim to do so for the good of the shareholders. The private ethic is socially known and even accepted to a degree, but not acknowledged. Public statements are made on the basis of the social ethic instead.

Problems of Partial Analysis

In cost–benefit analysis, we typically assume that the relative prices of goods remain unaffected by the choice made. This partial equilibrium assumption is not always valid. When we consider the possibility that the choices we make can alter the prices, a paradox can arise: we may prefer option B over A at prices prevailing under A, and yet prefer A over B at prices that prevail under B.[3] In other words, the grass is always greener on the other side of the fence. Fortunately, the chances that this paradox would occur are small.

Nonlinear Utilities

Even if we ignore the effect of choice on prices, another paradox can arise from the nonlinearity of agents' utilities. If twice as large an increase in cost does not result in twice as large an increase in utility, the social costs of moving from status quo A to alternative B may exceed its benefits, but, had B been the status quo, the social cost of moving to A may also exceed the benefits. The result—that the status quo may be superior to the alternative, irrespective of what the status quo is— arises not only from adjustment costs, but also from nonlinear utility functions of agents. However, nonlinearities of the utility of agents are simply ignored in most cost–benefit analyses.

Measures of Efficiency

Our discussion of concepts of efficiency has been abstracted from the organizational setting and practical considerations. These concepts are more useful in designing the system itself, rather than in predicting how a particular system will operate. In a social system or industrial organization, agents can be expected to enhance their own welfare by using whatever measure of performance or efficiency is used to determine their rewards. Researchers and scientists, for example, often seek their rewards in the mere fact of discovery and the acclaim that may follow. Salary, promotion, and tenure of university professors are tied to publication, which, in turn, depends more on innovation than usefulness. Engineers similarly strive for technical excellence and meeting production targets and schedules. In a bureaucratic organization, the number of documents processed, permits granted, invoices prepared, and other such criteria may provide measures of efficiency.

The performance of an organization as a whole is a function of the behavior of its participants. Individual behavior depends on measures of efficiency by which individuals perceive themselves to be evaluated. Accounting produces many of these concrete measures in organizations.

Mechanisms for Social Choice

The practical problem of social choice is solved by designing mechanisms for making social choice. Elections and markets are the two major nondictatorial methods. The outcome of nondictatorial mechanisms depends on the preferences of all individuals. In a *market* process, social choice is determined through price. Preferences are expressed through the willingness of individuals to make economic sacrifices in order to attain their preferred alternatives. The *voting* mechanism is employed when a unique choice must be made by a group or society as a whole, and where divergence of choice across individuals is not feasible. Although the market mechanism permits everybody to buy his or her own brand of coffee, the voting mechanism results in only one person being elected to the city council from a given district.

Should accounting choices be made by price in a market or by vote in a referendum? Markets and voting mechanisms are not mutually exclusive. A market can and often does exist for votes. On the other hand, the definition and operation of a market requires socially enforceable rules of exchange that must be arrived at by a voting process. Thus, the distinction between a voting and a market mechanism is not absolute, only a convenient analytical device. If both mechanisms are to co-exist, what should be the extent of the utilization of each? If the standardization of some aspect of accounting is considered desirable, some type of voting mechanism should be applied. In those areas in which the imposition of a single choice is not socially desirable, a market must be allowed to prevail.

In this chapter, we assume that this higher-level choice of which accounting areas are to be governed by market and by voting mechanisms has already been made. This issue is explicitly considered in Chapter 12. In the following section, following Plott and Sunder,[4] some of the problems associated with market and voting mechanisms are examined.

Limitations of Voting Mechanisms

Preferences of groups are unlike individuals' preferences. If we think of groups as individuals, or try to construct group preferences from the preferences of their individual members, results can be strange. We show three examples of how group preferences need not have any internal consistency, even if they are derived from internally consistent individual preferences.

The first example shows Arrow's Paradox:[5] even if the preferences of all individuals are transitive (if $x > y$ and $y > z$ then $x > z$ where symbol > stands for "preferred over"), preferences of the group as a whole, determined by their majority vote, can be cyclical ($x > y > z > x$). Consider a committee of three persons considering three options. The committee decides by majority rule, and the members of the committee have formed their personal preferences before meeting to resolve their conflict. In Figure 10.1, individual I prefers x over y over z; individual II likes y over z over x; and individual III likes z over x over y. The preferences of every individual are internally consistent.

If members of the committee vote to choose between options x and y, individual I votes for x, individual II votes for y, individual III votes for x. Under the majority rule, x beats y. If a vote is taken between options y and z, I and II vote for y, III votes for z, and y wins. In voting between x and z, I votes for x but II and III vote for z, therefore z wins. The group as a whole, using a majority vote, prefers x over y, y over z, and z over x. Transitive individual preferences can yield circular majority preferences.

Figure 10.1   **Effect of Agenda on Committee Outcome**

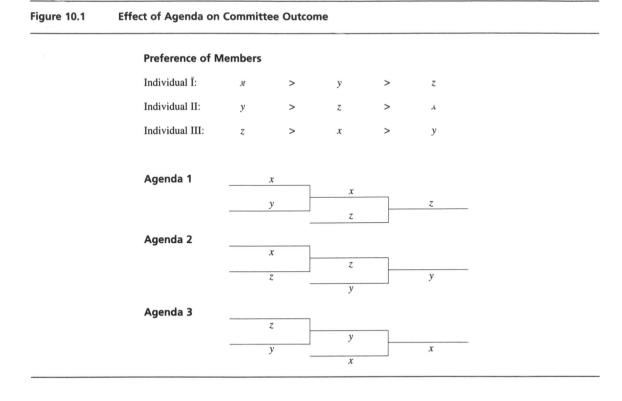

Preference of Members

Individual I:	x	>	y	>	z
Individual II:	y	>	z	>	x
Individual III:	z	>	x	>	y

Agenda 1

Agenda 2

Agenda 3

Another way of thinking of such results is that the outcome of the group process is vulnerable to the choice of the agenda—the order in which various options are pitted against one another and put to a vote. The outcome of the voting process can be quite different, depending on the order in which various proposals are paired up and put to a vote. For another example, suppose that the status quo is w, and z is proposed. It can be seen in Figure 10.2 that z is preferred to w by two out of three voters, so the system moves to z. Then somebody proposes y and the system moves from z to y. Then x is proposed and again a majority prefers x to y, so the system ends up at x. Using a democratic majority rule at each step, the system starts at w and ends up at x, even though every individual prefers w over x.

All known voting procedures cause problems demonstrated by these examples. Some rules assure a Pareto optimum, but they are all subject to procedural manipulation. As shown by the examples, the majority rule has problems on both counts.

Group choice is sensitive to the rules used. Consider a point voting system as a third example. If four alternatives exist, each voter is to assign four points to his or her best option, three points to the next best option, two points to the next best option, and so on. Points are then added, and the option with the highest total is chosen. Scoring systems like this are used for many purposes, including personnel

Figure 10.2   **Cyclical Group Preferences**

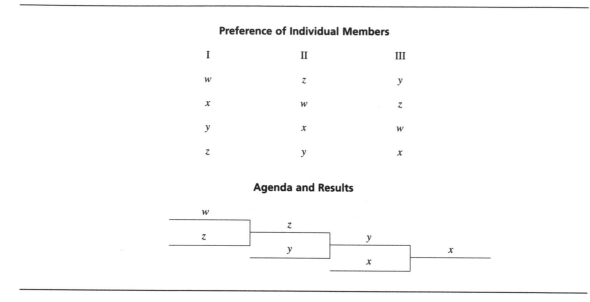

Preference of Individual Members

I	II	III
w	z	y
x	w	z
y	x	w
z	y	x

Agenda and Results

evaluation. The seven-person example in Figure 10.3 demonstrates the sensitivity of such choices to the set of options under consideration. With the four options (*w*, *x*, *y*, *z*), the total points are shown in the column labeled 1. In this case, *y* is the winner with 20 points, and it is followed by *x* and *w* with 19 and 18 total points, respectively. If the loser, *z*, with 13 points, had not been considered at all, the results would have been quite different. As shown in the column labeled 2, the choice would have been *w* with 15 points, followed by *x* and *y*, in that order. The addition or elimination of an unchosen option can cause the ordering of the other alternatives to be inverted by a committee. In other words, the group's preference can invert with the interjection or elimination of options.

Figure 10.3   **Point Voting System**

Individual Preferences over Options w, x, y, and z								Points	
I	II	III	IV	V	VI	VII		1	2
w	x	y	w	x	y	w	w	18	15*
x	y	z	x	y	z	x	x	19	14
y	z	w	y	y	z	w	y	20*	13
z	w	x	z	w	x	z	z	13	

*Highest total

Figure 10.4   Composition of a Single Issue Committee

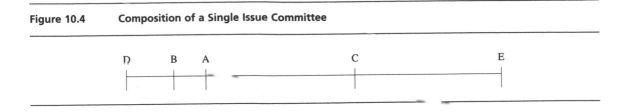

The core of a cooperative game (defined as the set of those choices that cannot be improved upon by any individual or by any subgroup of individuals acting on their own) is a good predictor of its outcome. This implies that people can manipulate groups that appear to be "fairly constituted." Balanced representation on committees is often a subject of protracted discussions. The idea is to obtain representation of all the extremes, to get proper information into the process by allowing all people to be represented. Let us suppose that we have a single issue, represented by the line in Figure 10.4, and a committee is to be appointed. We want the group to choose point A on the figure, but we cannot force it to do so. One strategy is as follows.

We choose someone for the committee whose preferences are like our own, that is, who likes point A best. Next, in order to make the committee look fair, we appoint people representing diverse groups. But each time we appoint someone whose preferences are to the right of A, we also appoint someone whose preferences are to its left. Even extreme positions can be represented as long as they are in equal numbers on either side of A. Point A is the core, and it will be the choice of the committee. The committee may look "fair," but you can see how representation determines choice.

Certain types of agenda are powerful determinants of group choice. Agendas that form a sequence of partitions can be used to determine, within limits, the choice of a voting group. Such an agenda partitions the options into two sets, and the vote is on which set to consider further. With one set eliminated by majority rule, the remaining options are again partitioned for a vote. The choice of options to be grouped into sets (the wording of the motions) is a powerful tool for manipulating groups that decide by vote.

This above discussion has centered on the problems of majority-rule voting. Similar problems of cyclicity or vulnerability to manipulation exist in other voting schemes. Buchanan and Tullock and Rawls provide tools to evaluate constitutions, rules, or processes.[6] Theoretical properties of voting processes may be altered by the political conditions in which they operate, adding uncertainty to the relative desirability of various voting processes.

Market Mechanisms in Accounting Standards

Market mechanisms can provide efficient solutions for the problems of the production and distribution of private goods. Standards for traded goods define the rules of the game by which the markets are governed. Product standards themselves are public goods. One can conceive of competition among alternative sets of rules of the market, such as a computerized stock exchange operated by the National Association of Securities Dealers versus the New York Stock Exchange with a trading floor. These alternative sets are public goods and no exchange market can exist for them. The choice of rules or standards must be arrived at by some social choice mechanism. To the extent that the form of exchange in the product market is left to be specified by the participants, they may overwhelmingly prefer one form over another. In such cases, one may use the evidence from the product market to introduce a new rule limiting transactions to the preferred form. Current accounting standards leave many aspects of financial reporting to the discretion of those who prepare, audit, or read the results. If a standard-setting body used evidence about choices made by reporting entities in making their decisions, it may be said to have used the market mechanism. Let us return to the problems of, and opportunities for, using markets to determine accounting standards.

Legal Rights and Markets

Markets facilitate the exchange of property rights. They require a socially accepted definition of these rights to function properly. This definition is arrived at by a political process. Conversely, the legal system relies on market choices for its effectiveness. Law defines the rewards and punishment associated with various types of behavior. It depends on people's desire to enhance their welfare for its effectiveness: rational people choose their actions in light of the rewards and punishments associated with the alternatives.

The interaction of the law and markets has interesting effects. When the cost of market transactions is zero, a change in the initial assignment of legal property rights may affect the distribution of wealth, but it leaves unchanged the equilibrium allocation of resources.[7] For example, if the operator and the neighbors of a steel mill could conduct mutual transactions without cost, the amount of smoke emitted from the chimneys of the mill would remain unaffected by whether legal liability for smoke damage to citizens lies with the citizens or with the steel mill. This apparently counterintuitive result follows from the fact that if the gain to the mill owner from emitting more smoke exceeds the damage to the citizens from so doing, the mill operator will be able to compensate the citizens for the damage and gain their consent to emit more smoke if the law makes the operator liable for damage. If, on the other hand, the law makes the citizens liable for the smoke damage, they will not find it economical to compensate the mill operator for the loss from reducing the amount of smoke emitted, because their gains from reduced smoke are not as large as the loss to the mill owner. Thus, the amount of smoke emitted from the chimneys in equilibrium remains unaffected by the assignment of legal property rights to clean air.

The same argument is applicable to standards that define property rights in information and accounting systems. If agents involved in a particular firm could make costless transactions among themselves, socially determined accounting standards would not have an effect on the accounting system of the firm. Standards can be effective only because the costs of such transactions are nonzero. Conversely, the rationale of socially determined accounting standards lies in firm-level transaction costs. When accounting standards are promulgated, it should have to be demonstrated that the problem cannot be handled at the level of the firm.

Summary

Social decisions on accounting affect many members of society in diverse ways. There are two basic approaches to defining socially desirable decisions. The Pareto criterion, which requires that a socially desirable decision not be harmful to any member of the society, is not easily met in practice. The social cost–benefit criterion is considered unacceptable by many, because it ignores the distributional effects of social choices. Its application may result in serious inequities. The practical application of both criteria is complicated by problems of uncertainty and by the time span over which the consequences of social choices are realized. There are no perfect mechanisms for making social choices. All mechanisms, whether they are based on voting or on market exchange, have weaknesses. In selecting ways of setting accounting rules and standards, it is useful to pay attention to the limitations of the instruments available to us.

Notes

[1] This section is based on Martin Shubik, "On Concepts of Efficiency," *Policy Sciences*, Vol. 9 (1978), pp. 121–126.

[2] See Richard M. Cyert and Yuji Ijiri, "Problems of Implementing the Trueblood Objectives Report," *Studies on Financial Accounting Objectives,* Supplement to *Journal of Accounting Research*, 1974, pp. 29–42; and William H. Beaver and Joel S. Demski, "The Nature of Financial Accounting Objectives: A Summary and Synthesis," *Studies on Financial Accounting Objectives,* Supplement to *Journal of Accounting Research*, 1974, pp. 170–187.

[3] E. J. Mishan, *Cost Benefit Analysis* (New York: Praeger Publishers, 1976).

[4] C. R. Plott and S. Sunder, "A Synthesis," *Studies on Standardization of Accounting Practices: An Assessment of Alternative Institutional Arrangements*, Supplement to *Journal of Accounting Research*, Vol. 19 (1981), pp. 227–239.

[5] Kenneth J. Arrow, *Social Choice and Individual Values*, Cowles Foundation Monograph 12 (New Haven: Yale University Press, 1951).

[6] James M. Buchanan and Gordon Tullock, *The Calculus of Consent* (1962); and John Rawls, *A Theory of Justice* (Cambridge, Mass.: Harvard University Press, 1971).

[7] R. H. Coase, "The Problem of Social Costs," *Journal of Law and Economics* (1960), pp. 1–25.

Additional Reading

Kormendi, R., and C. R. Plott. "Committee Decisions Under Alternative Procedural Rules: An Experimental Study Applying a New Nonmonetary Method of Preference Inducement." Social Science Working Paper Number 346, California Institute of Technology, 1980.

Melumad, Nahum D., and Toshiyuki Shibano. "The Securities and Exchange Commission and the Financial Accounting Standards Board: Regulation Through Veto-Based Delegation." *Journal of Accounting Research*, Vol. 32, No. 1 (Spring 1994), pp. 1–37.

ʼ11ʼ

Standardization
of Accounting

. . . .

Accounting standards are no different from many other kinds of standards in society. They prod individual behavior to something considered desirable by some criterion of social choice, or serve as guideposts for coordination among individuals. Benefits and costs are distributed unevenly, and few standards win the support of all. No mechanism for setting standards is beyond manipulation by interest groups who may capture them. The standardization of accounting affects not only the practice of accounting and auditing, but also what is taught in accounting classes. It is difficult to ascertain whether the origins of the wave of standardization that has swept the world of accounting since the 1960s lie in computers, in education of the previous generation of accountants, or elsewhere.

Rules and Economic Decisions

Accounting standards are a type of rules. Rules can be thought of as constraints to isolate *permissible* from *prohibited* behavior. Alternatively, we can think of rules as a system of rewards or punishments dispensed according to one's choice of action. Our choice of perspective on rules determines the distinction between volunteer and mandatory behavior in the presence of accounting standards.

Rules as Constraints

Rules define a feasible set of actions. What is not permissible under rules cannot be considered a feasible alternative. If the LIFO method of accounting is not allowed by the rules, inventory accounting must be restricted to the non-LIFO methods. The social ethic dictates that legitimate rules of society be followed by everyone, and this ethical consideration prevents individuals from considering options that violate the rules.

Rules as Payoff Functions

If rules are viewed in terms of a private or economic ethic, instead of a social ethic, they appear not as constraints on the opportunity set of individuals, but as payoff or cost functions. The violation of rules incurs a cost. Therefore, an economic decision involves choosing an alternative that provides maximum net benefit, after reckoning the cost of violation. In this framework, rules do not exclude any alternatives from the feasible set. They merely render some alternatives more or less attractive than others by attaching a reward or cost to them. A large enough cost of violation induces all agents to shun the proscribed alternatives, and has the same ultimate effect *as if* these alternatives were excluded from the feasible set of actions.

Economic analysis of the law proceeds from the assumption that laws alter the payoffs associated with various courses of action. For example, the law does not prohibit murder. If one commits murder, the law specifies that certain consequences are likely to follow. In economic terms, the problem of legislation is to analyze the consequences of various penalty schedules for behavior and then select the schedule that yields the most desirable pattern of behavior by rational agents subjected to these schedules. Economists can only identify the kinds of behavior people will engage in under various penalty schedules. Which of the many possible patterns of behavior is preferred by the society is a value judgment that lies outside the purview of economics.

Penalty schedules consist of two parts; one part is directly legislated, the other is not. Law defines the penalty on violations, conditional on the violation being identified. Because of uncertainties inherent in the enforcement and judicial system, some guilty persons go free and some innocent persons are punished. The expected reward or penalty associated with each course of action depends not only on the law, but also on the enforcement and judicial system. Both affect the choices made by individuals.

From an individual's point of view, enforcement and adjudication uncertainty makes each course of action appear as a bundle of risk and return. The chances of being prosecuted and found guilty of a violation and the magnitude of penalty specified by the law for those who are found guilty vary, depending on the violation. Rules are important to a person only in the sense that they alter risk–return bundles attached to various actions, not in the sense that they exclude some actions from being considered at all.

This intrusion of economics into social ethics may offend some. Society may be better off if individuals treated rules and laws as absolute prohibitions, and not as costs and benefits associated with their actions. In economics, absolute prohibition means that the cost of violation is large. Due to the uncertainties of enforcement and adjudication, it may not be socially desirable to impose large costs on those few who happen to get caught in the enforcement net. Unless enforcement of the law is perfect and automatic, the imposition of large penalties on violators induces those who are charged with violations to spend more resources on their defense.

Voluntary and Mandatory Behavior

A choice among accounting methods is labeled mandatory if it follows the issuance of a new rule or standard from an authoritative body such as the FASB or the SEC. Otherwise, it is called voluntary. The distinction between voluntary and mandatory behavior has no economic substance. We discuss this general problem before returning to their relevance to accounting standards and practice.

When a person is prevented from choosing an action by a legal constraint, the choice is called *involuntary* or mandated by the law in the sense that, in the absence of the law, that person would have chosen a different action. In economics, laws and rules are seen as incentives and costs, and the distinction between voluntary and involuntary behavior is less useful. Consider a simple example of economic decision making. One day you find that the price of eggs has increased, while the price of milk has remained unchanged since your previous visit to the grocery store. Given the new prices, your inability to alter them in any significant way, and a fixed budget, you may decide to buy more milk and fewer eggs. Your taste for eggs and milk, combined with the change in your economic environment (prices), induces you to alter your actions.

Second, consider a change in the legal speed limit from 60 to 55 miles per hour. The new law does not render it impossible to drive above 60 mph; it simply makes it more costly, depending on the level of enforcement efforts (police patrol cars, radar equipment, etc.), the judicial system, and the penalties. Given your inability to change the law in any significant fashion and considering the new cost–benefit ratio, you might be inclined to drive slower. Fast driving may no longer be worth the added cost.

What is the difference between these two examples? Since the change in the price of eggs is beyond the immediate control of the economic agent, as long as the agent is driven by personal preferences, this change can be said to have forced or mandated the agent to alter grocery decisions. In this sense, not only the change in road speed is mandatory, but all economic actions, driven by wants and environment, are mandatory, and nothing is voluntary.

However, the lack of free will is offensive to our self-image. We may define the grocery decision to be voluntary in the sense that the consumption of milk and eggs is freely or voluntarily chosen, both before and after the change in prices, and preference is nothing but an expression of free will. The same argument applies equally well to the choice of driving speed. According to this view, all human behavior is voluntary and nothing is mandatory.

Fortunately, classification of behavior as voluntary or mandatory is irrelevant to economic analysis. In the economic context, the terms *voluntary* and *mandatory* are mere rhetorical devices or emotional responses that imply value judgments.

Those who benefit from an increase in egg prices may find it advantageous to argue that the consumer still makes a voluntary choice after prices are raised. Those who are hurt by the lower speed limits (e.g., truckers) might decry the new law as coercive. In public debate among opposing interests, labels of *voluntary* and *mandatory* may be convenient weapons of attacking adversaries. They contribute little to scientific analysis.

Accounting standards, like other rules or laws, alter the costs and benefits of various courses of action. The labels *voluntary* and *mandatory* are frequently used in accounting contexts, but their use diverts attention from the economic nature of accounting choices. If a change in the interest capitalization policy of a firm, following the publication of FASB *Statement No. 34*, is labeled involuntary or mandated, shouldn't we also call a switch to LIFO during periods of high inflation mandatory? If external imposition is the essence of mandatory change, the FASB or the SEC are no more external than inflation is. Perhaps the essence of mandatory change is that they help avert the consequences of not responding to changes in accounting standards, such as audit qualification. But then decisions about LIFO, too, would qualify as mandatory, because the costs of not using LIFO in the environment of inflation must be paid to the tax collector in hard cash.

It is tempting to argue that accounting standards impose high costs on violators with such certainty that, for all practical purposes, standards are constraints on the feasible set of accounting choices. However, standards that appear to be mandatory in this sense rarely are. This has been demonstrated in the adjustments firms have made in response to *Statement No. 2* (which costs are classified as research and development, and in-house research versus contracting-out research work), *Statement No. 13* (redesign of lease covenants), and *Statement Nos. 8 and 52* (hedging of foreign exchange risk).

Classifying standard-induced accounting changes as mandatory obfuscates the economic nature of accounting decisions. It may be more fruitful simply to examine the effects of standards on the behavior of firms and agents.

Economics of Rules and Standards

Why have rules and standards? Why not be free to do what we want? What are the consequences of operating under rules? Standardization is widely practiced in all economic systems. Pieces of gold were cast into standardized pellets to serve as a medium of exchange millennia ago. All 110-volt electrical outlets take the same adapter. Appetites vary, but canned soup can be bought in only two or three different sizes at the supermarket. There are hundreds of standard-setting organizations in the United States, and thousands worldwide. Why is standardization so common?

Benefits of Standards

Standards save transaction and search costs. Without such costs, it might be optimal to use a 156-watt incandescent lamp in my living room and a 62-watt florescent lamp in the study. However, the costs of manufacturing, distributing, and retailing increase with the number of different sizes and types. Restricting our choice to, say, 25-, 40-, 60-, 100-, and 250-watt lamps carries the benefit of the lower price at which fewer sizes can be produced and sold. Consequently, standardization is widely practiced in manufacturing and construction industries.

Standardization applies to procedures, information, and news as much as it does to physical products. The standardized format of a newspaper makes it easier for the readers to locate the items of interest to them—stock quotation tables, exchange rates, and opinion pieces. A standard bus fare, unrelated to distance traveled, is cheaper to collect.

Costs of Standards

Although the benefits of standardization are shared by all, its cost must be borne by those persons whose preferred option is not chosen as the standard. The standardization of electric lamps to, say, five sizes increases the cost of nonstandard sizes. Those who are not adequately compensated for accepting a "suboptimal" solution to their problems oppose standardization.

Standardization affects innovation. The economic savings of standardization attract further development efforts to areas within the boundaries defined by the standards and help speed up innovation within these bounds. However, standardization raises the cost of radical innovation outside the standardized boundaries, and discourages it. Persistence of the inefficient QWERTY keyboard for roman-script typewriters is a good example of the conflict between standardization and innovation. More efficient keyboard layouts such as DVORAK are available now, but QWERTY standard is too deeply entrenched to be replaced easily.

Distribution and Equity

The immediate distributional effects of standardization can be quite inequitable. Those agents whose current products or practices are similar or close to the newly adopted standard earn a windfall, while others bear the cost of adjusting their products and practices to the new standard. Agents exert pressure to obtain standards so that their own adjustment costs are minimized.

Standards of quality specify the minimum acceptable level of quality. For example, Underwriters Laboratories issues standards for appliances, and the AICPA issues standards for accounting. The optimal standard from the point of view of each producer is equal to the quality of that producer's product, because such a standard maximizes the positive difference between the average quality of products that meet the standard and the quality of the producer's product.

Adjustment to New Standards

Introduction of standards induces agents to adjust their behavior. Ignoring this adjustment results in overestimating its effects. Windfall gains from the new standard dwindle as other agents change their behavior. Similarly, windfall losses cause agents to find new ways of avoiding the harm inflicted on them by a new standard. Predictions of perpetual windfalls and dire consequences, frequently made during debates on accounting standards, are rarely realized.

Adjustments to change are neither quick nor costless. Agents need time to learn the new environment and to search for and select new rules of thumb. Frequent changes in standards impose the costs of adjustment. Once agents have adjusted their behavior to a new environment, they do not look favorably on moves to disturb the status quo. It is not surprising that managers oppose virtually all proposals for new accounting standards.

Economic Theories of Standards

Each set of consequences of standardization forms the basis for an economic theory of standardization. Briefly, standards can be seen either as a means of limiting competition, or as a means of supplying industry-wide public goods. What are these theories, and to what extent are they applicable to accounting standards?

Monopoly and Limiting Competition

Organizations that set standards can limit competition in two ways. First, independent of the specific standards they choose, such organizations provide forums that can be used to conspire in restraint of trade in the industry. Public accountants who play a prominent role in setting standards could have used the Accounting Principles Board or the Committee on Accounting Procedure for this purpose. However, their professional association, the AICPA, provides a more convenient forum for collusion to restrain trade in the audit industry. Several provisions in the AICPA's *Code of Ethics* limited competition through restraints on advertising and on the solicitation of clients and employees of competitors. Many of these provisions were dropped under pressure from the Federal Trade Commission and the U.S. Department of Justice. The FASB, consisting of more diverse elements, is unsuitable for this purpose.

Second, standards themselves can be designed to limit competition. The most important threat to the stability of a cartel is hard-to-detect cheating by its own members. Setting standards for the minimum as well as the maximum limit on product quality is an attempt, not always successful, to cut the cost of monitoring by eliminating one dimension of non-price competition. Product compatibility and interchangeability standards (e.g., for cassette tapes) have this anticompetitive potential.

Accounting standards on disclosure have been limited to the minimum level of disclosure and do not specify a maximum level. Therefore, disclosure standards are free from anticompetitive potential on this account. However, emphasis on uniformity and comparability of accounting methods is similar to interchangeability standards in the manufacturing industry. We must evaluate their anticompetitive effect in the capital markets, because they may prevent individual firms from trying to devise financial reporting methods that investors may find more attractive than the extant standards.

Provision of Public Goods

Product compatibility and interchangeability standards are pure public goods because (1) anyone can use the standard, without reducing the opportunity for others to use it, and (2) no one can be excluded from using the standards. Most accounting measurement and disclosure standards are public goods. Their promulgation and enforcement promote social welfare by reducing the resources that must be expended by the readers of financial reports to understand that data. This public good is produced through social coordination of choices made in individual firms.

For the sake of coordination, states must choose whether drivers should keep to the left or the right on the road. Accounting standards for measurement and disclosure involve more complex choices among options whose costs and benefits to various agents are neither identical nor obviously known. While coordination is one of its important elements, the standardization of accounting is not a pure coordination game, which Hardin discusses.[1] Setting accounting standards also requires judgments about their relative efficiency.

Accounting Standards

Edey and Baxter identify four types of accounting standards: (1) standards of disclosure and explanation of accounting policies, (2) standards of uniformity of layout and presentation of financial statements, (3) standards of disclosure of specific facts and uncertainties, and (4) standards of accounting measurement.[2]

The first type of standard is a higher-level standard. It concerns the *disclosure* of what accountants do. The last three types concern what accountants *do* to prepare the financial statements. The difference between the first and the latter three types is analogous to the difference between standards for *labeling canned food* and standards for the *canned food* itself. Higher-level standards are easier to defend. Even if standards for contents cannot be agreed upon, it might be possible to justify standards for labeling. Standards on disclosure and explanation of accounting policies have been less controversial than those on accounting policies themselves, as evidenced by the history of accounting for the investment tax credit, depreciation, inventory, oil and gas exploration outlays, and stock-based employee compensation.

Enforceability of Standards

Useful standards themselves must be enforceable, either implicitly or explicitly. If we cannot know, either before or after the fact, whether a firm complied with a standard, it has little effect. Two attempts by the SEC illustrate the point. The SEC encouraged firms to disclose their earnings forecasts and their underground reserves in the oil and gas industry and, by extending protection under a safe harbor rule, tried to overcome managers' fears of being held liable for incorrect forecasts and estimates. Both experiments failed, because the managers had no incentives to publish any meaningful numbers and investors had no way of evaluating their accuracy.

Market Argument

In a world without accounting standards, each firm would arrive at a custom-designed accounting and reporting system through negotiations among the participants. Any conflicts among the agents would be resolved through direct negotiation and, where direct negotiations were not feasible, through the functioning of markets for the resources that agents contribute to and receive from the firm. For example, if investors want inflation-adjusted accounting data, managers have the incentive to provide such information as long as the value of such data to the investors exceeds the cost of preparing such data, and managers are the low cost producers of the data. For firms that choose to provide such data, investors will be willing to pay a higher share price (equal to the cost saving to investors from not having to produce inflation-adjusted data themselves or not having to buy it from other sources). This will lower the firm's cost of capital and provide higher compensation to the managers. The scarcity of firms who are willing to meet the supposed investor demand for such data suggests that no such demand exists, and that requiring publicly held firms to produce and distribute such data is a waste of the firm's resources. Standards benefit only those who earn their living by setting, policing, and enforcing them. The best accounting standards, according to this argument, are no accounting standards.

This market argument can be applied to the three lower levels of accounting standards and to the higher-level standards that concern the disclosure of accounting policy. If investors want to shoot craps in the stock market, there is no social reason to prohibit them from doing so through socially determined accounting standards.

A special variation of the market argument is that the current law, in bundling the shareholders' rights to vote and to receive residual resources and financial reports, unnecessarily constrains firms' accounting choices and induces an inefficient allocation of resources. The law of corporate property rights could be redefined to unbundle the right to accounting reports from other shareholder rights, yielding a more efficient resource allocation. Then, the firm would only produce information that could be profitably sold to private buyers.

Argument for Market Failure

According to this argument, accounting standards must be socially determined and enforced with the help of sanctions and penalties for their violation. This will furnish correct and adequate information about the firm to various nonmanagerial agents, enabling them to make efficient decisions. Markets cannot be relied upon to ensure that each firm, left to direct negotiation among its own participating agents, shall arrive at an efficient accounting system. Managers have too much power and control over the accounting system and, unless this control is constrained by socially determined standards, inefficient accounting methods will be chosen. Investors and other agents have little effective control over the behavior of managers who choose accounting methods to advance their own interests. Until accounting standards were issued to require publicly held firms to disclose inflation-adjusted accounting data, they did not make such disclosure. This nondisclosure is an example of the failure of market forces to yield efficient systems.

Efficient standards can be set, the argument goes, by a body of experts, supported by competent advice. An appropriate institutional mechanism can adequately identify the consequences of alternative standards and identify socially efficient options on the basis of external criteria, such as relevance, verifiability, understandability, timeliness, and neutrality.

A Synthesis

What should be the role of the market and voting mechanisms in determinating accounting methods? Voting mechanisms are natural choices when a single option must necessarily be chosen by society. However, the selection of a single method of accounting for all firms is not *necessary*. It is not obvious that the use of a single method of depreciation by all firms is superior to the use of two or more methods. Perhaps markets can also help determine accounting methods.

Setting socially efficient standards is a demanding task for a centralized institution. It has to be designed to have a reasonable chance of yielding something close to the social optimum. A centralized planning mechanism must gather data on the cost–benefits and preferences of agents, as well as induce them to reveal information truthfully, without engaging in strategic behavior. This is an unattainable task. The standardization of accounting methods to the exclusion of market-based mechanisms offers no panacea.

Complete reliance on markets to determine accounting methods is equally infeasible. In spite of a popular conception of markets as a place where freedom reigns, all markets require an enforceable system of rules or laws that define property rights to be exchanged in the market, and for settling transactions. Since only a single set of rules can govern transactions in an orderly market, the rules for a market must be defined by voting mechanisms if they are to be democratic. Rules of organization distinguish a market from anarchy.

Just because it is feasible to create a market for a resource does not mean that such a market will exist. Nor will it function perfectly just because it exists. The costs of conducting transactions in a market must be exceeded by the gains made from trading for the market to exist. These costs must be sufficiently small for the market to approach perfection. The market argument just given makes two logical leaps: (1) the existence of a factor market is possible; therefore it must exist under any level of transaction costs; and (2) if a market exists, we can assume that its outcome will be the same as if the cost of conducting transactions in the market were zero.

In the presence of market transaction costs, it is possible for accounting standards to improve social welfare. Due to imperfections in the properties of voting mechanisms, not all standards will be improvements on the solutions derived from imperfect markets. The rejection of extreme arguments for and against standards leaves us in the broad middle ground. The relative desirability of standards and market solutions to specific accounting problems must be worked out, item by item.

Institutions for Setting Accounting Standards

As we discussed in the preceding chapter, the criteria for social efficiency are weak and incomplete in theory and difficult to apply in practice, because different people know different things, they do not necessarily agree on what they know, and they do not necessarily reveal truthfully what they know. Institutions attempt to circumvent this problem by emphasizing *procedures* for decision making.

Models of Social Institutions

Social choice mechanisms can be classified into six categories: common law, market, referendum, legislative, judicial, and bureaucratic mechanisms. In practice, elements of two or more such systems are combined to design a social institution. Most of them have played some part in accounting.

The common law or grass-roots approach to making social decisions is the ultimate in decentralization. It is also slow. It is ineffective in making choices among technical alternatives not understood by lay persons. Pacioli's accounting text could be seen as common law rules of accounting. Societies that do not have publicly owned enterprises are well-served by this system. The introduction of more complex organizations, such as large publicly held enterprises, places demands on accounting systems that cannot easily be met by the common law approach.

Markets can provide efficient solutions for problems of production and the distribution of private goods. Standards for the traded goods define the rules of the game by which the markets are governed. As rules of the game, product standards are public goods because all agents can share in their benefits once they are implemented. It is possible to have two or more markets, operated by different rules, compete against each other. Various stock exchanges in the United States compete in this manner. These alternative sets of rules are public goods, and no exchange market can exist for them. The choice of rules or standards is made through other social choice mechanisms. Current accounting standards leave many aspects of financial reporting to the discretion of those who prepare, audit, or read financial statements. If a standard-setting body used evidence about choices made by reporting entities in making its decisions, it might be said to have used the market mechanism.

In a referendum, voters speak for themselves. Referenda are effective when alternatives can be simply stated so that they are readily understandable by the constituents, such as limiting members of parliament to four elected terms of office. When formulating alternatives itself becomes important, or when the consequences of technically complex alternatives are not easily comprehended by the constituents, direct voting is not effective as a social choice institution. The technical nature of accounting precludes the use of referenda to set accounting rules.

Constituent groups select or elect their representatives to speak on their behalf in legislatures. A legislature takes action only if it can agree on something within its rules of order. If, for example, majority support cannot be mustered for any of the proposals on the table, and the legislature's rules of order require a majority support to pass a resolution, no resolution is passed. Debate in legislative bodies is frequently partisan, because the representatives are expected to, and do, argue in favor of the interests of their constituents. Attempts to protect one's own turf are considered ethical in legislative settings. Several elements of legislative structure characterized the manner in which the Accounting Principles Board (1959–73) was constituted and functioned in the United States.

The judiciary is different from the legislature. Judges are expected to listen to partisan arguments and then impartially decide on the basis of law or equity. Unlike legislators, judges are not supposed to have a partisan interest in the issues placed before them. Also, unlike the legislative system, they cannot just agree not to do anything. They must decide one way or the other on the issues presented before them.

Judicial and legislative mechanisms are frequently accompanied by bureaucratic support. Some standard-setting mechanisms are purely bureaucratic. The FASB, for example, combines elements of judicial and bureaucratic mechanisms. Bureaucracies face the difficult problem of control. Frequently, they are motivated by maximizing their measured and reported performance. In the absence of performance data of some type, bureaucracies may waste resources. However, defining performance criteria (e.g., the number of standards issued) is almost as bad, if not worse, because bureaucracies may be induced to pursue such criteria independent of the effect of their actions on social welfare.

The Force of Standards

As we move from common law to bureaucratic mechanism, fewer people are directly involved in making decisions, and more of the power of an organization, whether governmental or private, is harnessed to enforce the decisions. The involvement of fewer people in the process makes it possible to move quickly and decisively to change the standards. For example, it is possible for the SEC to issue a ruling on an accounting issue in a matter of days, while the FASB would take months, if not years, to arrive at a decision. This faster response time is associated with a greater chance of making errors because some relevant consideration may escape the attention of the limited number of people who make the decision.

The effectiveness of standards depends on how they are made, as well as on how they are enforced. At one end of the spectrum, standards may be enforced by an implicit social or professional obligation to conform to the norms of the community (as is often the case with common law). At the other extreme, an agency may be empowered to enforce standards through an explicit threat of punishment for those who fail to conform (as is the case with the pronouncements of the SEC). The enforcement of standards through such organized agencies does not necessarily yield a more desirable result, for two reasons. First, the threat of substantial punishment induces violators of the standards to spend more time and resources to conceal and defend their actions. More lawyers are hired to pick holes in the wording of standards. Second, this nit-picking feeds back into the process of setting standards, pushing them to becoming more detailed and technical. Since the 1960s, there has been a tendency in the United States to enforce standards through more explicit threats of sanctions. The result of that threat is increasingly detailed and technical standards.

The Capture of Institutions

The actual operation of social institutions does not always conform to the intent of their original designers. Even though the rule makers may invite and encourage all constituents to participate in the process, only those who benefit sufficiently from participation can be expected to do so. For others, it may not be economical to participate individually. They may act collectively if (1) the costs of organizing are small, (2) these costs can be collected from the beneficiaries, and (3) somebody takes the initiative to do the organizing. When such organizing does not take place, which is often the case, social institutions are captured by interest groups that have the greatest stake in them, more often by default than by design. In the United States, the Committee on Accounting Procedure and the Accounting Principles Board were committees of the AICPA. For the first few years of its life, the Financial Accounting Standards Board also had to have a majority of its members from the auditing profession. The SEC does not seem to have been captured by any single accounting interest group so far.

The Effects of Standards

Instead of preparing a meal from scratch, we often find it efficient to use some standard, partially processed ingredients. Likewise, in constructing a house, it is often efficient to use some prefabricated parts. Accounting standards are like prefabricated parts for the construction of the contract set. The existence of standards reduces the cost of search and negotiation that participating agents must incur to arrive at agreed-upon contracts.

On Accounting Systems

The standardization of financial accounting makes it possible to design the contract sets in modular units. This system of modules is more evident in external reporting where these costs are relatively high. The Uniform Commercial Code and various labor laws accomplish a similar use of modules in contracts between buyers and sellers, and between employees and employers, respectively. For other contracts, it is possible, or even necessary, for the agents to negotiate the contracts one-on-one. This is especially true for contracts of various managers in the firm. Accordingly, there have been few standards set in that area of accounting.

On Accounting Education

The standardization of accounting affects what is taught in accounting classes and how it is taught. As Baxter predicted, this effect need not be, but often is, harmful to the quality of accounting education:

> [The official recommendations on accounting] naturally appeal to the feebler type of teacher, who finds it easier to recite an official creed than to lead a brisk argument. . . . If an official answer is available to a problem, why should a teacher burden his examination candidates with other views? . . . Thus the recommendations tend to rob our young men's education of its power to enrich and stimulate. . . . [T]heir minds will be less fit to solve the new problems of tomorrow; and such fitness is no bad test by which to judge an education.[3]

The proliferation of accounting standards in the United States, since the sixties has led to greater emphasis on official pronouncements in accounting textbooks. There is no other reason for the elephantiasis that afflicts intermediate accounting textbooks.

Official and authoritative stipulation of the meaning of terms used in accounting also tends to place unnecessary limits on the finer shades of meaning that can be explored in classrooms to understand a concept, as opposed to memorizing a definition. Kitchen points out:

> Stipulation by authority is not without disadvantages and foremost among these is the risk that clear and original thought may be inhibited in the degree that authoritative definitions receive unthinking acceptance, to the extent that they set an official stamp on some particular dogma, or in so far as they lean towards over-simplification and ambiguity.[4]

These negative effects of standards on education are not unavoidable, but teachers of accounting have to be especially vigilant to avoid them.

On the Auditing Profession

The standardization of accounting makes the job of auditors easier and reduces the role of auditors' judgment in certifying financial statements. It becomes easier and less costly to train auditors to perform their task. The downward trend in the price of auditing services may be an indication of this effect. Standardization replaces the judgment element of expert auditors' work by technical knowledge. Since it takes a long time to develop judgment, this may appear to be an advantage. However, in the long run it will reduce the price other agents are willing to pay for the auditors' services.

Summary

Accounting rules and standards can be seen as incentives to induce various agents to behave in a manner expected by others. Standards, per se, cannot be good or bad. Each must be examined for its effect on the welfare of various agents in society. We need to balance the advantages of setting and enforcing standards against the costs and other consequences they impose on society.

Notes

[1] Russell Hardin, *Collective Action* (Baltimore, Md.: Johns Hopkins University Press for Resources for the Future, 1982).

[2] H. C. Edey, "Accounting Standards in the British Isles," in W. Baxter and S. Davidson, eds., *Studies in Accounting*, 3d ed. (London: Institute of Chartered Accountants of England and Wales, 1977), p. 294; and William T. Baxter, "Accounting Standards—Boon or Curse?" *Accounting and Business Research* (Winter 1981), pp. 3–10.

[3] William T. Baxter, "Recommendations on Accounting Theory," *The Accountant* (10 October 1953), reprinted in W. T. Baxter and S. Davidson, eds., *Studies in Accounting Theory* (Homewood, Ill.: Irwin, 1962), p. 423.

[4] J. Kitchen, "Costing Terminology," *Accounting Research* (February 1954), reprinted in W. T. Baxter and S. Davidson, eds., *Studies in Accounting Theory* (Homewood, Ill.: Irwin, 1962), pp. 399–413.

Additional Reading

Benston, George J. "The Value of SEC's Accounting Disclosure Requirements." *Accounting Review*, Vol. 44 (July 1969), pp. 515–532.

Benston, George J. *Corporate Financial Disclosure in the U.K. and the U.S.A.* D. C. Heath Limited, 1976.

Cuccia, Andrew D., Karl Hackenbrack, and Mark W. Nelson. "The Ability of Professional Standards to Mitigate Aggressive Reporting." *Accounting Review*, Vol. 70, No. 2 (April 1995), pp. 227–248.

Kripke, Homer. "The SEC, the Accountants, Some Myths and Some Realities." *The New York University Law Review*, Vol. 45 (December 1970), pp. 1151–1205.

Leftwich, Richard. "Market Failure Fallacies and Accounting Information." *Journal of Accounting and Economics*, Vol. 2, No. 3 (December 1980), pp. 193–211.

Manne, Henry G., ed. *Economic Policy and Regulation of Corporate Securities*. Washington: American Enterprise Institute, 1969, pp. 23–79.

Manne, Henry G. "Economic Aspects of Required Disclosure under Federal Securities Laws." In *Wall Street in Transition: The Emerging System and Its Impact on the Economy: The Charles C. Moskowitz Lectures*, New York: New York University Press, 1974, pp. 21–110.

Moonitz, Maurice. *Obtaining Agreement on Standards in the Accounting Profession. Studies in Accounting Research No. 8.* American Accounting Association, 1974.

Pacioli, Luca. *Summa de Arithmetica, Geometria, Proportioni et Proportionalita*. Reproduced and translated by John B. Geijsbeek in *Ancient Double Entry Bookkeeping*. Houston, Scholars Book Co., 1974.

Spulbur, D. *Regulation and Markets*. Cambridge, Mass.: MIT Press, 1989.

Stamp, Edward, and Christopher Marley. *Accounting Principles and the City Code: The Case for Reform*. London: Butterworth, 1970.

Stigler, George J. "Public Regulation of Securities Markets." *The Journal of Business*, Vol. 37 (April 1964), pp. 117–142.

Sunder, Shyam. "Why is FASB Issuing So Many Accounting Standards?" *The Wall Street Journal* (27 April 1981), p. 24.

Sunder, Shyam. "Political Economy of Accounting Standards." *Journal of Accounting Literature*, Vol. 7 (1988), pp. 31–41.

Watson, Henry. "The Economics of Standards Organizations." University of Chicago, Working Paper, November, 1980.

Wong, Jilnaught. "Economic Incentives for the Voluntary Disclosure of Current Cost Financial Statements." *Journal of Accounting and Economics*, Vol. 10, No. 2 (April 1988), pp. 151–167.

Zeff, Stephen A. *Forging Accounting Principles in Five Countries: A History and Analysis of Trends*. Champaign, Ill.: Stipes Publishing Co., 1972.

◢12◣

Government, Law, and Accounting

●●

Government plays three distinct roles in accounting: as a contracting agent in other organizations, as an organization itself, and as a super organization that defines the templates for contracts of other organizations that operate within its jurisdiction. As a contracting agent in most firms, the government collects taxes and supplies them with public goods and services.[1] Government may participate in firms as a supplier of private goods and services (electricity, nuclear fuel), as a customer (ordnance), as a lender (U.S. Small Business Administration), and even as a shareholder (e.g., Continental Illinois Bank, Lockheed, and Crown Corporations in Canada). As a contracting agent, government affects accounting systems in its roles as the tax collector and sometimes a monopsonist customer. These and a few special characteristics of accounting systems that arise from the government's role as a contracting agent in various firms in society are discussed in the first section of this chapter.

In its second role as a firm, the citizens and organizations within the government's jurisdiction are the agents whose mutual contracts define the government. Like other organizations, government, too, must design and operate an accounting and control system to efficiently execute and enforce these contracts. The special features of accounting and control systems to serve government and other non-business organizations are the subject of Chapter 13.

In its third role, the government is a superfirm, a superset of contractual arrangements, meant to set the laws or rules that define the environment under which other firms operate. Coase states:

> The government is, in a sense, a super-firm (but of a very special kind) since it is able to influence the use of factors of production by administrative decision . . . It is clear that the government has powers which might enable it to get some things done at a lower cost than could a private organization. . . .

From these considerations it follows that direct governmental regulation will not necessarily give better results than leaving the problem to be solved by the market or the firm. But equally there is no reason why, on occasion, such governmental administrative regulation should not lead to an improvement in economic efficiency. This would seem particularly likely when, as is normally the case with the smoke nuisance, a large number of people are involved and in which therefore the costs of handling the problem through the market or the firm may be high.[2]

Just as a firm substitutes certain market transactions among individuals by administrative action and rules, the government or superfirm also replaces certain transactions among individuals and firms by laws, regulations, and administrative actions. Just as some, but not all, market transactions can efficiently be replaced by administrative action within organizations, some, but not all, transactions among individuals and firms can be replaced by organization of the superfirm or government in the form of laws and rules. The government defines the environment of accounting for individual firms through laws that govern the charter of firms, the sale of securities, accounts and audits of firms, the discipline and training of auditors, the publication of financial reports, and other information. The role of government as a superfirm is discussed in the second section of this chapter.

The Government as a Contracting Agent

The government occupies at least one, and often many, contractual slots in firms. Tax collection is the best known and the least admired of these roles. The rights of the government as a tax-collecting agent are defined by statutes and subsidiary regulations. In this role, the government has the general obligation to provide public goods (such as the provision of a legal framework of property rights, judicial and police protection and enforcement, communications, and certain utility and municipal services) to society as a whole. The government has no reciprocal obligation to contribute resources to any specific firm. How does the *tax collector* role of government shape the accounting system of business firms?

The Government as Tax Collector

Governments levy taxes on income, property, production, sales, import, export, and employment. Instead of negotiating directly with numerous taxpayers, the government announces rules for the determination of taxes owed, and allows each firm to adjust its actions and affairs to these rules. The government must anticipate how taxpayers might adjust their activities in response to the tax laws. For example, higher payroll taxes may induce firms to hire fewer people. Indeed, many features of tax laws—subsidies, deductions, credits, and exemptions—are deliberately designed to induce changes in the economic behavior of the taxpayers. Although the ability of government to unilaterally change the tax laws makes it appear otherwise, the actual tax liability of a firm is a joint result of choices made by the firm and the government. In this limited sense, the government's contract as tax collector is customized in individual firms.

The accounting system of the firm helps determine its liability to the government. Income taxes owed are computed from revenue and expenses, with exemptions, credits, and surtaxes for specified types of transactions. As is the case for determinating other entitlements, a firm must maintain an adequate system of records to support its tax return. Primary evidentiary documents and bookkeeping entries constitute the foundation of the firm's accounting system. These primary data may be aggregated variously to prepare tax returns, financial statements, and managerial performance reports. Maintaining a common primary accounting database presents obvious economies in costs of data collection, entry, storage, and audit. When the cost of creating and maintaining a primary database declines sufficiently, it is possible that the tax accounting system of the firm may be completely separated from the rest of the system. However, at the level of primary data, the additional cost of auditing a second system yields few advantages.

Accounting systems for tax and financial reporting are interrelated. Proprietorships and closely held firms do not need financial statements to provide "unbiased" estimates of wealth or income—these statements may only increase the taxes owed to the government. In such organizations, minimizing taxes is a primary criterion in designing the accounting system. The proprietor may also prepare informal statements for personal use.

Financial reporting is more important in publicly held firms because the body of shareholders is diffuse, and accounting rules for reporting to this diffuse body must be selected efficiently to solve the agency problem between shareholders and managers and other agents. These accounting rules are not necessarily efficient for the enforcement of the contractual relationship between the firm and the tax collector.

It would be prohibitively costly for tax collectors to negotiate and enforce a separate accounting contract with each firm. It is useful to think about the rules of tax accounting as tax collectors' attempts to economize on such costs without sacrificing too much tax revenue. Where measurements of resource flows used in accounting for financial reporting are relatively objective, the tax collector accepts the financial accounting methods for tax purposes. The accounting rules for wages and perquisites of administrative employees are an example of this type. In certain areas, financial standards permit a range of practices, but once an acceptable method of accounting is picked by the firm, managers have little discretion in its application. In such cases, the tax collector allows individual firms to pick their own accounting method and accepts it as the basis for tax computation if one or both of the following conditions are fulfilled: The firm must use it on a consistent basis over time, and the method must be included in the generally accepted accounting principles. Accounting for inventories is an example of this type.

Finally, managers exercise significant discretion in certain aspects of accounting for financial reporting. In such cases, the tax collector must specify a reduced-discretion accounting method for tax purposes to preserve revenue and minimize the costs of tax adjudication and enforcement. Financial accounting standards allow much discretion in accounting for leases, and the income tax authorities use their own rules to determine tax liability. No formal financial accounting standards exist for depreciation and revenue recognition, and the tax collectors specify their own reduced-discretion methods of accounting.

Accounting methods for financial and tax reporting overlap and influence each other. Tax laws and rules have a direct effect on financial reporting. Depreciation accounting became prevalent in U.S. nonregulated industries only after the Internal Revenue Act of 1913 introduced taxation of income and allowed a deduction for depreciation in computing taxes owed. Prior to 1913, few industrial firms systematically recorded depreciation in their financial statements. LIFO has been allowed for tax purposes since World War II. To discourage the loss of tax revenue, the government does not permit the use of LIFO for tax purposes unless it is also used for financial reporting. A large number of firms adopted LIFO in years of high inflation, especially during the 1970s. In 1954, when accelerated depreciation was first permitted for tax purposes, a large number of publicly held firms switched their tax and their financial reporting method to accelerated depreciation.

Financial reporting methods also affect tax accounting. To collect revenue with minimum effort, the government takes a free ride on financial reporting methods as long as the loss of revenue to managers' discretion is not too high. Tax collectors try to minimize the differences between tax and reported amounts subject to the tax revenue constraint. The taxpayer, on the other hand, is interested in minimizing taxes through the judicious choice of accounting options subject to the cost of accounting constraint. The tax-paying firm, in selecting its reporting policy, must also consider the possibility that the tax collector may try to exploit this publicly available data and increase the firm's tax liability. A good example is the U.S. Tax Reform Act of 1986, which included half the difference between reported and taxable income in the computation of the alternative minimum tax liability.

Determining the corporate income tax requires comprehensive involvement of accounting and control because corporate income is affected by practically all the transactions of the firm. However, there are other taxes where a firm's liability depends on some specific parts of the accounting system.

Property, production, and sales records help determine property, excise, and sales taxes, respectively. The custom duty on import and export is usually collected through physical inspection at the port of entry or shipment, and the role of accounting systems in payment of these taxes is to ensure that invoices on which these duties are imposed are properly prepared. The payroll accounting system is designed to ensure proper collection from employees and remittance to the government of the employees' and employer's share of the payroll taxes (e.g., Social Security and unemployment insurance). U.S. pension laws impose detailed accounting and disclosure requirements on employee pension plans, and employers risk losing corporate income tax deductions for pension costs if they fail to meet these requirements.

Different taxes are levied by different governmental units. Customs duties are levied by federal governments, excise, income, and sales taxes by federal and many state and local governments, and property taxes by local governments. Different governmental units do not necessarily coordinate the accounting requirements for their respective levies and they are occasionally in conflict, especially at coordinate levels of government. A corporation may face conflicting accounting requirements in different tax jurisdictions. Taxing authorities in states with higher marginal rates of taxation often suspect that the firm may be shifting income to other states and may therefore seize on financial reporting and other data to assess their share of taxes. The problem becomes even more difficult for multinational corporations, which must deal with the tax laws of many sovereign states. The tax laws of different countries can be consistent only by design. Some bilateral tax treaties simplify the taxpayers' task but they do not eliminate the accounting problems that arise from interaction between tax laws and financial reports. National tax jurisdictions can be even more paranoid, often rightly so, that multinational firms operating within their boundaries use transfer prices to siphon off their taxable profits to low-rate tax havens, depriving the governments of taxes due to them. They may impose tax accounting requirements that extend beyond the usual concerns of tax accounting and extend into cost allocation and transfer prices among subsidiaries and divisions of the firm.

The Government as Customer

The government buys many goods and services. When it purchases in the open market, it plays no special role in the accounting system of the vendors. However, a substantial proportion of government purchases, especially for defense, occurs through bilateral monopolies or monopsonies in which the government is the only or major buyer of those goods or services. The developmental nature of weapons systems requires large investments by vendors in the face of substantial uncertainties about their feasibility and ultimate cost. The government effectively underwrites these development projects and buys on cost-plus-profit contracts. This contractual form directly involves the government in the cost accounting system of the firm. In 1973, the U.S. government created the Cost Accounting Standards Board (CASB), which wrote accounting rules, primarily for defense contractors, to define the participation of the government in the accounting of its vendors.

The Government as a Superfirm

Many agents with diverse interests enter into mutual contracts to form a firm when they believe they can advance their welfare by doing so. Each individual can be, and often is, a member of many different firms, sometimes in a different capacity. The government, too, is a special type of firm. The participation of all citizens and their other organizations in government is automatic. One can refuse to participate only by moving to another jurisdiction and becoming a participant in a different government. Common law and statutes define the rights and obligations of each participant. General obligations include taxes, obedience to the constitution and laws, and, occasionally, military service. Special obligations to the government might be accepted by individuals in exchange for special rights. General rights consist mostly of public goods and services. Special rights include private goods that are either produced under economies of scale by the government or received through redistribution of wealth in society.

At the time of entering a firm, an agent may face uncertain returns, even a positive chance of undesirable outcomes. The choice to participate is based on a whole bundle of possible consequences. If they were allowed to unbundle the rights and obligations, agents might accept the rights and reject the obligations, making the contract set infeasible. In stable contracts, the rights of each participant are in equilibrium with the obligations.

If the value of rights is equal to the value of obligations, why would anyone want to enter into such an arrangement? At first it may look like the apparent paradox of the third law of motion: the force applied by object A on B is exactly equal to the force applied by B on A. If the horse and cart always apply equal force on each other, why should the horse pull the cart, and not the other way around? Of course, whether and in which direction the cart moves depends not on what forces *it applies* on other objects but on what forces are *incident* on it. Whether an agent accepts a set of rights in exchange for a given obligation depends not on what these obligations are, but on how much more or less desirable is this set of rights compared to others for which the obligation can be exchanged. In other words, it depends on the opportunity cost of one's resources.

Business firms operate in the legal–social–economic environment defined by the superfirm called the government. Individual economic agents transact in the superfirm as well as in individual business firms. There is a continuum of organizations of increasing size and diversity—from family, neighborhood, city, state, nation, to the world—in which individuals participate. Agents' participation in government and business organizations, and their effect on agents' welfare, may differ in degree, but not in nature.

It is tempting to apply loaded terms, such as *mandatory, involuntary,* and *coercive,* when it comes to fulfilling one's obligations in a contractual arrangement. But such terms are used when the resolution of uncertainty is adverse (the realized obligation of the agent exceeds its expected value). Settling a bet gone sour can hardly be called coercive or involuntary, just because the contract involved is labeled government.

As shown in the previous chapter, the distinction between voluntary and involuntary economic behavior is tenuous. A government action may induce an individual to choose option A instead of option B. We may refer to this change in individual choice as having been mandated by government and, thus, involuntary. An action of the firm may similarly render one option more attractive than another for an investor, manager, or employee. The firm would then be said to have mandated that choice. The argument is applicable to all environmental factors that could cause behavior to change, and to all organizations. It renders the set of voluntary choices empty.

A distinction is sometimes made between private sector versus public sector mechanisms for setting accounting rules and standards in discussions of accounting standards and related laws. Voluntary standards are said to be associated with the private sector, while the term *mandatory* is reserved for standards issued by the government.[3] When we think of government as a superfirm, this distinction becomes less clear. The difference between private-sector rule making (e.g., by the FASB) and the public-sector rule making (e.g., by the SEC) is in the degree of representativeness, scope, and power of the organization that sets the rules and standards.

A body that is more representative of the various types of agents it affects is more public. In this sense the FASB is more public than its predecessor bodies, the Accounting Principles Board and the Committee on Accounting Procedure, which consisted of the members of the professional association of public accountants. The "publicness" of a social mechanism depends not on whether its expenses are paid for by the exchequer, but on how well it represents the interests of the relevant publics.

Being part of the government does not necessarily make an organization effectively public, and being outside the government does not always make it private. Governmental regulatory agencies are known to have been captured by narrow interest groups.[4] On the other hand, reasonably representative public conflict resolution mechanisms can exist outside the government. The presumption that a government body is also a public body is not always correct.

Each type of transaction can conceivably be organized in the market or in organizations of varying scope or size. Whether and which accounting rules are best left to the market—agreed upon at firm level through its charter or shareholders' resolutions, determined at the industry level by industry associations, or determined economy-wide by a public body—is a matter of economics, not ideology.

The Charter of Firms

In the United States, state laws govern the charters of most limited liability firms. A large proportion of publicly held firms have come to be chartered in the state of Delaware. Consequently, laws of that state have become especially important for the larger, publicly held firms.

Since the special privilege of conducting business under limited liability is conferred by the government, the laws that govern the charter of such limited liability firms have been designed to protect the interests of lenders and others who conduct business with such firms. The law defines legal capital, surplus, dividends, and the like, and prevents shareholders from transferring creditors' wealth to themselves through dividends, purchases of treasury stock, and so on. State laws rarely specify the detailed financial reporting methods and requirements. Since the vast majority of limited liability firms are closely held, the inclusion of additional accounting requirements in the state charter laws would be quite inefficient. A large part of the burden of additional financial reporting requirements would fall on the privately held firms, whose shareholders hardly need to be protected from themselves.

The Sale of Securities

When a firm's securities are sold publicly, the cost of direct negotiation between a diffuse, unorganized group of investors and the firm is large. It is more efficient to choose the rules that govern the market transactions between firm and investors, or between insider and outside investors, at the societal level. Accounting and disclosure rules for publicly held and publicly traded firms are specified by the stock exchanges and the government. Since securities are traded in a national market, the federal government sets the rules. In the United States, the SEC sets the accounting and disclosure rules for publicly held firms.

As we discussed in Chapter 11, it is difficult to ascertain which accounting rules are efficient. People do not always reveal their preferences truthfully, and various social choice mechanisms are vulnerable to manipulation. With a few notable exceptions, the SEC has confined its rules to requiring prompt and adequate disclosure of accounting policies and important economic events of the firm. The SEC has largely refrained from requiring the use of specific accounting measurement methods. In the 1970s, it deviated from this general policy in the case of accounting for leases, inflation, and oil and gas exploration. The disclosure requirements have been far less controversial than the specification of accounting measurement methods.

Certification, Licensing, and Discipline of Auditors

State laws govern the entry of individuals to the auditing profession. The laws that govern entry to various professions are said to save the public from the unscrupulous and the incompetent. Such legislation does raise the average quality of professional services sold in the market. Whether such legislated action is socially efficient is controversial, especially because its enforcement is controlled by professionals who are securely within the fence themselves.

The laws of the United States that govern the certification, licensing, and disciplining of auditors vary across the fifty states. This variety provides a healthy environment for trial and error and the evolution of laws through competition among states. Dodd and Leftwich present a similar argument for state laws governing the charter of corporations.[5] Kaplan argues that if the disclosure laws were set by states instead of the federal government, a healthy competition could prevent bureaucratic excesses.[6] But this argument cuts both ways. The capture of regulatory institutions by interest groups occurs when the general public fails to coalesce into effective opposition because the benefits of doing so are small compared to the cost of organizing.

The cost of organizing has a fixed component, making it less likely that the public will organize at the state level to resist special-interest legislation. Thus, the state-regulated apparatuses for disciplining auditors and other professionals often remind one of the fox guarding the henhouse. In the United States, state boards of public accountancy are dominated by the state CPA societies.

Since the federal securities laws gave U.S. public accountants the exclusive franchise to audit the financial reports of publicly held corporations, the disciplining of firms (as distinct from individual auditors) that audit such corporations has fallen within the jurisdiction of the SEC. Over the past half-century, the SEC has gradually nudged the audit profession to (1) accept a more objective criterion for auditor independence, (2) move audit programs from bookkeeping audit toward field audit, including direct verification of inventory and receivables, (3) develop specific and detailed audit standards, and (4) create the Public Oversight Board and a system to monitor the quality of work done by the audit firms that practice before the SEC.

These changes have been gradual. When the SEC was created in 1934, it was not unusual for an auditor to be a member of the board or even a major shareholder of the client. In the 1970s, the SEC pressured audit firms to limit the sale of advisory services to their audit clients to reduce the chances of compromising auditor independence.

The expansion of the scope of audit started with the McKesson & Robbins case in 1938. Under the Foreign Corrupt Practices Act of 1977, an audit now includes a review of firms' internal controls. The creation of the Public Oversight Board, which organizes quality control measures for audit firms, was also triggered by the Foreign Corrupt Practices Act.

Summary

In most firms, the government plays the role of a major contracting agent as tax collector, customer, or vendor. In these roles, the government has substantial influence on the design of a firm's accounting and control. In addition, the government acts as a superfirm to set the rules by which various individuals and organizations in its jurisdiction interact. State and federal laws and standards relevant to accounting can be thought of as template contracts for firms. They save everybody the cost of negotiating contracts from scratch. In this role, the government produces public goods to increase the efficiency of social–economic exchanges. Finally, the government itself can be seen as an organization or firm that requires its own control system to implement and enforce the relevant contracts. This problem is discussed in the next chapter.

Notes

[1]Public goods can be provided to additional beneficiaries without incurring additional cost and they cannot be withheld from some people without affecting the others. Few goods are purely public or purely private, and I use these labels in relative terms. See Mancur Olson, *The Logic of Collective Action* (Cambridge, Mass.: Harvard University Press, 1965).

[2]Ronald H. Coase, "The Problem of Social Cost," *Journal of Law and Economics*, Vol. 3 (October 1960), pp. 17–18.

[3]Robert S. Kaplan, "Should Accounting Standards Be Set in the Public or Private Sector?" in John W. Buckley and J. Fred Weston, eds., *Regulation and the Accounting Profession* (Belmont, Calif.: Lifetime Learning Publications, 1980), pp. 178–196.

[4]R. A. Posner, "Theories of Economic Regulation," *Bell Journal of Economics and Management Science*, Vol. 5, No. 2 (Autumn 1974), pp. 335–358.

[5]Peter Dodd and Richard Leftwich, "The Market for Corporate Charters: Unhealthy Competition vs. Federal Regulation," *Journal of Business*, Vol. 53 (July 1980), pp. 259–284.

[6]Kaplan, op. cit.

Additional Reading

Anderson, Matthew, Urton Anderson, Richard Helleloid, Edward Joyce, and Michael Schadewald. "Internal Revenue Service Access to Tax Accrual Workpapers: A Laboratory Investigation." *Accounting Review*, Vol. 65, No. 4 (October 1990), pp. 857–874.

Berger, Philip G. "Explicit and Implicit Tax Effects of the R&D Tax Credit." *Journal of Accounting Research*, Vol. 31 (Autumn 1994), pp. 131–171.

Buckley, W., and J. Fred Weston. *Regulation and the Accounting Profession.* Belmont, Calif.: Lifetime Learning Publications, 1980.

Downs, Thomas W., and Keith A. Shriver. "The Analytical Derivation and Empirical Test of a Tax-Adjusted Fundamental Value Model." *Journal of Accounting Research*, Vol. 30 (Supplement 1992), pp. 77–98.

Fellingham, John, and Mark Wolfson. "Taxes and Risk Sharing." *Accounting Review*, Vol. 60 (January 1985), pp. 10–17.

Guenther, David A. "The Relation between Tax Rates and Pretax Returns: Direct Evidence from the 1981 and 1986 Tax Rate Reductions." *Journal of Accounting and Economics*, Vol. 18 (1994), pp. 379–393.

Halperin, Robert, and Bin Srinidhi. "U.S. Income Tax Transfer Pricing Rules for Intangibles as Approximations of Arm's Length Pricing." *Accounting Review*, Vol. 71, No. 1 (January 1996), pp. 61–80.

Harris, David G. "The Impact of U.S. Tax Law Revision on Multinational Corporations' Capital Location and Income-Shifting Decisions." *Journal of Accounting Research*, Vol. 31 (Supplement 1993), pp. 111–140.

Klassen, Kenneth, Mark Lang, and Mark Wolfson. "Geographic Income Shifting by Multinational Corporations in Response to Tax Rate Changes." *Journal of Accounting Research*, Vol. 31 (Supplement 1993), pp. 141–173.

Petroni, Kathy R., and Douglas A. Shackelford. "Taxation, Regulation, and the Organizational Structure of Property-Casualty Insurers." *Journal of Accounting and Economics*, Vol. 20, No. 3 (December 1995), pp. 229–254.

Scholes, Myron, and Mark Wolfson. *Taxes and Business Strategy: A Planning Approach.* Englewood Cliffs, N.J.: Prentice-Hall, 1992.

Shackelford, D. "The Market for Tax Benefits: Evidence from Leveraged ESOPs." *Journal of Accounting and Economics,* Vol. 14 (1991), pp. 117–145.

Thomas, Jacob K. "Corporate Taxes and Defined Benefit Pension Plans." *Journal of Accounting and Economics*, Vol. 10 (1988), pp. 199–237.

Accounting for Public-Good Organizations

$\bullet$

Not all organizations have shareholders or residual claimants. In this chapter we examine the structure of, and control in, organizations without shareholders. They represent a significant part of the economy in all countries of the world. Differences in structure of organizations arise primarily from the economic characteristics of their output markets. When the discipline imposed by output prices is weaker, the modification of contracts and decision rights becomes necessary to maintain control. Differences in accounting and control systems across a variety of organization types can be understood and explained by the nature of their output. The preceding chapters have focused on organizations whose output is a pure private good. In this chapter, we shall center on the other polar case of organizations whose output is a pure public good. As a practical matter, few organizations lie at either extreme.

Nomenclature and Classification

Organizations in which individuals or other organizations have an equity claim are called for-profit, commercial, or open corporations. Equity claims are capitalized and traded. The right to trade is included in the shareholder's contract. The existence of a residual interest and the alienability of this interest from the shareholders who own them are the characteristic features of such organizations. These alienable residual interest organizations are called business firms, and have been discussed in the preceding chapters.

The primary concern of this chapter is accounting and control in the large number and variety of organizations that are not business firms. Governmental organizations at federal, state, and local levels are a part of, or are constitutionally linked to, the sovereign organization of the land. Local government units, for example, include counties, townships, municipalities, school districts, and special districts for water, sanitation, port, industrial development, and soil conservation. There are more than 80,000 governmental units in the United States alone.

Not-for-profit organizations include many hospitals; colleges and universities; community health, welfare, and social service organizations; cultural, trade, and professional associations; museums; and organizations for scientific research and development, performing arts, and religion. Some of their functions are shared with, or partly supported by, grants from governmental organizations. Both not-for-profit and governmental organizations could be called non-business organizations except that both can, and often do, engage in businesslike activities—the sale of private goods or services for a price—and even compete with business organizations. For our purposes, all these organizations can be conveniently grouped under the label Non-Residual Interest Organization (NRIO), because they do not have alienable residual interest. In contrast, Hansmann defines the presence of profit distribution constraints as the distinguishing economic characteristic of the not-for-profit organizations. He does not consider governmental organizations.[1]

When organizations are seen as a set of contracts, the description of NRIOs as not-for-profit organizations is somewhat misleading. The profit of each agent is his or her gain in welfare from participation. This gain or profit accrues to all agents, albeit in different forms. The not-for-profit label is inaccurate even if a narrower concept of monetary profit is used. Employees, lenders, and vendors receive cash and make money on their transactions with such organizations. The difference between the for-profit and the so-called not-for-profit organizations is not the monetary nature of profit, but the presence in the contract set of shareholders who have a residual interest. The absence of such interest characterizes the contract set of such organizations, and we shall call them NRIOs for this reason. Why is such interest absent?

Economic Characteristics of NRIOs

Like other organizations, NRIOs, too, are contracts among rational economic agents. What are the special characteristics that influence the design of their accounting and control systems? Briefly, they produce public goods, or private goods sold in markets in which they have substantial market power, and therefore face little product market discipline that typically confronts business organizations. The absence of residual rights reduces the flexibility of an organization in the presence of uncertainty. In business firms, shareholders absorb the risk associated with claims to residual wealth, making it possible to design the contractual entitlements of other agents to be relatively rigid. In the absence of residual interests, all contracts must yield some to absorb shocks of uncertainty.

Markets for Resources

The two types of organizations face different product markets. Business firms such as General Motors produce private goods for paying customers. They must convince their customers that their product is worth the price. Customers can withhold revenue if they are not satisfied. Customers can effectively discipline such organizations. NRIOs, on the other hand, either produce public goods,[2] or are natural monopolies. Public-good-producing organizations have beneficiaries, not customers. Beneficiaries cannot discipline the organization by engaging in negotiated exchanges or by withholding revenues as the customers can. The lack of competition attenuates the ability of customers of natural monopolies to discipline them through the price system.

To provide public goods, capital must be raised either from taxes (e.g., national defense) or donations (e.g., public broadcasting). Individual beneficiaries cannot be charged for goods provided to them, and borrowed capital can only smooth the interperiod imbalance between taxes and contributions on one hand and the cost of producing these goods on the other. Neither tax nor donated capital is raised through the market mechanisms that govern the capital resource flows of business firms.

Thus, NRIOs and business firms face different environments in the product and capital markets. Though the labor market is similar for both types of organizations, the product and capital markets necessitate different contractual forms, managerial incentives, and accounting and control systems.

Agents

Buyers of salable goods and services probably constitute the most numerous class of agents in NRIOs. The sale of postage stamps, hunting licenses, car parking, university education, symphony tickets, and hospital care are examples of such contractual arrangements. Individual transactions of this type are hardly distinguishable from transactions of business firms. The delivery of output and the receipt of its price are exchanged practically simultaneously, the exchange rate is posted or negotiated in advance, and there are no major uncertainties in measuring the contribution of each agent to the organization and the agent's entitlement from the organization. Therefore, NRIOs account for such transactions in the same manner as business firms, using cash registers or invoices and the associated bookkeeping and internal controls.

The provision of public goods and services is a special preserve of NRIOs. Most NRIOs provide some public goods, whether or not they provide private goods and services. National defense, flood control, clean and lighted streets, accounting standards, and basic scientific research are examples of public goods. Emergency medical care, national parks, and judicial, religious, and child welfare services are often provided free of charge, or at subsidized prices, even though they are not pure public goods. Consumers of public goods do not make explicit payments linked directly to what they receive from the NRIOs. Their entitlement from the organization is defined in general terms and they do not have a right to enforce this entitlement directly because, as individuals, they cannot withhold any resources from the NRIOs. Accounting and control plays no significant role in the enforcement of the rights of the beneficiaries of public goods.

To pay for the unreciprocated outflow of resources to the beneficiaries of public goods, government organizations gather their capital either as taxes or as grants or revenue sharing from superior units of government. Governmental and nongovernmental organizations borrow from private investors. Nongovernmental organizations also receive contributions, donations, or grants from individuals, business firms, foundations, and governments.

Since NRIOs as well as business firms borrow capital from the same markets under similar conditions, the measurement of the input of creditors, their entitlement to interest and principal, and financial information about the organization is similar. Bookkeeping for debts is also similar; they appear as credits in the financial statements. The commonality of markets from which debt capital is raised induces a commonality of accounting for debt across organizations. Indeed, following the financial problems of the New York City government in the early 1970s, most of the demand for introducing business accounting practices into governmental organizations has originated from their bond-holders.

Citizens at large receive public goods in exchange for their collective tax contributions. The obligation of taxpayers to contribute taxes arises either from specific transactions (e.g., sales, income, excise taxes, and customs duties) or accrues with time (e.g., property and wealth taxes). Neither type of tax is an individual quid pro quo for the public goods received.

To measure the taxpayer obligation arising out of specific transactions, the government would theoretically need to keep account of all relevant transactions of all taxpayers. Even with the help of computers, this would be a formidable task. Tax collectors substantially rely on taxpayers' own accounting records, retaining the right to audit the accounts in order to control cheating. Accounting requirements for taxes accrued with time are less onerous, and governments often maintain records of individual property transactions and values to measure taxes due on them. In any case, revenue records constitute an important part of the governmental accounting system.

Not-for-profit organizations receive at least a good part of their capital from membership dues, contributions, donations, legacies, and so on. A part of such contributions, especially for membership dues, represents the price of goods or services available for sale (e.g., admission to concerts), while the balance is a donation. Donations do not give rise to an immediately identifiable financial obligation to the contributor. A contributor may receive a position on the governing board, a nameplate, fame, or gratitude. The out-of-pocket financial cost (as distinct from opportunity cost) of these obligations is relatively small and difficult to quantify, and the accounting system is not used to measure and report such entitlements.

Thus, the role of an accounting system in measuring entitlements is largely confined to one out of the three major classes of capital contributors—the creditors. Considering that so many aspects of the designs of the accounting systems of business firms is driven by the need to measure the entitlement of shareholders, it is hardly surprising that, in the absence of equity interest, the accounting systems of NRIOs differ in significant respects.

Managers supply their skills to NRIOs in exchange for compensation, just as they do in business firms. However, the absence of two important factor markets, markets for capital and products, leads to significant changes in the form of managerial contracts, and the role of accounting in managerial performance evaluation and control.

To recapitulate our discussion of business firms in Chapters 3–5, the inducements of all agents, except the shareholders and the top managers, are fixed as a function of their measured contribution. Shareholders are entitled to the residual resources. Because the contribution of top managers is difficult to measure, their entitlement is made to depend partly on the shareholders' entitlement. The income number is not only the residual entitlement of the shareholders, but also a vital clue to the continued viability of the organization under the current contractual arrangements. Income informs all participating agents about what is likely to happen at the next contract negotiation. To the extent that business firms transact in reasonably well-functioning resource markets, each agent can bargain directly to protect his or her interests. The dependence of top managerial compensation on income, combined with a partial external audit, ensures that the top managers will pay heed to shareholders' interests. It also induces them to exercise appropriate control over the middle- and lower-level managers to behave in like fashion by devising appropriate controls and incentives for them. The self-enforcing characteristics of this arrangement minimize the need for nonmanagerial agents to participate in the design of middle- and lower-level controls. Income at the top, and income-like surrogates at the lower levels of management, are crucial for effective control in business firms.

In NRIOs, no single class of agents bears a substantial part of the operational risk by accepting the residual as their entitlement. In the face of uncertainty, all agents share the risk. Suppliers of resources that are acquired from relatively well-functioning markets can protect themselves from risk-bearing. The absence or weakness of product markets in NRIOs forces their beneficiaries to bear a greater part of the risk.

The input of managers to NRIOs cannot be evaluated on the basis of the residual. It is relatively easy for the managers to boost the residual by cutting back on the supply of public goods. Because the product is not sold through bargained transactions, beneficiaries cannot withhold revenue from the organization. The evaluation of managers on the basis of the residual would induce them to minimize the public goods produced and distributed to the beneficiaries. This reduction defeats the purpose of the benefactors of the organization, who would be inclined to cut back their capital contributions to the organization. This sequence of events would end in cessation of the production of the public good and the dissolution of the organization. If benefactors of the organization are willing to pay for the continued provision of the public goods it produces, it would be counterproductive for them to evaluate their hired managers on the basis of the residual income. Thus, NRIOs require an alternative design (relative to business firms) for their managerial performance evaluation and accounting system so that they can continue to produce the public goods in equilibrium.

One such alternative is to evaluate NRIO managers on the basis of unit cost of output: the lower the unit cost, the better the assessed performance of the manager. Although the absence of benchmarks for comparison due to the monopolistic nature of the NRIOs' product markets renders this criterion impractical for evaluating top management, it can be used for the evaluation of the lower-level managers. Unfortunately, the governing board of NRIOs may have no independent data for setting standards of cost performance. Furthermore, it is difficult to get a reliable measure of the quantity and quality of many NRIOs' output. In the absence of competition and reliable benchmarks, unit cost standards simply lead to deterioration in the quality of public goods.

A solution to the problem of control in NRIOs turns out to be quite similar to the solution employed by business firms for the evaluation of middle-level managers. There is some similarity between the organizational units run by the middle-level managers of business firms and the top managers of NRIOs. The former often transact in factor markets internal to the firm, and these internal markets share the imperfections of the external markets in which NRIOs operate. Goods processed by one division of a business firm may be received from another division and dispatched to a third, all inside the same corporation. Often, these intermediate goods have no external markets, and they are transferred at negotiated, budgeted, or standard prices without reference to any competitive market price. Similar weaknesses exist in "markets" in which NRIOs "sell" their products. A division manager in a business firm receives capital from the corporate management at a cost that may have no reference to the cost of capital determined in a competitive market. Similarly, NRIOs receive tax and donated resources outside the discipline of a competitive market, and are therefore controlled through budgets, segregation of funds, and multiple performance criteria. The weakness or absence of product market discipline in NRIOs forces their governing boards or legislatures to play an extensive role in controlling the details of their activities, something that the board of directors of business firms do not do. Differences in the accounting and control systems of the two types of organizations originate in this functional necessity.

Characteristics of Accounting in Public-Good Organizations

What are the special features of the accounting and control systems of public-good organizations? Defining the accounting entity for such organizations is more complicated. Most of these entities use fund accounting to prepare segregated statements of stocks and flows for each of their activities. Accrual accounting is not always used, and when it is, the criteria for recognizing revenue and expense vary. The most glaring differences appear in accounting for long-term assets and liabilities, especially in the depreciation of fixed assets. Even for closely related accounting entities controlled by the same governing apparatus, the consolidation of financial statements is not necessarily more desirable. The role of a budget is more extensive in governmental units than in business firms. Finally, in spite of the large number of agents who interact with each organization of this type, the financial reports of NRIOs rarely receive broad exposure and remain largely confined to a narrow circle of experts. These differences are not mere historical accidents. They arise to help implement and enforce the distinct contract sets of business firms and NRIOs.

Entities and Funds

The separation of accounts into several classes called *funds* is a distinctive feature of the accounting and control methods of NRIOs. Each fund is associated with a specific public good or service included in the mandate of the organization. Even if resources in two or more funds are managed by the same governing boards, legislatures often place restrictions on their use and transfers across activities. These restrictions prevent the managers from treating the resources in various funds as if they belonged to a single pool. Business firms rarely impose such restrictions on their managers. Two or more such funds may still be operated by the same manager for the sake of administrative economy. However, the lack of fungibility creates multiple accounting entities within a single organization. While all NRIOs segregate funds to some degree, this segregation is enforced more strictly in government organizations.

Since the segregation of funds arises from the restrictions imposed on managers, a key step in understanding fund accounting is to understand the reason for such restrictions. It is difficult to specify unambiguous criteria of performance evaluation for the managers in the absence of well-functioning markets and a residual interest in the firm. As a result, agents who deal with the organization through poorly functioning markets protect their interests by seeking representation on the governing body and by placing appropriate restrictions on managerial discretion.

To fix ideas, let us look at the recommendation of the National Council on Governmental Accounting for the use of eight types of funds under three categories:[3]

Government Funds

General Fund: to account for all resources except those accounted for in another fund.

Special Revenue Fund: to account for revenue restricted to specified uses by law or administrative action. This fund does not include special assessments, expendable trusts, or major capital projects.

Capital Projects Funds: to account for financial resources segregated for major capital facilities, excluding those financed by enterprise funds or special assessments. A separate fund is usually created for each major project.

Special Assessment Funds: to account for the financing of public improvements or services that benefit identifiable properties or parties against which special assessments are levied. Long-term liabilities are included in this fund.

Data Service Funds: to account for the accumulation of resources for and the payment of interest and principal on general long-term debt. The general long-term debt itself is not a part of this fund.

General Fixed Asset Account Group: a set of accounts carrying the general fixed assets, excluding proprietary and fiduciary fixed assets.

General Long Term Debt Account Group: a set of accounts carrying the general long-term obligations, excluding proprietary, fiduciary, and special assessment long-term liabilities.

Proprietary Funds

Enterprise Funds: to account for natural monopoly and any other operations in which cost is recovered from the customers through the direct sale of goods or services. Fixed assets and long-term debt related to these operations are included.

Internal Service Funds: to account for goods and services provided by a service department within the organization to other departments (e.g., computer service, transportation). Both fixed assets and long-term debt related to these operations are included in this fund.

Fiduciary Funds

Trust and Agency Funds: resources held by a governmental unit as trustee or agent for individuals, nongovernmental organizations, or other governmental units.

Expendable Trust Funds

Non-Expendable Trust Funds

Pension Trust Funds

Agency Funds

A similar separation of funds is found in the accounts of nongovernmental NRIOs, though the classification is simpler.

Current Unrestricted Fund: analogous to the general fund for governments.

Current Restricted Fund: to account for resources that have been designated by the donor for specific use.

Endowment Fund: analogous to nonexpendable trust funds of governments. Income, and sometimes the principal of these funds, is available for restricted or unrestricted use.

Custodian Fund: analogous to agency funds of governments.

Annuity and Life Income Funds: to account for resources segregated to make periodic stipulated payments to named beneficiaries.

Loan Fund: revolving fund to advance student loans in universities.

Land, Building and Equipment Fund: to account for the acquisition, renewal, and replacement of fixed assets.

Governing bodies restrict the use of resources to ensure that the public goods are produced in agreed-upon quantities and provided to agreed-upon parties. Segregated financial reports enable the constituent agents of the organization to assess the fulfillment of its mandate to provide specific public goods to specific constituencies. This segregation is particularly important for those agents who transact with the organization through relatively weak markets. Special revenue, special assessment, trust, agency, and loan funds are of interest to specific classes of agents. Unless they are segregated from the rest, these agents would find it costly, or even impossible, to obtain this information elsewhere. In contrast, labor and nonmanagerial employees, whose interests in business firms and NRIOs are essentially similar, can and do privately negotiate for their wages and benefits. The part of the financial statements that concerns them directly is their pension fund. No other separately reported special funds have a special significance for this class of agents.

Consolidation and Detail

In 1993, AT&T, consisting of many separate legal entities, employed 308,700 people, had a gross revenue of $67 billion, and used twenty-three pages (including ten pages of an explanation of the company's operations) to present its operating results and financial position. In the same year, a city with gross revenues of $4 billion and only 50,000 employees needed more than two hundred pages to report its results. Is there an economic explanation of this difference, beyond a facile condemnation of bureaucratic inefficiency?

First, consider the possible incompetence of managers as an explanation of detailed disclosure of data by NRIOs. They simply failed to do the additional work to aggregate data. But disclosure of additional detail can only bring additional scrutiny and criticism to managers. In governmental as well as nongovernmental organizations, managers rarely disclose more than what they have to, unless it serves their own interests.

A second possible explanation is that the managers of these organizations were required to disclose greater detail by their contracts. In business firms, bookkeeping entries are adequate to serve most of the interests of all agents, except the investors for whom financial statements are prepared by aggregating these entries. Parties other than the investors are not usually represented on their boards of directors. In NRIOs, on the other hand, many classes of agents have representation on the governing bodies, and they all seek to scrutinize organizational performance from their own point of view. They direct the managers of such organizations to prepare multiaspect reports. Financial statements oriented to income and owners' equity satisfy the shareholders, but not the variety of agents who have a stake in NRIOs. These agents would be unable to protect their interests in the absence of detailed reports. If it does not serve their interests, they will abandon the organization, leading to its dissolution.

NRIOs have been criticized for their failure to present consolidated financial statements of all entities within the control of the same management. If business firms can do it, why can't the NRIOs?

A brief answer is that consolidation is useful when the resources of the consolidated entities are fungible or their transfer is within the control of the managers. Consolidation is carried out in business firms as well as in NRIOs when the management has such control. When management's control over resource transfers is weak or absent, neither business firms nor NRIOs consolidate. Such control is absent in mutual funds managed by the same managers and in the government. Neither type of organization produces consolidated financial statements. It is possible to prepare consolidated statements for the governmental units with some computational effort. Even after appropriate eliminations, they would be no more useful to the participating agents than the consolidated statements for a family of mutual funds would be to agents who hold shares in only one or two of these funds.

Recognition and Accrual

NRIOs' procedures for recording transactions and their criteria for recognizing revenue differ from the practices of business firms. These differences can be understood in terms of the imperfection of the markets in which the former operate, and the consequent external budgetary control imposed on their transactions.

Business firms recognize revenue when (1) the service to be performed has essentially been completed and (2) the amount to be received can be estimated reasonably accurately. These criteria assume that revenue is earned by delivering goods or services in direct exchange transactions. NRIOs that are natural monopolies use similar revenue recognition criterion and match expenses to revenues. However, if their output is a public good, there is no direct transaction, and the link between revenues (taxes, contributions, wills, legacies, fines) and the outlays necessary to produce and distribute the public good is remote. NRIOs are often criticized for their failure to use accrual accounting. How can the accrual method be used in the absence of direct exchange transactions when such transactions form the very basis of the accrual method?

Tax revenues are recognized when received in cash, except in those instances (e.g., property tax) where the amount due from an individual taxpayer can be estimated in advance and billed. In this latter case, tax revenue is recognized in the period in which it is levied. Contributions or donations, are recognized as revenue when pledged (subject to an allowance for uncollectibles), unless uncertainty associated with collections is too large and recognition is delayed until cash is collected. Commercial practice is followed in recognizing revenue from direct exchange transactions. Fundamentally, revenue recognition criteria in NRIOs are no different from those in business firms when revenue-generating exchange transactions can be identified.

Unlike business firms, the revenue of an NRIO is not a gross increase in the shareholders' equity or entitlement. It is a gross increase in the resources controlled by the organization for a specified fund or purpose. Although the accounting term used in both types of accounting systems is the same, its meaning is quite different.

This difficulty becomes more acute in accounting for the resource outflows. Since the accounting and control of business firms is oriented to the measurement of all resource flows in order to arrive at the net change in resources (income) the shareholders are entitled to, resource outflows are recorded as either assets or expenses, depending on when the revenue corresponding to this outflow is recognized. When an organization is engaged in producing public goods, there is no immediate link between resource outflows and inflows. In the absence of better criteria, the receipt of cash becomes the point of recording resource inflow, while the disbursement of cash becomes the point of recording the outflow of resources. Actual practice differs from the cash basis when the receipt and disbursement of resources in forms other than cash (pledge of donation for inflow, receipt of ordered supplies from the vendor to be paid for in cash for outflow) is a reasonably accurate predictor of cash flows that will follow. NRIOs retain the term *revenue* for resource inflow. The matching criterion that links revenues to expenses is dropped. This linkage, so crucial to accounting for business, is severed in NRIOs, and *expenses* is replaced by *expenditures*. Note that expenditures are not the same as disbursements, but in many cases, there is no difference between the two. For public-good-producing organizations, there seem to be no accounting alternatives that are clearly superior to this practice.

Fixed Assets, Depreciation, and Long-Term Liabilities

To understand NRIOs' accounting for fixed assets and long-term debt, it is useful to start with an explanation of how and why such resources and obligations are accounted for by business firms. Businesses record the acquisition of assets at cost and the issuance of debt obligations at cash proceeds. These transactions have no immediate effect on the residual interest (i.e., the entitlement of the shareholders).

As the remaining service potential of the fixed asset declines with time and use, the original acquisition cost is gradually amortized to reduce the shareholders' residual interest in resources of the firm. The statistical inaccuracy of reported changes in residual interest due to mechanical depreciation rules (e.g., straight-line depreciation) is the price a diffuse body of shareholders pays to obtain objective information. Managers have incentives to understate depreciation because managerial compensation is often linked to net income. Accounting blocks managers from misleading shareholders into believing that their residual interest in the firm is substantial while the plant is reduced to a rusting heap of junk. In calculating product costs, depreciation is entered as an estimate of the long-run opportunity cost of capital plant and serves as a basis of production and marketing decisions by the management.

The natural monopoly NRIOs' accounting for fixed assets is similar to the accounting practice of business firms. Although they have no residual interest, they face similar product pricing and managerial evaluation problems. In the production of pure public goods, however, all three rationales for traditional fixed asset accounting disappear—there is no residual interest, goods are not sold through negotiated transactions for a price, production-investment decisions are made by the governing bodies of these organizations instead of by the management, and managerial compensation is not linked to the residual or surplus. NRIOs have no practical advantages from adopting business firms' accounting practice for fixed assets. Without fixed assets and depreciation in the accounting system, business firms will not operate efficiently. This is not so for the public-good-producing NRIOs, and they should not be expected or be forced to use the fixed asset accounting practices of business firms.

NRIOs cannot return to the taxpayer to finance capital projects as business firms can do by selling additional stock. NRIOs set cash aside from their annual tax collections to meet the cost of capital projects, renewals, or replacements. Not surprisingly, depreciation is widely seen in these organizations as a means of setting cash aside to replace capital facilities.

Budgets, Appropriations, and Encumbrances

Unlike the boards of directors of business firms, governing bodies that control NRIOs approve budgets that give detailed and specific directions to managers in various spheres of activity. Budgetary comparisons also provide a multidimensional basis for the performance evaluation of managers. While the use of budgets for evaluation of middle- and lower-level managers in business firms is relatively recent, their use in the government is quite old. Variations on this technique—performance budgets, the planning programming budgeting system (PPBS), and zero-based budgeting—all originated in the government sector.

Unlike business firms, budgets in governmental organizations are integrated into the accounting system and bookkeeping. Item-by-item appropriations approved by the legislature are entered into the account books as the amount available for spending on each item during the year. As these appropriated funds are committed (e.g., by placing an order for supplies with a vendor), an encumbrance entry is made in the account to avoid the possibility of making commitments that may cause expenditures to exceed the appropriation in any account. This feature of accounting and control ensures that the will of the governing body is not thwarted by executive error or design.

The preparation and approval of detailed budgets outside the executive branch of government, and the integration of budgets into the accounting system, are designed to ensure that the organization's actions correspond closely to the expectations of the contracting agents. In public-good-producing organizations, the discipline of the budget is the substitute for the absent discipline of the marketplace. Budgets constrain the behavior, creativity, and innovation of managers. Managers in NRIOs receive fixed salaries, but no performance bonus or stock options. They do well for themselves if they stick close to the budget and take a hostile stance toward risk and deviations. The system is deliberately designed to discourage innovative behavior, given the distributional consequences of deviation from the budget in such organizations. The compartmentalization of resources through fund accounting is a part of the design to achieve this end.

NRIO and Business Accounting Interaction

Accounting systems of businesses and NRIOs are interdependent. Organizations that produce private goods as natural monopolies have been pressured to introduce accrual accounting concepts. When public-good-producing organizations branch out into private-good business, they often lag in adjusting their control system to the private-good environment. The difficulties of applying accrual concepts to the making of public goods are real, but replacement of cash accounting by accrual systems to record private-good transactions is delayed by the inertia of past practice.

NRIOs are often asked to produce consolidated financial statements to provide readers with an overall perspective across all fund entities. Unlike the demand for accrual accounting in private goods NRIOs, this demand is not well-founded. Business accounts are consolidated across legal entities because the economic substance (of control) is supposed to dominate the legal form of separate entities. Accountants in governmental bodies object to consolidation, not because they prefer the legal fine print to economic realities, but because the legal limitations on the control and discretion of managers on various funds often transcend the appearance of common control. The dominant economic characteristic of NRIOs as well as the *substance over form* criterion call for separation of funds if their use is not fungible.

The preceding chapters assumed that each participating agent strives to design his or her own contractual (including accounting) participation in an organization in such a way as to maximize personal welfare. Every aspect of accounting systems does not serve all agents. In segregated funds statements, at least, each agent can find what she or he wants. Consolidated statements of a business firm furnish a better picture of an agent's residual interest to the shareholder. In NRIOs, bondholders who may lend to the organization as a whole are the only such beneficiary of consolidation.

Interaction between NRIOs and business accounting has been a two-way street. Financial reports of NRIOs, known for their length, detail, and complexity, are forbidden territory for all but the experts. Business financial statements have grown in length, detail, and complexity with the size of such organizations. As more and more agents demand various types of information through a nonmarket mechanism (e.g., the FASB), they slowly yield and issue pronouncements that cumulatively add to the complexity of financial statements. Unless the securities regulators (e.g., the SEC) change their stance, it may be only a matter of time before annual reports of large publicly held corporations vie with the federal budget for honors in length and complexity. Fortunately, the SEC has approved the use of summary financial statements in annual reports, allowing the full set of financial statements to be included in the 10-K filings.

Business firms have not only borrowed budgeting as a tool for managerial control from the NRIOs, their increasing size and complexity is leading them to use similar techniques to ensure legal and policy compliance within the organization. The Foreign Corrupt Practices Act of 1977 made it illegal for publicly held corporations in the United States to fail to maintain adequate internal controls on the firm's resources. Such controls have always been required in governmental accounting systems.

Summary

The control requirements of organizations that produce public goods or produce private goods under conditions of natural monopoly are fundamentally different from the control requirements of those that produce private goods and sell them under competitive conditions. Many of the differences among the accounting and control systems of these three types of organizations can be understood in terms of the economic characteristics of the markets in which they transact and the consequent differences in the design of contracts. Nothing is perfect, and it is always possible to improve any system, including the accounting for NRIOs. However, the differences between accounting methods of NRIOs and business firms do not constitute prima facie evidence that the former are defective and should be altered to conform to the latter.

Notes

[1]Henry B. Hansmann, "The Role of Nonprofit Enterprise," *The Yale Law Journal*, Vol. 89, No. 5 (April 1980), pp. 835–898.

[2]Pure public goods are defined to have two properties: (1) marginal cost of producing the public good for consumption of one additional person is zero and (2) no one can be excluded from consuming the public goods. While few goods and services are purely public in this sense, many are public at least in part.

[3]National Council on Government Accounting, *Government Accounting and Financial Reporting Principles, Statement No. 1* (Chicago: NCGA, 1979).

Additional Reading

Accounting Principles and Reporting Practices for Certain Nonprofit Organizations, Statement of Position 78-10. New York: AICPA, 1969.

A Financial Information System for Municipalities, Vol. 1— General Introduction; Vol. II—The Classification System; Supplement—Proforma Statements, Ottawa: Dominion Bureau of Statistics, 1970.

Anthony, Robert N. *Financial Accounting in Nonbusiness Organizations: An Exploratory Study of Conceptual Issues.* Stamford, Conn.: FASB, 1978.

Audits of State and Local Governmental Units, 2nd ed. New York: AICPA, 1978.

Beedle, A. *Accounting for Local Government in Canada: The State of the Art.* Research Monograph No. 2: Vancouver: Canadian Certified General Accountants' Research Foundation, 1981.

Chan, James L., ed. *Research in Governmental and Non-Profit Accounting.* Vol. 1 (1985). Greenwich, Conn.: JAI Press, 1985.

Davidson, Sidney, David Green, Walter Hellerstein, Albert Madansky, and Rowan L. Weil. *Financial Reporting by State and Local Government Units.* Chicago: University of Chicago, 1977.

Drebin, Allan R. "Governmental vs. Commercial Accounting: The Issues." *Governmental Finance*, No. 3—Special Issues, Vol. 8. Chicago: Municipal Finance Officers Association, November 1981.

Drebin, Allan R. "Is Accounting That's Good for General Motors Good for Detroit?" *The Government Accountant's Journal.* Spring 1981.

Drebin, Allan R., James L. Chan, and Loran C. Ferguson. *Objectives of Accounting and Financial Reporting for Governmental Units: A Research Study*, Volumes I and II. Chicago: National Council in Governmental Accounting, 1981.

Financial Accounting Standards Board. *Objectives of Financial Reporting by Nonbusiness Organizations. Statement of Financial Accounting Concepts No. 4.* Stamford, Conn.: FASB, 1980.

Financial Accounting Standards Board. *Recognition of Depreciation by Not-For-Profit Organizations. SFAS No. 93.* FASB: August 1987.

Financial Reporting by Governments. Toronto: CICA, 1980.

Financial Reporting for Non-Profit Organizations. Toronto: CICA, 1980.

Granof, Michael H. "Governmental Standard Setting in Perspective." *Journal of Accountancy* (March 1979), pp. 56–63.

Lambert, A. T. *Royal Commission on Financial Management Accountability: Final Report.* Hull, Quebec: Ministry of Supply & Services, 1979.

Mautz, Robert K. "Financial Reporting: Should Government Emulate Business?" *Journal of Accountancy* (August 1981), pp. 53–60.

Skinner, R. M. *Canadian University Accounting.* Toronto: CICA, 1969.

Steinberg, Harold I. "A New Look at Governmental Accounting." *Journal of Accountancy* (March 1979), pp. 46–55.

Vatter, William. *The Fund Theory of Accounting and Its Implications for Financial Reports.* Chicago: University of Chicago Press, 1947.

Epilogue

All seven wonders of the world are physical objects we could see or touch. Humanity has always measured the accomplishments of its civilizations by "hardware," from the Great Wall of China, the Pyramids, and the Taj Mahal to Apollo 13. Yet, the world is not ruled by brilliant engineers. The greatest accomplishment of man is organization that made the Great Wall and Apollo 13 possible. Although stories of bravery of Alexander the Great are legend, arguably what made him so great was his organizational skill, not his skill with the horse or the sword.

Organization design and operation are the unappreciated "software" of human civilization. Getting hundreds of individuals, who are free to choose and pursue their own goals, to build a jet airliner would be virtually impossible without this software, in spite of their engineering skills. Accounting and control is a key element in how organizations are put together, operated, maintained, transformed, and dissolved. Returning to the computer metaphor, if resources and humans are the hardware of organizations, accounting and control are their operating software. Software connects various parts of the computer in their proper relationship, and makes it possible for it to function. Accounting and control servces a similar function in organizations.

Thinking about organizations as sets of contracts among people makes it easier to see the enabling function of accounting and control. Because organizations come in hundreds of sizes and forms, so do accounting and control systems. A broad survey of their varieties and extent is a good starting point to build a theory of accounting and control.

Index